LEARNI.

Learning in Christ's School

Babes, Children, Youth, and Fathers

RALPH VENNING

THE BANNER OF TRUTH TRUST

THE BANNER OF TRUTH TRUST
3 Murrayfield Road, Edinburgh EH12 6EL
P.O. Box 621, Carlisle, Pennsylvania 17013, USA

★

'Learning in Christ's School' first published in 1675
Reprinted in 1823
First Banner of Truth edition
© Banner of Truth 1999
ISBN 0 85151 764 1

Typeset in 10½/12pt Linotron Plantin
at The Spartan Press Ltd,
Lymington, Hants
Printed and bound in Finland by
WSOY

By the same author:
The Sinfulness of Sin

CONTENTS

And I, brethren, could not speak unto you as unto spiritual, but as unto carnal, even as unto babes in Christ. I have fed you with milk, and not with meat: for hitherto ye were not able to bear it, neither yet now are ye able.

1 Corinthians 3:1-2

For when for the time ye ought to be teachers, ye have need that one teach you again which be the first principles of the oracles of God; and are become such as have need of milk, and not of strong meat. For every one that useth milk is unskilful in the word of righteousness: for he is a babe.

Hebrews 5:12-13

I write unto you, little children, because your sins are forgiven you for his name's sake. I write unto you, fathers, because ye have known him that is from the beginning. I write unto you, young men, because ye have overcome the wicked one. I write unto you, little children, because ye have known the Father. I have written unto you, fathers, because ye have known him that is from the beginning. I have written unto you, young men, because ye are strong, and the word of God abideth in you, and ye have overcome the wicked one.

1 John 2:12-14

PUBLISHERS' FOREWORD

'Babes', 'little children', 'young men', and 'fathers' form the 'classes' in the school of Christ which Ralph Venning describes in these pages. These he presents as the stages in the renewal of human life leading up to the 'academy of heaven'. We find them referred to in 1 Corinthians 3:1–2; Hebrews 5:12–14 and 1 John 2:12–14.

These pages are filled with scriptural references and allusions, and while Venning's exegesis may be questioned from time to time, that does not undermine the value of this thoughtful look at spiritual growth. Recognizing themselves in these portraits, readers will be thankful, humbled, and spurred on to further progress in the grace of God.

Noting the eagerness of the newborn, the delight of the little child, the vigour of the young, and wisdom of the mature, cannot but challenge mediocrity; seeing their foibles, weaknesses, and vulnerability will, on the other, challenge presumption. The book contains a much needed message for today.

The text is followed by an analysis of the structure of the work. Also included here are two prefaces which appeared in the 1823 edition, one by friends of Venning and one by the author himself.

This study of the process of restoring grace complements another treatise by Venning, *The Sinfulness of Sin*, also published by the Trust.

PREFACE by James Barron and John Collins

The following advertisement was intended as an epistle to the reader, before the author's own was found.

This treatise as it is now published was left by the worthy author when he went to his rest. Its excellence and usefulness will best become evident in its reading. It is pre-eminent beyond many of the practical discourses lately printed, in that its scope is unique and not treated, at least to such length, by any before it.

The several degrees or states through which Christians pass to the measure and stature of the fullness of Christ are here insisted upon and clearly explained, according to the rule of faith and with great experience.

The greatest part of the discourse concerns those that make up the greatest part of true Christians: the weak ones, or babes. Here will be found things of a comforting character, which will contribute much to their establishing and promote their advance to a greater degree of grace, till they come to the assurance of the love of God by the witness of the Spirit which the children enjoy. What is laid down in reference to the witness of the Spirit, some may differ with in their conceptions. Yet the author's caution against delusions are such that no person will have a reasonable ground to make any exceptions.

The young men have attained to a strength of grace whereby they are made conformed to Christ, who was in all things tempted as we are, yet without sin. What is said about their handling of temptation will be of great encouragement to many in their present warfare.

As to the last state of Christians, fathers, the author has said very little. Those who were acquainted with him might judge him to have attained to that degree of Christianity, which lies in the highest experience of the mysteries of the gospel. Yet, through modesty, he leaves that for others to supply.

And so you have the legacy of that good man, who served Christ in his generation.

The spiritual advantage of Christians is all that is aimed at in the publication, and accordingly it is recommended to them by the author's very good friends,

James Barron
John Collins

AUTHOR'S PREFACE

Reader,

Though that which I here present may look like a novelty, I hope it will prove to be old truth. For though I confess I have not met with any that have treated the several degrees of saints this distinctly, I must say I was led to consider them by persons of great name and worth, both ancient and modern, who have now and then hinted at them in their writings. These gave me occasion to inquire more fully into this subject and accordingly to preach upon it many years ago in Southwark and, I bless God, not without good reception and success, as I have reason to believe.

On the first three states I have spoken at length, but very little on the last, of fathers, not being willing to venture beyond my line or measure, only hinting in general what may be gathered from the Scripture. What I have said concerning them I submit to the judgement of my elders and betters. I hope they will find me moderate and modest in my assertions, and that the assertions conform to the analogy of faith and agree with the tenor of Scripture, both in truth and in expression.

I shall say nothing more of the treatise, for I hope it will speak for itself. My only desire to God is that it may be blessed to every reader, either for conversion or for edification. If God pleases to grant my prayer, it will be a matter of thanksgiving not only for them, but also for me, their servant in and for Christ Jesus.

Ralph Venning

PART ONE

Introduction

That there are degrees of grace, and consequently that there are Christians of several degrees, is granted by all; but it seems not to be so clear to some pious and learned men how many sorts there are and whether they are to be ranked into several distinct classes. Yet this, with submission, I humbly offer and hope to demonstrate by the Scripture's light, which is the light of the Spirit by whom it was given.

That there are lambs and sheep (*John* 21:15–17); that there are strong and weak (*Rom.* 15:1); that there are spiritual and babes (*1 Cor.* 3:1); or perfect and babes (*Heb.* 5:13–14), the Scriptures undeniably assert and experience confirms. And why there may not be more than two sorts, I can see no reason to disbelieve. Indeed, there seems to be a great deal of reason to believe it. The Apostle John names three: 'fathers', 'young men' and 'children': and the Apostle Paul names a fourth, 'babes', for though they are as carnal, they are still in Christ (*1 Cor.* 3:1) but are a degree below children, as I intend to show in the following discourses.

RANKS OF SAINTS – NOT MEASURED BY AGE

To clear the way, I shall examine 1 John 2:12–14, and consider whether it asserts that there are certain classes of saints. I hope to show that there are three distinct classes, which are marked by their particular attain-

LEARNING IN CHRIST'S SCHOOL

ments, and not by natural years or by the length of time of Christian profession. Scripture never measures by the latter rule, or else it could not point out any gradual apostasy in any saints, as in Ephesus (*Rev.* 2), or any standstill, as among the Hebrews (*Heb.* 5).

For though with the ancient there usually is wisdom, grey hairs are not always wise, as Elihu said (*Job* 32:7–9). The wise are always old, but the old are not always wise. It is not how long they have stood or how many years they have been in Christ, but their enjoyments, experiences, proficiency, and fruitfulness that place them above some others. Some may be in Christ before others, yet outgrown by others who came in long after them. Most of the older disciples were outgrown by Paul (*1 Cor.* 15:8–10), a younger brother, one born out of due time, as he speaks of himself, who yet laboured more abundantly than them all. So, many that are last shall be first.

Some that are young in years may be fathers in experience and attainments, when others that are old and aged as to time may be young and raw in knowledge and practice. Some are only children when they are old, and others may be men when they are young, as Timothy was. He knew the Scriptures from the cradle, as it were, or from a child. By allusion, some are like David: a youth, and yet of more true valour and worth than Goliath, who was a man of war from his youth.

The apostle tells us of some who, if time had been the measure, might have been teachers of others and attained to a great degree, but were such pygmies and babes that they needed to learn the ABC of religion. They were dull of hearing and had very weak stomachs and poor digestion (*Heb.* 5). It clearly follows, then, that many may be of long standing in Christ, may be old, fathers in years, and yet be only babes in understanding

[4]

and ability to digest the strong meat of the gospel. Other men that are only babes in time, newly newborn, may be men in Christ, as Paul was in a little time. And out of the mouths of those who are babes and sucklings in time, there may be more perfect praise than from older persons of many years' standing.

It is true, grey hairs found in a way of righteousness are a crown of glory, and usually the older the wine is, the better. As for many of God's saints, their works have been more at last than at first, and their latter end better than their beginning. Father Abraham, Father Job, Father Moses, Father Paul, and some others, were fathers not only for age but in grace.

In Acts 21:16 mention is made of Mnason, an old disciple who was another Gaius, one who gave hospitality to the apostles and saints. But he is not called an old disciple, I suppose, merely for his age, but because he was as much a disciple as he was old. Faith and obedience ran along and kept pace with his age, that as he grew in years, so he did in grace. He was an old disciple, well taught and able in the school of Christ. It was a great commendation to Andronicus and Junia, not only that they were in Christ before Paul, but that they were of note, eminent, and renowned for their religion (*Rom.* 16:7). And it was the great praise of the church of Thyatira that her last works were more than her first.

But it was not so with all who were of equal age and standing with these. Some were ever learning but learnt only a little, ever doing yet did little. The widow's mite was more than the contribution of those who cast in much. Philadelphia, having little strength, did effectually more than Ephesus, of whom great things are spoken (*Rev.* 3:8; 2:2–3). Every man in Christ is not a man in Christ Jesus; he may be a child or perhaps only a babe. In this text of John, there are children that were fathers, children that were young men, and children that were but children, and some others that were only babes, for under these four heads all are included.

'LITTLE CHILDREN' – ALL TRUE CHRISTIANS

To clarify this a little more, let us note: Two different words are used for 'little children' in three verses. Verse 12 has *teknia*; and *paidia* is in verse 13. *Teknia* includes young men and fathers, who are distinguished from *paidia* in verse 13. *Teknia* in verse 12 therefore applies to all; and that is how Mr Cotton[1], Grotius[2], and Zanchius[3] understand it.

The name *teknia* designates all true Christians, because by the ministry of the apostles they were begotten, or born again, to Christ and to God. This word does not denote any distinct state as the other three do: fathers, young men, and *paidia*, little children. All these words the apostle uses only this once, except *paidia* once more in verse 18. But the word *teknia* he uses seven or eight times in common to them all. And accordingly, the privilege of forgiveness of sins is in common to them all, the youngest as well as the oldest, the babe as well as the father-saint, though it is not known by or manifest to them all alike.

The apostle uses the diminutive often and speaks to them not as *tekna*, children, but *teknia*, little children.

[1] John Cotton (1584–1652), New England Puritan clergyman, theologian and writer. A.B. (1603) and A.M. (1606), Trinity College. B.D. (1613), Emmanuel College, Cambridge. Emigrated to Massachusetts Bay Colony 1633.
[2] Hugo Grotius (1583–1645), Huig de Groot, Dutch jurist, theologian, and statesman. Attended Leyden University at the age of 12. LL.D. University of Orleans.
[3] Zanchius (1516–1590), Girolamo Zanchi, Calvinist pastor and theologian. Taught at Strasburg (1553–63) and University of Heidelberg (1568–1577).

This may be an allusion to the custom of the Jewish teachers of calling their scholars 'little ones'. It notes how tenderly he loved them, and how dear they were to him, as having begotten them by the preaching of the gospel. Paul calls the Corinthians beloved sons (*1 Cor.* 4:14–15), and the Galatians he calls little children (*Gal.* 4:19). The Saviour, too, calls his disciples little children (*John* 13:33); and John, who was the beloved and loving disciple, uses this word.

FATHERS, YOUNG MEN, LITTLE CHILDREN

In verses 13 and 14 we have three distinct classes of Christians, the character of each of them being their proper and particular attainment.

Firstly, the 'fathers', who had the most exact and perfect knowledge of him who was from the beginning, that is Christ Jesus (*John* 1:1–2), the everlasting Father, as Christ is called (*Isa.* 9:6), who is the same today as yesterday and will be forever (*Heb.* 13:8), the Alpha and Omega, the beginning and the ending, who is and who was, and who is to come, Jehovah (*Rev.* 1:8). And this is repeated in verse 14.

Secondly, the 'young men', of whom it is said that they have overcome the wicked one and that they were strong (verse 14), that the word of God abode in them in strength, like Joseph's bow (*Gen.* 49:24).

Thirdly, the 'little children', of whom it is said that they have known the Father as their heavenly Father who has loved them.

BABES

Interpreters generally understand these verses to speak of all the orders of Christians, and that there are no more

[7]

than these three; that all saints are either little children, or young men, or father saints. But, with respect, I believe that there is a fourth, inferior to or younger than the youngest of these. They are and are called babes, who do not yet know the Father as such, as the little children are said to do.

The babe-saint is expressed in Scripture again and again, and is of a lower form than the little children, as, God willing, will be shown later, when I speak of the characteristics of each state. For the present I mention only this in general: The fathers are so called, whether older or younger for years, from their great experience and wisdom, having gone through each of the inferior states. The young men are marked by their strength of faith, by which they overcome the evil or wicked one. The little children have their character from knowing the Father, which notes a state of assurance. And the babes eat milk, the first principles of repentance and faith, and desire after growth. All this is evident from the several places of Scripture where these distinct classes are mentioned with these very names. We shall examine them all, God willing, in the following chapters.

GENERAL APPLICATION

Having given a general account of my intentions, I shall for the present speak a little first to all, and then to each of the different classes.

(i) To all:

a) Love one another without favouritism, without pretence, and with a pure heart fervently (1 Pet. *1:22*). But love not the world nor the things of the world, the lusts of the flesh, the lusts of the eye, and the pride of life (*1 John 2:15-16*). The apostle obliges all of them to these two things, because their sins were forgiven them (2:12), and obliges each of them according to their particular privileges: the fathers, because they have known him that is from the beginning; the young men, because they are strong, and are conquerors; and the children, because they have known the Father. Seeing these things are so, love one another, as I said before, and love not the world, which is what I now say.

b) Let no one measure himself by another or make comparisons, either for lifting up or casting down. Some of the Corinthians (*1 Cor.* 4:6–8) were apt to be puffed up because they supposed themselves to have attained more than others, which is an ill sign. Though they were high in gifts, they were low in grace, for they were babes. Therefore the apostle ruffles their fine feathers with this quick interrogation: 'Who makes thee, whoever thou be, who makes thee to differ? And what hast thou that thou didst not receive? Now, if thou didst receive it, why dost thou glory, pride thyself and boast, as if thou didst not receive it?' Grace gives us no leave to be proud or to despise or undervalue others.

On the other hand, there are some poor souls, and I believe there are some among the Corinthians, that are apt to become discouraged when they compare themselves with others. When a dwarf stands by a giant, a man of low stature by a tall one, as David by Goliath, he seems to be nobody; yet he is a man, a perfect man, in spite of the vast difference between them. Many poor souls, when they see themselves outstripped in knowledge, faith, love and patience by some that came into Christ long after them, are apt to think that they are not saints because they are not saints such as those.

This seems to be the case of some of the Corinthians. There were some who were only as the foot, the very lowest member of the body, and were therefore too inclined to think that they were not part of the body. For the apostle says to them: 'If the foot shall say, Because I am not the hand, I am not of the body, is it therefore not of the body? And if the ear shall say, Because I am not the eye, I am not of the body, is it therefore not of the body?' No, you should by no means say so; it is a complete *non sequitur.*

So if you should say, 'Because I am not a father, I am not a child of God,' it does not follow. You may be a young man, and if not that, then a babe in Christ. Begin lowest; do not stretch yourself beyond your measure. And do not let any be proud if they have gone beyond others, to be puffed up and despise the weak.

c) Let everyone be thankful and bless God for what he has attained, be it more or less. Are any of you cedars in Lebanon when others are but shrubs as the hyssop on the wall, or as the lilies of the valley? Are any of you, like Saul, taller than your brethren by the head and shoulders? Are you crowned with the grey hairs of wisdom and righteousness? Have you overcome the wicked one? Have you lain in the Father's bosom? Give God the glory, who gave you the grace. Are others of you recently come in, or of but little and low stature? Are you only babes in Christ? Yet despise not the day of small things. Let none of his mercies or consolations be small to you, who are less than the least of them all. It is great mercy to be one of Christ's, even one of his little ones.

Our Lord Jesus chose twelve to be with him as his family, of whom three were admitted to be his confidants, Peter, James, and John; and of these three, John was the darling. He was the disciple whom Jesus loved with a particular love and was admitted to lie in his bosom. Now if you are not a John, thank him if you are a Peter or a James; if not of them, thank him that you are one of the twelve (but not Judas); if not one of the twelve, then one of the seventy, for he afterward enlarged the number, to do him any service abroad. Bless him that you are a member of his body, though an ear or a foot; that you are a star in his firmament, though not of the first magnitude, but the very least of all.

David had his worthies, and the lowest was honourable, though he attained not to the first three (*2 Sam.* 23:23). And among the thirty-seven, Uriah the Hittite was the last (23:39). Even if you are last, it is a mercy to be one of the thousands of Israel. Though you do not sit at the king's table, bless him if you are a door-keeper to behold his goings out and comings in. Bless him that you are one of the little flock, though you are not the principal or the choicest, but the least of it.

If you have learnt the ABC of godliness, the first principles of the doctrine of Christ, bless him for it. You do not know how soon he may teach you to spell and to read more clearly the deeper lessons, that your joy may be full. He takes notice of the kindness of your childhood, of your lisping and attempts to walk, and he will perhaps take you by the hand and teach you to go from class to class, till you come to be one of the uppermost in the school of Christ. And then he will remove you into the University (the holy Academy), where the spirits of just men made perfect will welcome you and be glad of your company. Then you will be of the society of Christians, of them that are in Christ indeed, and will live with Christ forever, which is the best of all.

At present, if you are not worth thousands, rich in grace, bless him that you are worth anything, worthy of his calling, and made acceptable to partake of the inheritance of the saints in light by being delivered from the power of darkness and translated into the kingdom of his dear Son (*Col.* 1:12–13). Though he has not made you a father, bless him that he has made you a son, though as yet you are still a babe. He that blesses God for a little is in the right way to be blessed with more.

d) Let everyone that is not a father aim to be so, and let everyone that is a father aim at being more so. As there is a growth from one degree to another, press forward to the utmost degree of perfection, as St Paul did (*Phil.* 3:12–17). Do not be content with being babes, but grow from there to be little children, and from there to be young men, and from there to be fathers, and so to be perfect men in Christ Jesus (*Eph.* 4:13–16). Go from strength to strength till you appear before God in Zion above.

Grow in grace and in the knowledge of our Lord and Saviour Jesus Christ (*2 Pet.* 3:18). Immediately before this, the apostle says, 'Take heed that you fall not from your steadfastness.' But lest you should think it enough not to be apostates, or to be steadfast, he adds in the same breath, 'But grow in grace.' So, the charge is not only to be steadfast and immovable, but to abound, be always abounding in the work of the Lord (*1 Cor.* 15:58).

The Apostle Peter would not have us think that to be newborn and so to partake of a divine nature is sufficient. He says, 'Besides this, add to your faith virtue, knowledge, godliness, etc.' And if these things are in you, is that enough? No, but if these things be in you, and abound, then an abundant entrance shall be administered to you into the everlasting kingdom of our Lord and Saviour Jesus Christ (*2 Pet.* 1:4–11). Do not content yourself merely with so much grace as will bring you into heaven, the haven of happiness, but that you may enter in with full sails, with full conviction and assurance.

e) Do not let the weak envy the strong, though they may emulate them; and do not let the strong despise the weak, but help their faith and joy. Babes are apt to become jealous, resentful, and sullen if others fare better than themselves. But this ought not to be so, for God may do with his own what he pleases and give to everyone as he will. Many of this kind are like David's brother Eliab, who attributed David's inquisitive boldness to the pride of his heart, and did not consider that it was of the Lord, who had chosen and preferred David before himself, who was the older brother (*I Sam.* 17:28; 16:6–7). This was the very reason for the grudge against his brother David. Saul was also jealous when David's victories increased and the ten thousands ascribed to him (*I Sam.* 18:5–8). Thus it is with weak Christians. They are apt to envy their superiors and betters the very grace of God. But let envying as well as wrath be laid aside, so the apostle says to babes (*I Pet.* 2:1–2).

On the other hand, do not let the strong despise the weak, but bear with and bear their infirmities, which is to fulfil the law of love and of Christ (*Gal.* 6:2–3, *Rom.* 15:1–7). This honour is due to these weaker vessels, for God has bestowed it upon them. He has so tempered the body that the hand cannot say to the eye, 'I have no need of you,' or again the head (it is strange, for the head is Christ; yet his Church is his fullness [*Eph.* 1:23]); much less can any of the members say to the feet, 'I have no need of you.' Moreover, those members of the body which seem to be most feeble, are not only convenient, but necessary. And not only do we give, or ought to, but God himself gives more abundant honour to that part which lacks (*I Cor.* 12:12, 21–24).

It is said (*Prov.* 22:2) that the rich and poor meet together (in the same body) and the Lord is the maker of them all. He that made him poor and you rich could have made him rich and you poor. And as it is now, the rich need the poor as much as the poor need the rich. So do not despise the poor and low. Job tells us that he did not despise (or even dare to despise) the cause of his manservant or maidservant, though they contended with him, for, as he says, he could not answer for it to God, who made and fashioned his servant in the womb as he did himself (*Job* 31:13–15). Excellent arguments!

Well then, do not let the babe envy the young men or others. In a great court many times there is a special favourite whom all the rest are apt to envy because they are not favoured and honoured as he is, though they also are in the same court. Everyone would be the only one. And that is so too often in the court of heaven upon earth, the Church. Jesus Christ, the king of saints, takes one or another (as John) to be his bosom favourite, and the other ambitious courtiers cannot bear this. They look upon such a person with resentment, as Peter did upon John (*John* 21).

When Christ Jesus, after making sure of Peter's love, told him not only what he must do but suffer also, and nothing of that nature was said concerning John, Peter seems to take it ill and is unable to resist asking, 'And what shall this man do?' That was from envy, for Christ takes him up on it with an angry 'What is that to you?' (*John* 21:15–22).

When some poor souls – babes that they are! – see children-saints made so much of and enjoying the light of God's countenance and lying in his bosom all the day long; when they see young-men saints making great conquests and obtaining victories over temptations; and when they hear father-saints telling long stories of their acquaintance with Christ through every turn, and what variety of experiences they have had in all conditions, and by contrast see how little joy, victory, and experience they themselves have, they are apt to envy and regret the others' enjoyments and glory.

And on the other side, the fathers hear the younger ones speak of experiences, lisping and speaking half words, and see how short they fall of their attainments; the young men see the children baffled and led into captivity by temptations; the little children see how ignorant the babes are, and that they do not know their Father. At such times the rich and strong are apt to deride or undervalue the poor and weak as unworthy of their company. It is all too common with those who know much to know it too much, and for those who are wise and rich, but so often in their own eyes, to have very low thoughts and speak meanly of their inferiors. But it should not be so with saints. If it is, it is their infirmity, not to give it a worse name. Therefore, let not him that eats strong meat despise him that eats milk, nor let him that eats only milk envy him that eats strong meat, that I may allude to something the apostle says in another case (*Rom.* 14:3).

f) Seeing there are several degrees of saints, let all be willing that each may have a share at a sermon, or in an epistle. At least allow that some may be spoken to at one time and some at another, for we cannot speak to all at once. Some must have patience in a queue, for all cannot be served at one time; and so it is in this case. Some when they come to a sermon think nothing is worth hearing but what is spoken to their case, and truly there are almost as many minds as men. If it is not a sermon for humbling, says one; for consolation, says another; for exhortation, says a third; it is worth nothing. So one is for Paul, another for Apollos, and a third for Cephas; some for Barnabas and others for Boanerges; some for the law and others for free grace; some for faith and others for works. Fathers are for antiquities, young men for wars, children for love tokens, and babes for milk. But, my beloved, all should wait for their meat and portion in due season.

g) Everyone should endeavour to make the best use of what they hear and read. All Scripture is profitable and is written for everyone's learning. If fathers are spoken to, it is of use to the younger sort to incite them to aspire to such attainments and experiences. Therefore the apostle resolved to go on and to expound fully, strong meat and doctrine, though his hearers were but babes (*Heb.* 6:1). If the younger sort are spoken to, it is of use to fathers, to call to remembrance what once they were (for such were some of you), and also to stir them to thankfulness that God has advanced them to a state of which it may be said not all saints have such honour, and to say as David did, 'Who am I, O Lord God, and what is my house, that thou hast brought me hitherto?' (*2 Sam.* 7:18).

I have heard of an eminent person who had been with others at a sermon, and when some complained and seemed to be offended because the preacher was a Boanerges and threatened wrath and the flashes of hellfire to sinners, he told them it was one of the sweetest and most comforting sermons that he had heard in a long time: 'For,' said he, 'I bless God I am delivered from it all.' This is to make a good use of a sermon? Do you that are saints hear sermons preached to show sinners the misery of their condition? Then bless God that has converted you. Do you that are sinners hear sermons preached to saints to show their privileges and happiness? Then pray to God to make you saints also. Thus everyone may make a good use of every sermon they hear. Do not be offended and say, 'I would have done as well to stay at home, what does this concern me?' Oh, let no one say so. No concern to you! There is no truth, no doctrine that does not concern you more or less, be you sinner or saint, be you a father, young man, little child, or babe.

(ii) A few words to each in turn:

a) To fathers, I entreat you to lay aside childish things, and let it not be said of any of you that you were once a man but

[16]

twice a child. It is not comely for aged persons to play the child, or to play with children. The apostle says: 'When I was a child, then indeed I spoke as a child, I understood as a child, I thought as a child; but when I became a man I put away childish things' (*1 Cor.* 13:11). The aged men and women should be sober and grave, teaching and giving examples to the younger ones (*Titus* 2:2–4). So Paul counsels: 'Brethren, be followers of me, and mark them that walk so, as you have us for an example, for our conversation is in heaven' (*Phil.* 3:17,20). This (it seems) was written by him when he was Paul the aged, when he was prisoner at Rome, and he calls himself Paul the aged as well as a prisoner (*Philem.* 9).

Fathers and old men love to tell stories, so recount your experiences to the younger sort, and tell them (as David did his children) what God has done for your soul. Tell them how God converted you, how God carried you on step by step, from faith to faith, and from one degree to another, till you became fathers in Israel.

I might add also, do not disdain to learn, for St John writes to you fathers also concerning brotherly love and not loving the world, as if you had not properly learnt these things.

b) To young men I say, Be strong in the grace that is in Christ Jesus and the word that abides in you. Acquit yourselves like good soldiers of Jesus Christ, as Paul says to the young man (*2 Tim.* 2:1–3). And do not entangle yourselves with the affairs of this life, so that you may please him who has chosen you to be soldiers. The fathers are for counsel, but you young men for war; they steer the vessel, but you must fight; the glory of young men is their strength. Be strong then in faith, for from this is your victory by which you overcome the devil and the world (*Eph.* 6:16, *1 John* 5:4–5). And flee youthful lusts (*2 Tim.* 2:22), for they war against your souls(*1 Pet.* 2:11). From these we see it is not cowardice but courage to run and flee away, even in young men who are strong and soldiers.

Take heed of pride also, to which young and strong soldiers are very prone. Young and strong men frequently boast how they can vault, leap, and perform feats of activity and arms, and of what victories they obtain. Well, though your marrow be in your bones (*Prov.* 3:8), that is, the word of God abiding in you, do not be lifted up, for pride goes before a fall. A man's pride shall bring him low, however high and strong he is (*Prov.* 29:23). And the helpers of pride or strength shall stoop under him because of God's anger (*Job* 9:13). For God resists the proud; therefore you younger ones be clothed with humility (*1 Pet.* 5:5).

c) To the children-saints I say, Be obedient to your Father, whom you know and know to be loving.   Be loving also to your brothers, whom you are to love for your Father's sake; and whom, if you love not, you love not the Father (*1 John* 4:20–21; 5:1–2). The fathers are for knowledge, the young men for strength, but you are for love; your state and age is proper for love.

d) To the babe-saints I say with the apostle (1 Pet. 2:1–2), As newborn babes, desire the sincere milk of the word, that you may grow by it.   You have tasted, and as yet only tasted, that the Lord is gracious. Milk is your proper food, desires your proper acts. These are for your growth; and tasting, that is, experiencing, is to encourage your appetite and desire. Desire milk then, that you may grow stronger and taller.

FURTHER CLARIFICATION

Before I treat each class separately, there are several

[18]

premises to be laid down in order to understand the subject better:

(i) There is a vast difference between the least or lowest of saints (babes) and the highest of men (philosophers and moral men) who are mere men and unconverted.

Socrates, Seneca, and others are great examples of how far men may go by nature's help; and Paul, before his conversion, how far a man may go by the help of the law (*Phil.* 3:6). And yet the least saint in the school of Christ outgoes and surpasses all these (*1 Cor.* 1:13–31; 2:6–10), for he is taught of God (*Matt.* 11:25). And though he is but a babe, still he is in Christ; and though he is as carnal, he is not a carnal man (*1 Cor.* 3:1) as all are that are not in Jesus Christ. No, he is a new creature. Gold, though in the ore, exceeds the best of clay and earth. So a babe-saint, which is gold in the ore, exceeds and excels all other men who are but clay and of the earth, earthly.

The philosophers tell us that the least fly has more excellence in it than the highest heavens, because it is a living thing and moves from an internal principle of life which the heavens do not have. And the wisest of men, Solomon, tells us that a living dog is better than a dead lion. All of this testifies that the value of any being is in its life, and the more life the more value.

Now men that are not converted are dead in sins in which they walk, as the prodigal was (*Luke* 15:32), and all were (*Eph.* 2:1–3). And it is said of the Gentiles again, that they were alienated from the life of God (*Eph.* 4:18). But the least, the babe-saint, is made alive, for he breathes (prays), as it was said of Paul as soon as he was newborn (*Acts* 9:11). These babes have life, life more abundantly, for in a measure they partake of the divine nature and life.

[19]

It is primarily upon this account (among others) that the righteous is better than his neighbour who is not righteous (*Prov.* 12:26). The least saint is better than the best man in the parish that is not a saint. By way of analogy, I may refer to what our Saviour said of John, that he was among them born of women one of the greatest, yet that he who was the least in the kingdom of God was greater than he (*Matt.* 11:11). So, I may say that the least and lowest of saints born of God is greater than the greatest that is only born of a woman. Those who believe in Jesus have this honour to be called, and to be, the sons of God; who are born not of blood, nor of the will of the flesh, nor of the will of man, but of God. Surely they are most highly descended who are born from above, or of God (*John* 1:12–13, *James* 1:18).

Of his own will he begot us, that we should be the first-fruits (or, the most excellent) of his creatures. For as man is greater than all the creation of God, except angels (*Psa.* 8:4,8), similarly, of all men, the saints are the first-fruits. And in some respect they are advanced beyond the angels (*Heb.* 1:14), for the angels are their attendants and ministers; they learn from the Church the manifold wisdom of God (*Eph.* 3:10). And though Christ is head over the angels, he is not their head as he is the head of the Church, which is his body (*Eph.* 1:22–23; 5:23). The best of men are but men at best, but grace makes men more men than they were, and more than men.

(ii) As there is a great difference between saints and men, so there is disparity between saints and saints.
They (as the stars) differ from one another in glory. All saints are excellent, but they are not equally excellent (*Psa.* 16:3). All of them do virtuously, but some excel the rest. In the human body there are some members that are far more noble than others; there are principal and vital,

and there are the less important and incidental. Indeed, all members of Christ's body are vital and necessary. Yet some are more so than others and in their functions and operations far excel the rest, as the eye does the ear, and the hand the foot (*1 Cor.* 12).

And the apostle tells us (*2 Tim.* 2:20), in a great house (such is God's Church) there are vessels of gold and vessels of silver, and also of wood and earth, some of them to honour and others to dishonour, referring not only to the differences between common and special grace among men and believers (*Rom.* 9:21), but to the true members of the body (*1 Cor.* 12:23) who are called less honourable.

Now no man doubts that vessels of silver and gold are more excellent and honourable than those of earth and wood. There are some that are wooden saints and earthen saints, in comparison with some that are silver and others that are golden saints (*1 Cor.* 3:12–15). Yet this I say also: The highest of saints do not so far exceed the lowest, as the lowest exceeds the highest of men. For the saints compared one with another differ only in degree, while saints and men differ in kind. Gold in the ore is not so much inferior to the most refined and pure gold, as clay and earth are inferior to gold in the ore.

(iii) There are things common to all the saints of whatever degree.

They are all born of God, all his children, all taught of God from the greatest to the least (*Heb.* 8:11, *1 John* 2:20–27), including the (*paidia*) little children, to whom St John last of all addressed his speech (*1 John* 2:18). The babes are in Christ Jesus as well as the Father, though not so well rooted and grounded in him (*1 Cor.* 3, *Col.* 2:6–7). The sins of all of them are forgiven alike

(*1 John* 2:12). All are gracious, though some have more
grace than others, just as all men are rational, though
some are more rational than others. The reality of
grace is common to all, though growth in grace is, in
some respects, more peculiar to some.

They are all brothers, brought forth in the image of
God and created according to him (or his likeness) in
righteousness and holiness of truth. You may see the
Father's image in the babe's eye. Though only newly
born, they are newborn and new creatures.

In short and finally, they are all members of the body,
the foot as well as the hand, the ear as well as the eye (*1
Cor.* 12). Though the stars differ from one another in
glory, they are all stars. The fathers, the young men, the
little children, and the babes also have this in common,
that they are of God's family and of the household of
faith, the sons of God. They are all in Christ's school,
though not all in the same class.

*(iv) As there are things common to all, so there are some things
specific and particular to each state.*

There are things specified of the fathers which cannot be
said of the young men; things specified of the young men
which cannot be said of the little children; things said of
the little children which cannot be said of the babes. And
there are things said of the babes which cannot be said of
them that are not yet newborn though there is still too
much in common with babes and carnal men, because
the babes are not yet thoroughly cleansed, but are as
carnal and walk as men.

There is something in the best saints that may be
found in every one; but there is something in some that
cannot be found in all. The apostle gives these three
classes particular attributes: That of fathers is wisdom;
that of young men is valour; that of little children is love.

And St Paul tells us that the babes eat only milk, that is they repent and believe (a little faintly), to which St Peter adds desires (*1 Pet.* 2:2).

It is true indeed that the highest and greatest contains the less, but the less does not contain the greater, much less the greatest. So, the father knows all the four states, for he has passed from a babe to a little child, to a young man, and from there to a father. The young man knows three states, for he has passed from babe to little child to young man. The little child knows only two states, being gone no further than from a babe to a little child. The babe is acquainted with only his own state, at present, and does not know what it is to be anything that is proper to the other three. He knows only this: He is passed from death to life, from being a sinner to being a saint, though a weak one.

(v) The disparity of difference between saints is not in their gifts but in graces.

And the disparity is not in common, but in special grace; and not only in accessory and complementary graces, but in principal and fundamental ones proper to each state. It is possible for persons to be rich in gifts yet poor in grace, as the Corinthians were. They came behind in no gift (*1 Cor.* 1:7). They were full, they were rich, they reigned as kings. They were wise, strong, and honourable, at least in their own esteem (*1 Cor.* 4:8–10), and yet were babes and as carnal (*1 Cor.* 3:1). Therefore the apostle showed them a more excellent way than that of gifts: grace, and specially the grace of love (*1 Cor.* 12:31; 13:1–3).

Apollos was a very eloquent man, mighty in the Scriptures and instructed in the way of the Lord. He was fervent in spirit, teaching zealously, diligently, and boldly, yet he needed to have the way of God expounded to him more perfectly (*Acts* 18:24–26). The Corinthians came behind in no gift, yet came behind and fell short of many a grace. The measure of a man's excellence, then, is not to be taken by what gifts of knowledge and eloquence he has, but by what grace he acts.

Again, this measure is not to be taken from common, but from special and saving grace, and not from profession but from practice. There is common faith, and the faith of God's elect. There were foolish as well as wise virgins. There are seeming as well as truly religious persons. The stony-ground hearers made a fair show in the flesh, and the thorny brought forth fruit, but not to perfection. They did not know the root of the matter, or the grace of God in truth, for that brings forth ripe fruit (*Col.* 1:6).

There were some that through the knowledge of Christ had escaped the pollution of the world, but licked up their vomit, showing that their nature was not changed, but they were dogs still. And they wallowed again in the mire; though they were washed, they were sows still and not really converted so as to have a saving work within them (*2 Pet.* 2:20–22). Surely, says the apostle, they that went out from us were not of us (*1 John* 2:19). He speaks of 'them' as distinguished from 'us', using the word 'us' five times, and 'they' six times, in that one verse.

Yet again, the measure is not to be taken from accessory graces, which contribute chiefly to the well-being, the comfort and refreshment, or (if I may so speak) the recreation of Christians, as joy, delight, and rapture; but from the graces which are essential and proper to each state. Wisdom and much experience is for fathers, strength and the word abiding for young men, love for children, and repentance for babes. Now, as any person acts out of the substantial and fundamental graces of any state, such is his state; and as he passes from one to another, such is his advance.

(vi) As this difference is to be measured by graces acted upon, so it is made by the grace of God working and actuating these graces in us.

It is grace that makes the difference, not only between saints and sinners but between saints and saints. That it makes the difference between men and men in taking one and making him a saint while leaving the other in his sins is clear (*Matt.* 11:25, *Rom.* 9:13–24, and many other places). And it is as clear that grace and the good pleasure of God make the difference between saints also, so that one has more grace and acts upon it more than another (*1 Cor.* 4:7; 12:11,18).

Indeed, God works all things according to no counsel but the counsel of his will, and who shall say to him, 'Why hast thou made me thus?' His wind blows where and how it will; and as he shows mercy to whom he pleases, so it is with what and how much he pleases. The first and the later increase is of God. He gives five talents to one, two to another, and only one to a third, and it is not the man but the talent that brings in the gain.

The apostle, when he had said, 'I live', corrects himself with, 'Not I, but Christ liveth in me, and my life is by faith' (*Gal.* 2:20). And when he says he laboured more abundantly than them all, he seems to recall it, and says, 'Not I, but the grace of God which was bestowed upon me, and was with me, to assist and enable me' (*1 Cor.* 15:10, *Luke* 19:16).

It is observable how Paul alters his language when he speaks of what he did in a state of nature, and what he did in a state of grace. At first he attributes all to himself: 'I was this, and I did this' (he was always very proficient); 'I profited more in the Jews' religion than many of my

[25]

contemporaries that were of my standing' (*Gal.* 1:14). But when he is converted, though he laboured more than any of his seniors, he is not arrogant and assuming but modest and thankful: 'Not I, but the grace of God that was with me. Though by nature I was forward and zealous, yet as to this work and labour, I have reason to attribute it and pay my gratitude not to nature, but to grace.'

As it is of grace that one is taken and another left, so it is of grace that one is promoted and advanced more than another. That John lies in Jesus' bosom, and that Paul grows so fast, is of God and of the grace of God. That one should be a father, and another who was in Christ before him should be a babe still, is of grace. One would think wise men should know most and strong men do most, yet by grace babes are wiser and the weak do more (*Matt.* 11:25, *1 Cor.* 1:25–31). It is a difference made by grace that the children of the kingdom should not enter, but publicans and harlots should. And in the body, if this is an eye, that an ear, this a hand, that but a foot, it is because God has set every member in the body as it pleases him. That this is a babe and only a babe (and so of the rest), our response is, 'Even so, Father, for it seems good in thy sight, it is thy will and pleasure it should be so.'

(vii) God has great and glorious ends in having people of several degrees in his Church, several members in the body, and several classes in the school of Christ.

Though God is not bound to give an account of any of his matters, he is pleased to be so condescending as to do it. As everything is beautiful in its season, so everything is beautiful in its place.

When God was about to erect the material temple, he made man and things fit to a purpose. There were stones and timber as well as gold, and vessels of several sorts and sizes. Some men worked in gold, some in purple and blue; some had one office and task, and some another.

And he did so when he erected a spiritual house and building (his Church, the body of Christ). And he continues to do so, but far more gloriously, so that everyone, all creatures, may utter glory to him to whom it is due (*Psa.* 29:9). The apostle alludes to this when he says: In whom (Christ Jesus) the whole building fitly framed together grows unto a holy temple in the Lord (*Eph.* 2:21). And: From the head, Christ, all the body by joints and bands having nourishment ministered and knit together, increaseth with the increase of God (*Col.* 2:19). And more fully: From whom (the head, Christ) the whole body fitly joined together and compacted by that which every joint supplieth, according to the effectual working in the measure of every part, maketh increase of the body to the edifying of itself in love (*Eph.* 4:16).

From all of this we see with what peculiarity and exactness of art (may I so speak) God has ordered every part in relation to the beauty and perfection of the whole. Here is beauty, harmony, communion, and edification, all meeting together.

The more pieces there are in any work drawn into a union, the more admirable is the work. When the queen of Sheba saw the house that Solomon had built, there was no more spirit in her; she was enraptured with admiration (*1 Kings* 10:4–5). How much more wonderful it is to see the variety and unity of the house of God! The first workmanship of God was so glorious; he brought together and united so many particles of dust into the body of a man. To frame such a curious piece out of dust was worthy of awe and wonder.

And a far greater beauty is drawn by God himself in the second creation: the whole mystical body, made up of such different members, as fathers, young men, little children, and babes, all united to so glorious a head as Christ is, and called his fullness. That in music so many sounds should melt into one, and in painting so many lines and colours should conspire to make one face, is admired even by artists. But alas! What is art to nature? And what is nature to grace? What body was ever like the body of Christ, so fitly framed together?

In 1 Corinthians 12, the apostle gives us a more particular account of God's design in the body and tells us that there is not one unnecessary member, no, not the most feeble (*1 Cor.* 12:15–26). And if these have such abundant honour bestowed upon them, what is the honour of the comely parts that have no need?

No need? What, though they do not need what the other parts do, do they have no need of one another? Yes, surely; for God has so tempered the body and has so set the members that the eye cannot say to the hand, 'I have no need of thee,' nor the head to the feet (oh, strange!), 'I have no need of you.' The foot and the ear are as much needed as the hand and the eye to make the body complete; smelling is needed as much as seeing and hearing. If there were only one sort of members, it would not be a body.

But what is the end of all this variety and disparity? It is that there should be no schism or division in the body, but that the members should have the same care one of another, as if it were for themselves (*Heb.* 13:3), as if the case were your own, for so it may be. If one member suffers, all the members may suffer with it, or if one member is honoured, all the rest may rejoice with it. Such a mutual assistance results from this united variety that it is far better, not only for the whole, but for each one, than if every one were for themselves (as the world is) and concerned for none else. Woe to him that is alone without the society and sympathy of others; but what a happy communion is made by the babes' desire, the little children's love, the young men's strength, and fathers' wisdom! And so that these may the better contribute to one another, God puts them into a body (*1 Cor.* 12:27).

What, alas, should the weak do, were there not some stronger to bear their infirmities (*Rom.* 15:1)? What should an overtaken one do, if there were not some spiritual ones to restore him with a spirit of meekness (*Gal.* 6:1)? And this they are obliged to do as if they were in their place and condition, considering themselves, for either they have been tempted, or may be, and therefore should bear one another's burden.

I may add also: What would the older sort do with all their strength and knowledge, if there were not others to be strengthened and taught? For the good of knowledge and experience is not only in possessing it, but in communicating it. The design of such men having more grace than others is not only to save them (less would do that) but to edify others also, as gifts of so great degrees of grace are given for a common good.

Paul was converted not merely to save him, but that he might be an example to them that should believe (*1 Tim.* 1:16). In his tribulations and temptations he was comforted not only for his own support, but for the consolation and salvation of others, that he might be able to comfort them who are in any trouble, by the comfort through which he was comforted of God (*1 Cor.* 1:3–6) with which he was more than acquainted (*2 Cor.* 11:23–29).

Thus then, we see that this body is so compact that the communion between the members is lively, sympathizing and helpful, as if it were everyone's own case. This indeed is the excellence of this great piece of God's work, that all the members are so joined that if you touch one all the rest feel it and have a sense of it, as the head also has if any of his members are abused (*Acts* 9:4–5). Sculptures and paintings please the eye to look at, but they have no life or sense; if you touch one part, the rest are not concerned. But in this body, they rejoice together and suffer together according to the good or evil any members meet. If only a toe is trodden on, the head feels it and cries out, 'Saul, Saul, why persecutest thou me?' If Peter is in prison, the Church is at prayer.

The members of this body are partners in joy and sorrow. If they laugh, it is together; if they weep, it is together. As each member contributes to the making up and edification of the whole (*Eph.* 4:16), so each partakes of the enjoyments or sufferings of the whole or any part. And to this purpose God has framed harmoniously and admirably this body, made up of these members, babes, little children, young men, and fathers, all of whom are necessary to the edification and perfection of the whole structure.

(viii) Each of these ranks and states have a measure to which they are appointed and a degree at which they are fixed.
The foot is fixed to its place and measure, as are the rest of the members. So it is in this body, though with this difference: that some who yet are babes may become little children, and so go on from degree to degree. Yet there are constantly these fixed states of babes, children, etc., so that those appointed to be only babes go no higher. And so of children that do not come to be young men; and young men that do not become fathers. Though I cannot say that this or that person is fixed to be a babe or a little child and shall be no other, still I can say that the state of a babe, etc., is fixed, and that those appointed to be such proceed no further.

Some die young, as Jeroboam's son, who ran his race

almost as soon as he could walk. The thief on the cross died almost the moment, or hour, in which he was new-born. Yet he might have more grace and be of a higher degree than some that were converted before him and lived longer after. God says in this case as to the sea: 'Thus far shalt thou go and no further.' As he appoints times and habitations, so he appoints estates and riches, to which they cannot pass. There is the measure of the gift of Christ, and the measure of the stature and of every part, and of faith (*Eph.* 4:7,13,16, *Rom.* 12:3). And as God has appointed who shall be members, so also the growth of each member. For they increase with the increase of God, of his appointment as well as his blessing and production (*Col.* 2:19). They are not to be all of the same stature, but according to the measure that is allotted to them.

(ix) Everyone shall have grace suitable and sufficient to his state and degree: the father for his, the young man for his, and so of the rest.

God will feed them all with the food convenient for them, to allude to Agur (*Prov.* 30:8). A babe shall have babe's grace, babe's food and raiment, babe's portion. And all the rest shall have what is suitable to and sufficient for them. What will fit and suffice one will not fit another, but the God of all grace (of all sorts and degrees) will fit and furnish them all. As our fathers according to the flesh give to their children according to their age and capacity, so does the Father of spirits give to his children.

As for talents, the Lord gave to every man according to his ability what was suitable for that task, place, office, or necessity entrusted to him. In case of temptation, he will not allow them to be tempted above what they are able (*1 Cor.* 10:13). Of duties, he lays on them nothing but what is necessary to their state and condition (*Acts* 15:28). Our

Saviour would not put new wine into old bottles; he would not require his disciples to fast, which was at that time a duty too hard for them (*Matt.* 9:15–17). He would not lay men's duties on babes, or children; no, he has a special tenderness for his little ones. He (as Jacob did his flocks) drives them gently, as they are able to go, as he does also those that are with young. And if his lambs faint, he takes them into his bosom (*Isa.* 40:11). He does not, as the Pharisees did, bind heavy burdens; or if he does, he will put in his helping hand.

God keeps a good table. He has several dishes: milk for babes and strong meat for grown persons. He takes care in the first place that Peter feeds his lambs, and then his sheep (*John* 21). The mother surely does not forget her sucking child, though she does not neglect the rest. The weak little ones shall be made much of and have the breast or the spoon often, because they cannot digest much at a time. Precept shall be upon precept, line upon line, here a little and there a little (*Isa.* 28:9–10).

God will give all their portion in due season and divide his word aright among them, so they shall have suitable benefits. He will give the tongue of the learned to some, that they shall know how to speak a word in season to him that is weary (*Matt.* 11:28) and to others also, as John did to fathers, young men, and children. He will not break the bruised reed nor quench the smoking flax. Yet he will not coddle the sinners, but use the rod as well as rebuke them sharply, that they may be sound in the faith. As their case and condition is, so they are dealt with.

Our Saviour would not say more to his disciples than they could bear (*John* 16:12), and he taught his apostles to tread in his steps. When Paul found the Corinthians to be only babes, he spoke to them and treated them accordingly (*1 Cor.* 3:1–2). So he did the Hebrews (chapter 5) who were dull of hearing. It does harm, and not good, to preach to persons otherwise than their capacities are. There is a time for all things, for everything is beautiful in its season. Sometimes new and sometimes old things must be brought out of the treasury; sometimes promises, at other times threatenings. The best is that which is fittest and most agreeable. We must not study what we can best preach, but what the people can best bear; we must not teach a babe as we would a child or a young man. A word fitly spoken is like apples of gold in pictures of silver, both inviting and captivating, being lovely and desirable, because they are both pleasing and profitable.

Whatever we do, to be sure, God feeds his people with food beneficial for them, giving every one their portion suitably, which is the beauty of it. He knows what everyone needs and will supply it. The grace that Paul had already received might have been sufficient for others, or for himself perhaps in another case, but being buffeted by Satan he needed more. Accordingly, God told him, 'My grace shall be sufficient for thee; I will give thee more strength than thou yet hast.' That is how Paul understands it (*2 Cor.* 12:9-10) and accordingly rejoices.

If you are a babe he will feed you (though only with milk), and you shall not lack what is best for you. If you are a little child he will smile on you and show you his love. If you are a young man he will strengthen you, and you shall overcome the wicked one. If you are a father, he will stir up your memory and cause you to remember and tell others the stories of what acquaintance you have had with him that is from the beginning. If your work is great and temptations strong, he will not be an Egyptian taskmaster to you, but will enable you with strength in your soul. If you are a weakling, he will uphold and succour you. Whatever your state, his grace shall be sufficient for you.

(x) It is seldom that any of these (unless the fathers) are eminent in the exercise of all graces, at least all alike.

Though the seed and root of every grace is in everyone, they do not spring up and grow in all alike. Certainly the class of babes is not eminent in any grace, not even in those which are their proper acts and by which they are marked. Their repentance, desire, and faith are imperfect and weak, but they are true. The little children are for love, and live less by faith because they live by a conscious knowledge of (the love of) the Father. The young men are strong in faith. The fathers have gone through all these and are filled with assurance and the riches of its joy.

There have been some persons eminent in some special graces, as Abraham for faith, Job for patience, and Moses for meekness. But few have been eminent in all grace, which may show that there are few in the uppermost form (the class of fathers) in the school of Christ. All have grace in some degree, but few have all grace to a high degree. As it is in gifts, it is also in graces, often (*1 Cor.* 12:8,18,29). Some excel in one thing and some in another.

The highest estate is the fathers, the next the young men, and so downward. The lower the form, the less and lower is the grace, and I fear that many who pretend high (perhaps so high as to be above all forms) will be found to be as low as babes and that they need to learn their very alphabet again.

(xi) Some (those appointed to pass and proceed from one state to another) grow up faster than others.

Some that shall be children, young men, and so on, do not reach that state as quickly as others. It is not here as in our university degrees, where at some time after a certain standing persons may commence, though they are not of equal learning and proficiency, to be called Masters of Arts, though they be master of none; or Doctors of Divinity, though they have yet to learn. No, it is not so here: God does not give his grace as men do. Some grow up suddenly, others by degrees and more leisurely.

Paul starts up immediately, and is so proficient that he has the right hand of fellowship given him by James, Cephas, and John (*Gal.* 2:9). The Thessalonians grew exceedingly beyond expectation (*2 Thess.* 1:3–4). Others come on more slowly like some grain, first the blade, then the ear, then the full corn in the ear (*Mark* 4:18). As some are long in travail and have hard labour before they are delivered, so some are long at the breast before they are weaned, and it is a great while before they can walk or speak. Time is required for most, as the apostle hints (*Heb.* 5:12), but some shoot up and become men in far less time than others do.

The reason for this in general is the distinguishing grace of God, who causes the increase of some to be swifter than that of others. All increase and fruit is from him, but some he blesses more abundantly, waters them every moment, and pours out more of his Spirit upon them at the very beginning than others have all their life long. Such was the case of Paul, who had a huge stock bestowed upon him at the very first. So he that had five talents at the first had more than he that accumulated four after a long time. Some get the start so much at first that others cannot overtake them by all their industry.

God gives what and how much he pleases, yet usually does this when such men are appointed to great undertakings and sufferings as Paul was. This was told at his first conversion and was the reason why he was so filled with the Holy Ghost – to the amazement of them that heard him – and he quickly increased the more in strength (*Acts* 9:15–22).

Or else, God gives much when such persons have not only much work to do but little time to do it in, being newly called and converted, as those who came late into the vineyard but (it seems) worked as much as, and perhaps better than, those who came in before. And perhaps it is so with the thief on the cross, for he acted a great deal of grace in that little time, and had not only hope but assurance, too, of being with Christ in Paradise. So when there are great sufferings, God fills them full, as it were, at first, as Stephen was, who suffered death soon after (*Acts* 6:5; chapter 7).

(xii) But though some grow faster than others, each of them shall sooner or later grow up to that measure of the stature of Christ to which they are appointed.

The babe that is to be a child by appointment shall be so by attainment, and so of the rest. No saint shall die till he has attained the utmost of what he was designed to. As none of God's elect die before they are converted, so no converted ones die till they come to their maturity and ripen, like a shock of corn, for the harvest of God. God gathers only ripe fruits, though some are ripe sooner than others. And I may say, some are summer and others winter fruit. Some die young and others old, yet there shall not be an infant of days or an old man that has not fulfilled his years, but everyone shall attain to his full stature (*Isa.* 65:20).

Our Saviour could not, as he told that fox Herod, be perfected till he had finished his work. It was then that his hour came (*Luke* 13:32–33). When any saint, like him, has glorified God on earth by finishing the work God has given him to do – and everyone has his task set him and his work cut out to his hands (*Eccles.* 9:10) – then shall he go to be glorified, as Christ did (*John* 17:4–5). As he could not die till then, so then he would not but die.

David was a man of a public spirit and served his generation according to the will of God; and what then? He fell asleep. When his work was done he went to rest in the bosom of God (*Acts* 13:36), though his body saw corruption, which Christ's body (who was without sin) did not see. Indeed, David thought to do more work, to build the temple, but that was reserved for another. And so, having done his measure, he fell asleep.

So it was with Paul. When the time of his departure was at hand, he was ready to be offered. For, he says, I have finished my course, I have run to the end of my race, I have nothing to do but to die (*2 Tim.* 4:6–8). So, too, the reverend good old man Simeon could not die till he had seen the salvation of God – and could not but die when he had seen it.

This then is the thing in hand, that God, having begun a good work, will finish it before he takes any of his converted ones out of this world. He will bring them to their appointed stature. Some may die in the good old age of fathers; others while young men in their prime, after great and glorious achievements and victories; others in their childhood, while their love is fervent and strong; and others in their babe state, with the milk in their mouth. But everyone before the time of his departure shall finish that work which was appointed for him to do.

(xiii) These states are not so constantly fixed and immutable; sometimes for a season there may be a variation.
To avoid misgivings and objections, it is necessary that I set this forth. A babe may have a spring-tide now and then, but he ebbs quickly and comes to low-water mark again. The child of light and love may walk in darkness;

God may so hide his face, that the child may not know his Father. The young man conqueror may be buffeted again and perhaps led captive and made a prisoner to a temptation. A fit of forgetfulness or sickness may befall a father and make him forgetful, that he may seem to be a child again.

But these intermissions, risings of the low and fallings of the high, do not alter their state. No, God measures none by particular acts or cases, but according to their constant tenor and course. The Corinthians made a great show, were doing a great deal, yet were babes. Paul himself was buffeted because he was apt to be puffed up. He prayed thrice before he had any answer, and yet he was a father even at that time. There may be some unevenness in the high and low and yet no alteration of their states.

The love and works at the church of Ephesus were more at first than when our Saviour sent her that epistle. And the church of Thyatira, her works were more at last than at first. Yet we cannot conclude from the partial decay of the former or the advance of the latter which was best at the last, for one might repent and the other not hold fast, which were the duties called for. But this we may clearly see, that great beginnings of zeal may be discontinued and decay.

On the other hand, small beginnings may increase more and more to godliness. Some persons run without weariness, walk without faintness, grow without intermission. They meet with no rubs, are not held back by a difficult time as some others are. It is said of the Colossians that from the very day they heard of the gospel and knew the grace of God in truth they bought forth fruit (*Col.* 1:6); there was no decay but growth. But the Hebrews, like the idle servant, stayed at a standstill and were babes for a long time. And indeed, they met

[38]

with many a stumbling-block in their way, which the apostle endeavoured to remove in that epistle, that they at last might go on to perfection.

So there is great variety in these things, the first last, and the last first very often; the younger born is the elder grown in grace. But no one can conclude infallibly as to particular persons what their estate is at present or shall be for the future.

(xiv) Seeing no one knows and no one can tell him what he is appointed to, everyone should aim to attain the highest state. Strive as many a common soldier strives to be a captain, many a young student to be a master, and many an apprentice to be not only a free-man or common-council man, but an alderman. This I say that none may be idle or negligent, but pursue perfection. Great things have been attempted upon mere possibilities, and it may come to be.

If you are but a babe at present and have been so for many years, who knows but you may be a father at last? Let no one therefore say, 'I have listened to sermons, prayed, and waited so long, and yet I see no more comes than did at first; so I will take up with this portion which I have.' Oh, let no one say so. Who knows but that after you have been planted in the house of the Lord and become well rooted and grounded, you may flourish as the palm tree and grow up as the cedars in Lebanon? You may be fat and flourishing and bring forth more fruit in your old age than you did in your youth (*Psa.* 42:12).

If God waters you with the dew of his blessing, you will not only blossom as the lily but cast forth roots as Lebanon; your branches and beauty shall spread and be as the olive tree (*Hos.* 14:5–6). The cloud that was at first but a hand-width at last covered the face of the heavens, and there was an abundance of rain (*1 Kings* 18:44–45).

[39]

The water that was at first to the ankles ascended to the knees, and from there upward to the waist. At last it was a river to swim in and not fordable it rose so high (*Ezek.* 47:3–5).

The mustard seed is little, yet grows to a great tree. So are the workings of grace in many a soul growing up more and more to perfection. Many a man that began with little, yet being faithful and industrious, has become master of a great estate. Do not be discouraged because great things are difficult and you are but little in Israel. Who knows what anyone may come to? Therefore, press forward. Our degrees, like times and seasons, are in the Father's power and are hidden from us to make us the more watchful and industrious.

(xv) God usually builds us up by that which he brought us in by, his Word and Spirit.

While we behold the glory of the Lord in the gospel glass, we are transformed into its image from glory to glory by the Spirit of the Lord (*2 Cor.* 3:18). The same Spirit that convinces of sin convinces of righteousness, and of judgement and victory, too (*John* 16:8). The gifts given to pastors and teachers as well as those given to apostles are for the perfecting of the saints, the edifying of the body of Christ, till we all come to a perfect man, to the measure of the stature of the fullness of Christ (*Eph.* 4:13).

Now it is clear that every part of the body has its measure (4:16). But the gospel and the gifts of ministers are left to perfect this measure in everyone, till all come and make up the whole body complete, which body is the fullness of Christ, who fills all in all, or supplies what every part has (*Eph.* 1:23).

The apostle tells Timothy how useful the Word is to make every man of God perfect, for it is profitable for four things. These may refer to these four states, for surely it was to make not only the preaching men of God perfect, but the hearing ones as well (*2 Tim.* 3:16–17). It is profitable for doctrine, to teach even fathers themselves; for reproof of young men if rash and proud; for correction of little children if wilful; for instruction in righteousness, which refers to babes, of whom it is expressly said that they are unskilful in the word of righteousness (*Heb.* 5:13)

We are born again, not of corruptible seed but of incorruptible, by the Word of God, which lives and abides forever. And this is the Word which by the gospel is preached to you (*I Pet.* 1:23–25; 2:1–2). So then, lay aside evil and, as newborn babes, desire the sincere milk of the Word that you may grow by it. God brings us in and builds us up by his Word.

And this I say, that the preaching of the gospel may not be worthless in any of your eyes, as if when a man were once converted or had attained to some degree of grace he were past listening. Oh no, you see plainly, that by which God begets us he brings us up; we grow by the Word as well as are begotten by it. And this till not just one or two, but till we all – every one – come to our perfect stature, so that the whole body and every member is perfect and entire, lacking nothing.

Having cleared the way, I shall now, God willing and enabling, consider the several classes in order, using several Scriptures which are to be found on these subjects. I hope to find more of this sort than are ordinarily thought of, this being a specific subject that I have never yet seen addressed by any person.

PART TWO

Babes

From 1 Corinthians 3:1–2 and Hebrews 5:11–14

The word 'babe' is used sometimes in a natural and other times in a metaphorical sense. In a natural sense, a child in the womb is called a babe: The babe leapt in my womb for joy (*Luke* 1:44). A child newly born is called a babe, as our Saviour once was: Ye shall find the babe wrapped in swaddling clothes (*Luke* 2:12). It is used also to denote children, boys and girls: Out of the mouths of babes and sucklings thou hast perfected praise (*Matt.* 21:15–16). Though the word 'babe' often refers to one that cannot speak, these were speaking and praising babes, for they cried Hosannah to the Son of David, and are called children. Lastly, the term is used indefinitely for children under age that survive their parents: They leave the rest of their substance to their babes (*Psa.*17:14). Such babes we call orphans.

When applied morally, the word babe is used in a metaphorical sense, first by way of commendation and excellence. Brethren, be not children in understanding, but in malice (or evil) be ye children, be ye babes; but in understanding be men, perfect (*1 Cor.* 14:20). Thus to be babes as to unacquaintedness with evil is an excellence worthy of our ambition.

Secondly, babe is used to humble and disparage, to set out persons' deficiencies in understanding and other

[45]

attainments (*Isa.* 3:4, opposed to verses 2–3). So babe is opposed to men, or being perfect in understanding (*1 Cor.* 13:11; 14:20), and is joined with foolish (*Rom.* 2:20). It is the same as being a servant in bondage to the rudiments of the world, as opposed to the adoption of sons or having the Spirit of sons (*Gal.* 4:1–6). It denotes instability; such babes are tossed to and fro (*Eph.* 4:14). In these places the word should be translated 'babes', and not 'children', as sometimes it is. It shows an ignorance or unskilfulness (*Heb.* 5:13), as opposed to those whose senses are practised to discern, and consequently to approve what is best.

It is in this metaphorical and moral sense that I shall speak of babes, and it is perhaps worth observing that *brephos* is used only once in this way (as I remember), and that by St Peter (*1 Pet.* 2:2); *nepios* is the word so frequently used by St Paul. But by both words is meant the same state of persons, as is clear from the fact that they both mention milk when they speak of these babes.

These metaphorical babes (whether young or old for years) are of a lower rank than the 'little children' whom St John addresses. I may demonstrate this not only from the different words used so frequently (which is not inconsiderable), but from the characters and attainments of the two states, which is the best proof, indeed, it is undeniable.

The word which in John is rendered 'little children' is used once by Paul to denote want or weakness of understanding: My brethren, be not children in understanding (*1 Cor.* 14:20). It is therefore as clear as the sun that the little children which John speaks of cannot be meant in this verse, for John attributes to them the excellence of knowing the Father. They are called little children because of their knowledge, which notes an understanding that amounts to assurance.

[46]

But babes (in nature or in grace) do not know their Father. So from this very characteristic it is apparent that the rank of babes is below that of little children. Children are sons and know it, but babes, though they are sons, do not know it, do not have the assurance that they are so. In this sense they are not reprobates, but only without clear evidence of faith, as the apostle says to the Corinthian babes (*2 Cor.* 13:5–6). They sought proof of Paul's apostleship, and he required proof of their conversion, but they were less able to provide proof than he was. He was not without proof, but they were. So though they had grace, it was so weak in its actions that it afforded them no assurance, as strong and vigorous grace does.

The starlight of their grace is not clear enough in babes for them to find their way by it, and many times it is clouded, too, and the stars do not appear. And though grace lives in their hearts, the light and comfort of it may yet be lacking. For though every man can reflect upon his own actions, can discern his thoughts and affections, and can tell what he loves, fears and grieves for, he may still be questioning and doubting whether his love, fear, and grief is gracious, spiritual, and truly holy or not.

The reason he questions and doubts is that though the spirit which is in a man knows the things of a man, it is only by an extra light of the Spirit, who works grace in us and is given to enlighten us (*1 Cor.* 2:11–12), that anyone can know the true worth of these things, and whether they are given him by God. Now without this light or testimony of the Spirit (which the little children have, but babes have not), it is with them as with the natural man, who knows not the things of the Spirit (*1 Cor.* 2:14). But the spiritual man, by the light of the Spirit, judges all things wrought in him by the Spirit.

Now to babes, not being spiritual but carnal (*1 Cor.*

3:1), the apostle could not write of such things as he did to the spiritual (*1 Cor.* 2:13). Instead, he was eager to feed them with milk, for they were not able to bear strong meat, having weak stomachs (*1 Cor.* 3:2). They, like the Hebrews, could hear of and believe in Christ in some way, but to take him as Christ crucified, as the Great High Priest, as their righteousness, they had a great deal yet to learn and digest. This was the case with both the Corinthian and the Hebrew babes (*1 Cor.* 3:2, *Heb.* 5:10–11).

So then, by these distinct attainments and characteristics it is plain, I hope, that there is a class of babes in Christ who are a degree below the 'little children'.

I shall speak of babes first, because they are the beginning of the new creation of God. And I am apt to believe that the kingdom of God and of Christ, in heaven and in earth, is filled more with these than with any other sort. That is not to say more than all the other sorts together, but that there are more babes in Christ than there are children or young men or fathers.

Though I do not doubt that the little children spoken of by our Saviour in Mark 10:14 are meant in a natural and literal sense, perhaps the words may bear a testimony in a fuller sense than is commonly understood. 'Suffer the little children to come to me, and forbid them not, for *of such* is the kingdom of God': of infants or babes – for so *paidia* must there signify, Christ taking them into his arms (*Mark* 10:16). It is of infants, I say, (both in a natural and spiritual sense) that the kingdom of heaven consists, as well as, if not more than, of others.

Speaking on their attainments and characters, I shall consider 1 Corinthians 3:1–2 and Hebrews 5:10–6:3. In both passages the apostle uses the same words concerning them, and the explanation of the milk and meat in Corinthians is clear and full in Hebrews.

[48]

The apostle speaks much about the Spirit, spiritual things, spiritual men, and of the wisdom of God to them that were perfect (*1 Cor.* 2:6), that is, those who can judge and discern spiritual things (*1 Cor.* 2:15). Then at the beginning of chapter 3, he anticipates an objection that the Corinthians might make: 'Why then do you not preach such things to us?'

To this he answers that he would gladly and with all his heart do it, but that they were not spiritual, but as carnal, being babes, and did not have, neither before nor at present, the capacity to receive them: If you must know the true reason why I do not preach to you the deep mysteries of godliness, or the wisdom of God in a mystery, or the hidden wisdom of God (*1 Cor.* 2:7), it is not that I cannot or do not want to preach it, but that you cannot bear it. You would say that to eat his flesh and drink his blood and live by it was difficult teaching, as they did when Christ himself said so (*John* 6:53–60). And if you can hardly hear this without being offended, what if I should preach of his ascension, and the executing of the other part of his priestly office now in heaven, which is yet a higher doctrine and strong meat (as it is called in Hebrews 5:11–14)? If that offends you as the Saviour intimates it did them (*John* 6:60–62) how much more would this? For this reason, my brothers, I could not speak to you as to someone spiritual, but as to someone carnal, feeding you with milk (the very alphabet of Christ's doctrine). I am eager to preach to you, as to sinners and carnal unconverted persons, the very same doctrine that I did at first.

Let us see how this parallels the text of Hebrews 5. The author had told them that Christ Jesus being made perfect, that is, glorified, had become the author of salvation to them that believe in and obey him; that he was called of God a High Priest after the order of

Melchisedek; and that there were many more things to say (*Heb.* 5: 8–11). 'Why do you not tell on and speak out, then?' Why, because they are hard to be uttered, says he. This does not imply any defect or inability to utter them, as if he lacked knowledge or speech, but an incapacity in his listeners to grasp them, because they were dull of hearing. For though as to their standing they might have been teachers, yet as to their understanding, they needed to learn, to go over again the first principles. Like the Corinthians, they needed milk: to be taught and repent and believe as if they were scarcely converted, and as carnal.

Thus, both these Scriptures agree in the same subjects and attributes. I shall here briefly note a few observations from these two texts, to make our way more plain and smooth:

(i) There are some Christians, or persons in Christ, who are not men in Christ, but only babes.
They have the Spirit of Christ in a measure, or else they could not be his (*Rom.* 8:9). Yet though they have the Spirit, they are not spiritual in any high degree. They are in Christ Jesus, for otherwise they would not be newborn or new creatures (*2 Cor.* 5:17), but they are yet babes in Christ and the very next degree to carnal. They cry rather than speak; their voice is inarticulate and indistinct (*1 Cor.* 13:11).

They have been translated from death to life; they are not miscarried or stillborn. They have the beginning of life, and they just begin to live. There is joy in heaven that this man-child is born, though he is not yet grown up or thoroughly washed from his pollution. He is still in swaddling clothes and in a manger, if I may allude to what was said of Christ.

They have the image of God upon them, but not

[50]

perfectly stamped. The features are not yet discernible. Yet this you can say: It is not the devil's or the sinner's image. And God knows that it is his image, and Christ knows it to be the Father's image, for it is born not of the flesh, nor of the will of man, but of the will of God. They could not have the name of babes if they did not have the Father's image, though the image is not so visible to onlookers as that of the spiritual man is. The babe is a Christian in the smallest print, but the spiritual man is one in capital and golden letters.

(ii) Some persons may be only babes for a long time (Heb. 5:12), though they live under the best preaching in the world.
Indeed, some of those were under Christ's own ministry (*Matt.* 11:25). Many of the disciples were not better till Christ ascended and the Spirit descended.

The Corinthians had heard three of the best preachers on earth: Paul, Apollos, and Cephas (*1 Cor.* 1:12; 4:6), yet were only babes. The Hebrews had sat under similar ministry, but were babes for many years. Paul had begotten, or planted, the Corinthians. He was their father (*1 Cor.* 4:15) and had continued a year and a half teaching the Word of God among them (*Acts* 18:11). Apollos was their nursing father, who had come to Corinth and watered them after Paul's departure (*1 Cor.* 3:6, *Acts* 18:27). Yet from that time to the date of this epistle, they continued babes.

Philip was called by Christ Jesus in the beginning of Christ's first year of ministry, before his first miracle at the wedding in Cana (*John* 1:43; 2:11). Yet this Philip, who had lived with Christ all the time of his ministry, was yet, when Christ was about to leave the world, but a babe, for he did not know the Father. And this made Christ upbraid him (*John* 14:9): 'Have I been so long a time with you, and yet hast thou not known me, Philip?

[51]

He that hath seen me hath seen the Father, and how sayest thou then, Show us the Father?' Alas! Of how many listeners may many a preacher say, Have I been so long with you, and yet you do not know the Father! You do not have the knowledge of God, may it be spoken to your shame (*1 Cor.* 15:34). You are still in a babyish state, and not grown or advanced in faith, knowledge, or love.

(iii) These babes can eat milk, though nothing but milk.
The Corinthians had been nursed a year and a half and were not weaned, but were babes and sucklings still. They could eat only milk. Their stomachs were not able to bear strong meat, though their appetite might desire it. Christ Jesus, when telling his disciples the offices of the Spirit, stops and tells them, 'I have yet many things more to say to you, but you cannot bear them yet' (*John* 16:12). I could tell you what great things there are in mine and my Father's heart and purpose concerning you, but you are not in a condition to receive them till you have received the Spirit and grown up to a higher state.

Babes cannot understand mathematical and metaphysical demonstrations, but they can receive stories, illustrations and parables; and so Christ taught them (*Mark* 4:33). To tell them that there is joy in heaven at the conversion of a sinner will not go down with them unless taught by the parable of a lost and found sheep. Babes live by sense more than by faith.

The Hebrews understood little of the priesthood of Christ, which is strong meat, although the apostle illustrated it by their own shadowy priesthood which they had under the law. The apostle Peter spoke of the state of renewal in the new heavens and the new earth, of which his beloved brother Paul had also written. Among these things, some were hard to be understood. By whom? By the unlearned and unstable. And therefore he pressed them not only to steadfastness but to growth in grace, without which they would not attain to knowing the things hard to understand (*2 Pet.* 3:13–17).

But they could not eat strong meat, only milk. And though only milk, it was yet milk. This implies that they were not only alive, but had some little strength. They took in some nourishment and had some experience of the working of grace in them, though weak and faint. Says the apostle, I have fed you with milk. So not only did he give it to them, but though they did not thrive much, it kept them alive in their present weak state. What this milk is I shall next show.

(iv) These babes, as well as the spiritual ones, are called brethren by the apostle.

Though they did not have the right hand, still they had the left hand, of fellowship. He says, Though you are still weak, you and I are brethren. The spiritual Paul, and the Corinthian babes, who were as carnal, were brothers. Not only Paul, but Christ himself, the firstborn among many brethren, is not ashamed to call the babes, as well as others, brethren (*Heb.* 2:11–14). For Christ took the whole seed of Abraham (*Heb.* 2:16). And if any are Christ's, as those babes are, then they are Abraham's seed, and heirs according to promise (*Gal.* 3:29). The whole brotherhood have fellowship one with another, as have all the members of the body from head to foot.

These babes, then, have truth of grace, the root of grace is in them. God has put truth in their inward parts and written the truth of repentance, faith and love in their hearts. They are true-born, and not illegitimate, as the distinction is (*Heb.* 12:8).

But their grace is weak; it is grace in a low degree. It is

also mixed with much corruption, and strong corruptions demonstrate weak grace. Of all saints, the babe-saint has the least grace and the most corruption.

And (and this is to be noted of all the rest also), these babes are so-called not only because they are newly born, but because they continue in such a state. No state is measured by one or two acts, but from the tenor and course of their hearts and lives for some duration. We call no one a dunce or a bad scholar from one day's dullness, or for one mistake in an exercise, but when he is constantly dull and thick, as the Hebrews were, who were babes for a long time. It is the habit that marks this and every class.

THEIR FEEDING ON MILK

The attainment of these babes is expressed in both texts by their feeding on milk. Milk is the food of babes, and therefore, to better understand their state and attainment, we must know what this milk is.

In general, all the Word of God (the gospel) is called milk (*1 Pet.* 2:2). As newborn babes, desire the sincere milk of the word, that you may grow by it; this milk is for growth. The Word is not only for begetting (*1 Pet.* 1:23–25), but it is for nourishing and bringing up also, to a perfect stature (*Eph.* 4:11–16).

It is observed that Peter does not speak merely of the Word written in the Bible, but of the Word preached (*1 Pet.* 1:25). But then this word preached must be the sincere milk of the Word, not mixed and corrupted by the devices, inventions, and comments of Jews or Gentiles. This is what the Apostle Paul disclaims and speaks against (*2 Cor.* 2:17). We are not as many who corrupt or deal deceitfully with the Word of God, but we speak in Christ from sincerity in the sight of God. We have renounced the hidden things of dishonesty, not walking in craftiness, or handling the Word of God deceitfully, but by manifestation of the truth commending ourselves to every man's conscience in the sight of God. We are not hucksters like some others mentioned (*2 Cor.* 4:2:).

As this word must not be mixed with and corrupted by false doctrine and base ends, so this milk must not be sweetened with the sugar and honey of men's wisdom and eloquence. The apostle disowns and disallows this also (*1 Cor.* 2:4). My speech and my preaching, he says, was not with enticing words of man's wisdom. I did not use pretentious words to show wit and learning; I did not come with witticisms (*1 Cor.* 1:17) but in demonstration of the Spirit and power. So then it is not a sound of words, but sound and sincere doctrine or milk of the word by which we grow and thrive.

But more particularly, milk is used to denote weak nourishment, and is opposed to strong meat. And thus, milk means the first principles of the oracles of God (*Heb.* 5:12; 6:1), the alphabet of the Christian religion. Of this the babes have their mouths and bellies full but are weak and puny notwithstanding. So in these texts, milk represents the very foundation of repentance, which is that the kingdom of God (the Messianic dispensation) was at hand (*Mark* 1:15). Milk denotes preparation doctrine, the initiating doctrine, where the Jews and Christians agreed as a foundation to build upon. Now, what this doctrine was is expressed under several heads (*Heb.* 6:1–2): repentance from dead works, faith towards God, and others.

Some may object: Here is no mention of faith in Christ; can they be Christians in any degree, even only babes, who do not believe in Christ? To this I answer that those principles or foundation doctrines are called the word or doctrine of Christ (*Heb.* 6:1), and therefore this repentance and faith is not without respect to Christ. When the apostle mentions these two elsewhere, he speaks of Christ as the object of faith, testifying both to the Jews and to the Greeks repentance towards God and faith in our Lord Jesus Christ (*Acts* 20:21). This the apostle taught the Corinthians at first (*1 Cor.* 2:2; 15:2–3). In calling this the foundational doctrine, Christ must be included, for other foundations can no man lay (*1 Cor.* 3:11) because God has laid him and no other (*Acts* 4:11–12), and it is by him that we believe in God (*1 Pet.* 1:21). Moreover, we must remember that these were but babes, were unskilful in the word of righteousness, and were not without some confused notions.

Indeed, both God and Christ are the objects of faith. And though God is the ultimate object of faith, for Christ's design is to bring us to God (*1 Pet.* 3:18), Christ is the more immediate object. But nature teaches us to look to God, and revelations of grace teach us only to look to Christ. Therefore many persons, especially babes, are apt to have more recourse to God than to Christ. For the faith of babes is no more developed than theirs generally was under the Old Testament. They did not have such distinct notions of Christ Jesus as we under the gospel have, or ought to have, now that Christ is manifested to manage all affairs between the Father and us.

Therefore our Saviour bids his disciples to believe not only in God, but in him also (*John* 14:1). Accordingly afterwards, the apostles in their preaching direct men to believe in Christ Jesus. This is the excellence of knowing, or the excellent knowledge of Christ Jesus: to know him so as to be found in him, not having our own righteousness which is of the law, which babes too much seek after, but that which is by faith in Christ (*Phil.* 3:8–9).

This is what the apostle directs the Corinthians to (*1 Cor.* 1:30; 3:10–11). And to the Hebrews he sets forth Christ as a High Priest after the order of Melchisedek, the king of righteousness, and the Lord our righteousness.

I conclude, then, that their eating of milk is the receiving and practising of these principles, the beginning of the doctrine of Christ. In general, repentance and faith take in such things as a sense of sin, together with sorrow for and repentance from it; prayer for pardon; reliance on the mercy of God in Christ Jesus, which gives them hope; an obedience to ordinances, as baptism; and believing in the resurrection and eternal judgement.

But there are sealings of the Spirit, joys in the Holy Ghost, which the babes are not acquainted with. They attain only to what is necessary to salvation (*Heb.* 6:9). They have enough to keep them out of hell and to land them safe in heaven. But as to the well-being of a saint, that is, an assurance of the Father's love, which the little children have; strength of faith to overcome temptations, which the young men have; great wisdom from much experience, which the fathers have – of these they know nothing. They are God's building indeed (*1 Cor.* 3:9), but only the first storey just laid upon the foundation. Yet they, too, are the temple of God, and the Spirit of God dwells, though almost indiscernibly, in them (*1 Cor.* 3:16). They will, I say, have an entrance into heaven, because these things are in them, but not an abundant entrance, because these things do not abound in them, as Peter intimates (*2 Pet.* 1:8–11).

And all this is spoken of a state in which they may live and die and not reach beyond it.

GROWTH IN BABES

Before I proceed, it is necessary to clear up one objection

that may arise: If growth of grace is necessary to prove the truth of grace, how can these be said to grow, if they may continue in this state all their days?

You may remember how I premised that no one can tell whether he may be built up a storey or more higher, and therefore no one should be content to take up with this portion only, but press forward. Yet seeing there is such a state in which some may continue to abide, I first concede that growth of grace is indeed required of all as the evidence of its truth.

But then I say there are several kinds of growth; and as the state is, such is the growth required. There is a growth by addition, and a growth of continuation and perseverance and going on to the end; one kind of growth is required of the other states, but another is necessary to the state of babes. The others' growth is by addition (2 Pet. 1:5-11), but growth of babes is by abiding in grace. They learn the same lesson over and over, when others go on to new ones. Or they are like trees that grow continuing to bring forth the fruits of their kind (Gen. 1:11). But if a graft of a nobler sort were grafted onto them, then they would bring forth other and better fruit.

So, growth in babes is not an addition of new grace, but a renewing of and abounding in their first grace. This must be the growth of the Corinthians and Hebrews, or else there would be none at all, for they are the same after a long time as they were before. And therefore Paul asks the Corinthians only to prove, for the present, that they are in the faith, and that Christ is in them (2 Cor. 13:5). And he tells the Hebrews to give diligence to a full assurance (Heb. 6:11); yet supposing they shall not attain it, he often calls upon them to hold fast and not to apostatize. And if they do not advance, yet they might be saved by abiding in the present state, though they are babes (*Heb.* 3:6–14; 10:23–35). He tells them that the just shall live by faith, which they have. That is, they should continue believing to the end, and not draw back to perdition (*Heb.* 10:35–39).

To clarify this point, let us consider some other places which show that continuing in the same grace, or holding fast to what they have, is all that is required of some Christians (*Rev.* 2:24–25). It is said to them of Thyatira, who kept free from Jezebel's doctrine: I will put upon you no other burden, but that which you have already; hold fast till I come, keep your ground. Again, in Revelation 3:8,11–12, it is said to Philadelphia, who had but a little strength: Hold fast that which thou hast; and to him that overcometh, etc.

So perseverance in the little strength that any have carries the promise of salvation, and is all the growth of some saints. He that continues to the end shall be saved, and this is called overcoming, which has the notion of some kind of growth in it. And therefore it seems clear that the gain of babes is in not losing, and their growth in not decreasing. Or, if you would rather express it: The babes' growth is in reiterated acts, or abounding in acts of the same kind, which is a growth in degree. And, as I shall show shortly, their growth is also in desires after higher attainments: eating more and more milk, repenting more and more, and believing more and more, even to the end, increasing in these things to their fullness, and yet not in passing into another state.

Before closing this section, we shall look briefly at the covenant of God made with all saints, and the promises of God made only to some saints. The promises of growth by addition, I humbly suggest, are made not to all saints, but to saints expressing certain graces in duties to certain degrees. For instance, in Psalm 1:3 there is a promise of growth, but it is not made to every saint, but to those who delight in the law of the Lord and in his law meditate day and night. This meditation shall be to them as the watering of the river is to a tree.

But as for the covenant: As it gives grace, so it secures it. It is made with the lowest saint, and it ensures against falling away: I will put my fear in their hearts, and they shall not depart from me (*Jer.* 32:40). Christ prayed for Peter that his faith might not totally and utterly fail (*Luke* 22:32). This I speak for the encouragement of poor babes, that they may not stumble when they do not grow as others do. I would have them bless God that they grow with a growth suitable to their state. They rely and cleave close, they do not apostatize but hold fast, they persevere in eating milk till death do them part. They attain to the extent of the covenant, which is perseverance, and to the end of their faith, which is the saving of their souls.

BABES' ATTAINMENTS, IN GENERAL (FROM HEBREWS 6:1–2)

The apostle is not here telling the babes to lay aside the first principles, but is speaking of his own intention to go on to address other and higher matters, more complete doctrine suitable for grown saints. He calls these doctrines foundations, and therefore doubtless would not have them dug up, but would have more and higher storeys built on them, even to the laying of the top stone. At present he only names them to show what these babes had attained to.

These six principles are, as I may call them, six portions of milk, which the babes ate and were nourished by. The first two, repentance and faith, are internal graces working in them. The other four are proofs of this internal work. Two of these, their submissions to the ordinances of baptism and laying on of hands, are proofs of their conversion in the sight of men. The other two, their practical belief of the resurrection and eternal judgement, are proofs of their conversion in the sight of God.

And these should not be separated, for submitting to ordinances without believing in the resurrection and eternal judgement are not proofs of repentance and faith. No, for without this faith, the ordinance is in vain and men are yet in their sins (*1 Cor.* 15:12–17). And else what shall they do that are baptized for the dead, if the dead rise not at all? why are they then baptized for the dead? Baptism is submitted to in vain if there is no resurrection. Indeed, the very notion and design of baptism is to denote the resurrection from death (*Rom.* 6:3–5, *Col.* 2:12–13).

On the other hand, to believe in the resurrection and judgement, as the Jews did, without submitting to ordinances of baptism, etc., is no proof of conversion, either. Therefore, when our Saviour charged his disciples to preach the gospel, it is that he who believes and is baptized shall be saved (*Mark* 16:16).

So, all these principles together are the babe's attainment. I shall now speak on each as they appear in the text.

REPENTANCE FROM DEAD WORKS

Repentance is the first milk which they suck, take in and best of all digest. They repent not only for but from dead works, that is, the works done by those who are dead in sin (*Eph.* 2:1–3). They escape the gross pollutions which are in the world through lust.

The other portion of milk, faith, is harder for them to digest; it stays long in their mouths before they swallow. For, says the text, it is but faith towards God, it is only in orientation, in acting rather than acted. And the faith is not so much towards Christ as towards God – not excluding Christ, but they have less skill in exercising faith towards Christ than towards God. They are able to enact repentance better than faith.

(i) Repentance is the first milk that babes eat.
This will be seen by considering who are babes, and accounted babes, throughout the whole of Scripture.

Most of the people of God under the Old Testament were babes. There were indeed some fathers, for example Abraham. But there was, as I may say, only one of a sort, as Abraham the father of the faithful, Job of the patient, and Moses of the meek. There were also some young men who were strong and overcame the evil one, as Joshua and Caleb, who followed God fully; the word of God did abide in them.

But there were babes in abundance, as the apostle tells us (*Gal.* 4:3–4). When we were children (the word is 'babe' in verse 4), when we were under the law, we were in a state of bondage, more like servants than children (*Gal.* 4:7). And accordingly, the milk given these to eat was the doctrine of repentance, for Christ Jesus was under a veil and was represented to them mostly in types and shadows, and their faith was towards God and Christ.

The people of John the Baptist's time were generally just babes, and therefore he also fed them with milk, the doctrine of repentance, yet still directing their faith to Christ who was to come after him. His doctrine and baptism was that of repentance.

While Christ was in the world, most of the disciples were babes, as was mentioned above. And Christ himself gave them milk for their first feeding, yet mixed with faith (*Mark* 1:15): Repent and believe the gospel, which is called the beginning of the gospel of Christ (*Mark* 1:1, *Heb.* 6:1). They also believed in God, and our Saviour called upon them to believe in him also, as an advance of their faith (*John* 14:1-4). All at first conversion are babes, and to all these repentance is better known than faith for some time. The first doctrine preached to the first converts was repentance (*Acts* 2:38), and those appointed to be no more than babes feed on this milk all their days.

(ii) Babes digest repentance and are better at it than at faith and love.

They are best at repentance; it is their excellence, the chief of their attainments. Not that they are better at it than the saints of higher forms. But because the babes have more need of it, they are more skilled at it than they are at other graces, it being more their trade and occupation.

Most of the Jewish saints under the Old Testament were continually repenting and returning, a word in great use under that dispensation, and in weeping and mourning, which belong to repentance.

So it was in John's time: The fruits were to be such as were worthy of, or agreeable to, repentance as their highest pitch (*Luke* 3:8).

And in Christ's own time, Peter's weeping bitterly and other similar acts were found among the disciples, as the best of what they had attained to.

Also in Hebrews, this took first place, that they repented from dead works, the babes who still were unskilful as to the word of righteousness. The Corinthians, among whom were so many babes, were famous for repenting (*2 Cor.* 7:10-11).

(iii) Repentance includes: the sense of sin, sorrow and confession, and reformation.

a) The sense of sin: The first work of the Spirit is to give a sense of sin, which not only lets men see it, but makes them feel it, that they may sense what an evil thing it is to be a sinner. In lands where the gospel is preached, there are indeed some common principles, like seeds, scattered here and there in the hearts of men, before this powerful conviction comes upon them and the way is made for conversion. Such men know not only that there is a God, and that he ought to be worshipped, which the heathen also know, but that the will of God is the rule of worship; that this will and rule are revealed in the Scripture, where we learn what the good is which we ought to do, and the evil which we ought to leave undone; that he who transgresses this law sins; that whoever sins deserves the wages of sin; that every sinner stands in need of a redeemer and mediator; that Jesus Christ, Immanuel, the Son of God and the Virgin Mary, is this redeemer and mediator; and that salvation from Christ is by faith in him.

But though these principles are professed, and God makes use of them to work in men, they do not amount to a powerful and converting conviction without the Spirit of God giving them a particular application and sending them home. How many have this common notion that they are sinners, indeed, that they are such sinners, as swearers, drunkards, impure, etc., yet they are far from seeing the ugliness and feeling the burden of sin, so as to repent it? The conviction I speak of is accompanied with a sense called pricking of heart (*Acts* 2:27), caused most usually by some particular sin.

Experience tells us that men are convinced not of a bad nature, but of a bad life; the tree is known by its fruit. Hazael would not believe the prophet that he had such a perverse nature; no, nor Peter that he had such a treacherous heart, till sad experience made the conviction. It is by conviction of a *particular* sin, of either omission or commission, that men come to believe the more general corruption of their nature, and their confession and reformation begins there. And I think the examples of converted ones will demonstrate this. The sight and sense of sin which babes have leading them to repentance, then, is of sin in the fruit, more than in the root; of sinful lives more than of sinful hearts, though this also comes by degrees afterward.

The deceitfulness and desperate wickedness of the heart was a thing that not many were much convinced of (*Jer.* 17:9). No, nor were the disciples in Christ's own time, for our Saviour told them that they were without understanding in this point (*Matt.* 15:15–29). And the apostle cautions the Hebrew babes to take heed lest there be an evil heart of unbelief or any root of bitterness in them, more than they were aware of. Few babes know what is latent in their hearts. Peter told Christ upon occasion that he was a sinner, yet would not believe that his heart was as sinful as Christ told him he would find it to be.

Babes are generally as carnal and like other men in that they know they sin but do not know where it comes from. Therefore they commonly charge it upon the devil and his temptation, rather than upon themselves and their own corrupt natures, if not on God himself (*James* 1:13–15).

b) Sorrow and confession: The second step or degree of repentance is confession of and sorrow for sin, without which there is no true repentance. I put them both into one, because they go together. It is godly sorrow that leads to a full repentance, and this sorrow cannot be kept in. It is as coals of fire in the bosom, breaking out in confessions, lamentation, and self-abhorrence. As there is a sight and sense, so there will be sighs and groans in true penitents. A woman may as well be delivered of a child in a dream and without pain, as a soul repent without sorrow. And this sorrow is accompanied by confessions and complaints to God.

And this is how these things are in, and expressed by, babes: The thing which pinches most, and consequently comes first out in confession, is the particular sin they were convinced of. Take a new convert at prayers, and I warrant you, that you will hear him telling God sad, sad stories of what he was convinced of, be it good omitted, or evil committed, be it whatever sin.

I take it to be an infallible rule that according to the sight and sense, such is the sorrow and complaint. It is with these souls as it is with children playing in the dust: They are not so much concerned for all the rest, as for that which falls into their eyes. They brush off the rest without much ado, but at the dust in their eyes they fall crying. It is said of Paul, as soon as converted, Behold, he prays; and had you overheard him, doubtless you would have heard sad bemoanings of his persecuting the saints, a thing which stuck close to him, as a thorn in his flesh, all his days.

It is to be observed also that there is a great deal of legal bondage cleaving to their sorrow, as dross to gold. For as yet they mourn more for sin as against and a burden to themselves, than as against and a burden to God; more as it stands in the way of their own peace and salvation, than of the glory of God, though that also has a little place. Woe unto us, we have rewarded evil unto our own souls, they say in the Old Testament.

A grown saint, when he sorrows for sin, does not leave out the consideration of the evil it has done to himself, and God allows it should be so. Yet what goes most to his heart, as it did to David's (*Psa.* 51), is that 'against thee, against thee only I have sinned'. He could better bear his broken bones, his own shame and pain, than the sense that he had grieved and dishonoured his God.

But the weakness of poor babes, to which yet God will be merciful, is that whereas they heave a sigh now and then for God's sake, they heave many for their own. They are best at that which comes more naturally, at sorrowing for sin because they have wronged themselves. But faith and hope are altogether supernatural and so are more feebly acted out by them.

Again, you may observe that as the sight and sense of a particular sin first awakened them, so that one *alone* alarms them, and they think that no other sins, or even all the others together, are such a cloud between God and them as that one sin. And they are not so much interested in a general pardon, as in the pardon of that one sin. Indeed, they sometimes cry out in general, 'Wretch that I am! Who shall deliver me from this body of death?' But their most common complaint is of such particular sins and of the kind in which Satan generally has a hand. But as for the secret lurkings, or lust, the stealings away of the heart from God, private pride, worldly love, etc., these things, which are the great trials of grown saints, are taken little notice of by the babes.

Where they do sorrow, it is true they sorrow greatly and sometimes, like Rachel, refuse to be comforted. They are sometimes in danger of being swallowed up with overmuch sorrow and despair. There are two reasons for their sorrow and despair.

Firstly, they have a sense of sin, but not of forgiveness. They are convinced of sin, but not of righteousness. Now though the sense of a pardon does not take away all sorrow for sin, it takes away the excess of it, and also the curse and bondage. But because this is not fully understood by babes, they sorrow many times as men without hope.

Secondly, they find their corruption still strong and unsubdued, and so their sorrow continues to grow. Because their sin is not conquered, they think it never will be, but they shall one day perish. Though they have repented, the taste and bitterness of their former sins is often kept fresh and strong by Satan, and they fear and mourn desperately. But this sorrow itself needs sorrowing for, it is so base and mercenary; for they even think to make amends with God this way, repaying God with so much sorrow for so much sin, without looking to Jesus Christ, the propitiation and the advocate, as they ought.

Besides the confirmation of this gained from the experience of young converts, all is amply demonstrated by the story of the prodigal (*Luke* 15). After being long dead in sin, he comes to himself and is convinced of his wicked living and consequently of his own lost, undone, and perishing condition – which is the very hinge upon which he turns about to go to his father. The first sense is not of sin against God, though that comes afterward, but against himself. He resolves to go and confess his sin, and to bind himself to God and serve him for wages as a hired servant. But as soon as the father has kissed him and assured him of his love, though he goes on to confess his sin, he says not a word more of being a hired servant.

So these poor babes, they come to God in an emotional state and bind themselves like hirelings. They are afraid of being damned, and rather than be so, they will serve God with prayers and tears day and night. But after God has kissed them, they abide in the house as the sons that serve him, and not as servants.

The grown saints do much in a little, whereas babes do little, though they make much ado in all they do. Love

[68]

and faith do more in a day than fear will be able to do in many days or years.

c) Reformation: The highest degree of repentance is not only for but from dead works. There are reformation and fruits worthy of and suitable to repentance. Men that repent do not only say, 'What have I done?' and mourn for that, but, 'What, Lord, wilt thou have me to do?' And they submit to a way of obedience.

When John the Baptist called for fruits worthy of repentance (*Luke* 3:7–14), the people asked, 'What shall we do?' and the publicans, 'What shall we do?' and the soldiers, 'What shall we do?' To all these he gave directions to leave their former, their particular sins, and to lead new lives directly contrary to their former lives, which is the proper fruit of penitents. When they were pricked at heart (*Acts* 2:37) they cried out, 'What shall we do?' and the jailer (*Acts* 16), 'Sirs, what must I do?' and Paul himself (*Acts* 9), 'Lord, what wilt thou have me to do?' True penitents aim not only for humbling, but for reformation. They repent not only for but from dead works; the babes do so.

How, or in what sense?

Dead works are the sins they lived in before conviction and conversion, according to the course of the world and of the devil (*Eph.* 2:1–3). There are other sins which are deadly workings, for to be carnally minded is death (*Rom.* 8:6). But these cannot in a strict sense be called dead works, which are the sins of men dead in trespasses and sins. So, though grown saints mortify not only the flesh but the lusts and affections, too, the babes go scarcely further than leaving the works of the flesh, the sins in which they lived before conversion.

Thus did the prodigal. He spent no more of his time and substance on harlots and riotous living. Zaccheus began with mercy and restitution for any wrongs he had done to any (*Luke* 19:8). And so with Paul, from persecuting to preaching Christ (*Acts* 9). The jailer, from making wounds, turns surgeon and binds up the wounds which he had made (*Acts* 16). Throughout the Scripture you will find that babes become clean contrary to themselves; you shall not find them retaining the sins which they were first convicted as guilty of. This is their repentance from dead works.

So the first attainment of babes is their eating of the first portion of gospel milk, repentance from dead works.

Application

a) For those who have not repented, and so are not babes:

Alas! there are all too many who live under the preaching and profession of the gospel and are called Christians, who have not received into themselves this first spoonful of milk or learned the first principle of repentance from dead works. Though men profess the common principles which I named above, they have eyes and do not see, ears and do not hear, so as to understand with their heart, to be converted and healed. Their hearing and seeing does not affect their hearts; they are still without a sense and feeling of sin.

How many know drunkenness, uncleanness, and other things to be sins, and that they live in such sins, yet are not touched at heart? They never yet saw sin so as to feel it, or so felt it as to confess and be sorry for it, or never so confessed or sorrowed as to repent from dead works, to cry out, 'What have I done!' or 'Lord, what wilt thou have me to do?' They have done more than enough to undo themselves, have been told the way of recovering and saving themselves, and yet these things are but to them as idle tales. And we are to them (as Lot to his sons-in-law) like those that mock, that flatter them with promises or scare them with threatenings, as if we were not in earnest.

But in order that they may yet at last be awakened, and if God may yet give them repentance, I entreat them to consider these things:

(i) Consider this, that all the common principles which you have received from the light of nature, law, or gospel, will not be sufficient to justify, but they will condemn you (Rom. 1:18–21; 2:14–27). Our Lord Jesus Christ will one day sit in judgement upon men, and he will then convince and condemn them from their own principles. Men's consciences will be one of the books that shall then be opened, and they will be self-condemned.

For example: Suppose Christ Jesus asked these questions: 'Did you not believe and know that there was a God?' 'Yes, Lord, we did,' is the answer. 'Why then did you not serve him? Did you not believe that his word declared his will?' 'Yes, Lord,' says conscience. 'Why then did you not obey his word?' And so on. Men will be speechless and silent, having nothing to say for themselves, as he that came without a wedding garment. If your principles do not convince you now, they will condemn you hereafter, and you will cry out when it is too late, 'My perdition is of myself, even I being judge, I have rewarded evil to my own soul.'

(ii) Consider how many times God has been knocking at your door, and how long waiting to be gracious to you. How many times have you been smitten at a sermon and trembled like Felix? How often have you been almost persuaded, as Agrippa, to be a Christian? How many times have you purposed and promised to sin no more, and yet after all this, you have given up yourself to sin, and like another Ahab, sold yourself to work wickedness? How you have eaten, drunk, played and slept away the

convictions that have been upon you, how you have forgotten, or smothered and put off these things, saying, 'It is true, sin is an ugly thing, but it has its pleasure for the present; but there is time enough, and I intend to repent hereafter. Others are as bad as I, and yet we escape well enough.' Only a qualm and misgiving comes over us now and then, but it goes away again. 'Ministers must have leave,' you say, 'because it is their place to reprove sin, but God is merciful,' and so on.

Thus do many put off all convictions, and though they have been gashed and wounded, like dogs they lick themselves whole again, as they suppose. Yet, after all this, it pleases God to take more pains with you. Today he calls on you once more to hear his voice, lest you be hardened by the deceitfulness of sin, and by your impenitence and hardness of heart heap up wrath against the day of wrath. Oh, what goodness is this! Despise it at your own peril (*Rom.* 2:4–5).

(iii) Consider and know assuredly that if you die impenitent and in your sins, you are damned forever irrecoverably. If you harden your heart, God may harden it, too. If you give up yourself, God may give you up, too, and then you are in the suburbs of hell. You fill up your measure and heat the furnace seven times hotter while you are adding sin to sin. The signs of death are upon you, for such is a hard heart. And I have nothing to say but, The Lord have mercy on you; which if he has not, you will howl and cry and roar in hell: Oh, wretch that I was, that for a little sinful pleasure and worldly profit, which was only for a little time, I have undone, undone my soul, and that forever, alas, forever.

But now, if God blesses this to awaken you, that you in earnest say, 'What shall I do to be saved?'; if you are thirsty, then hear God's proclamation: Everyone that thirsts, come and buy wine and milk, without money and without price (*Isa.* 55). Take the waters of life freely (*Rev.* 22:17). Incline your ear and come. Hear, and your souls shall live. Do you hear him calling? Come to me, all ye that are weary and heavy laden, and I will give you rest (*Matt.* 11:28). He is calling you.

b) For babes, who have repented from dead works:

Do not despise the day of small things, but bless God that has brought you this far. As God has laid a foundation, so he will lay the topstone in due time (*Zech.* 4:9–10). In our text, Hebrews 6, this doctrine is called a foundation, and surely it is not laid in vain.

We come sometimes to a place where some great person is about to build a great house, and when we see only the groundwork laid, and a great deal of rubbish lying about it, we think little of it. But if we stay awhile till it is built upon, we perhaps admire the design and structure, too. God brought a good world out of the chaos which was first made, and so he also does in the new creation. The first work seems to be a confused business. But if we stay till the six days are over and God has finished his work, we shall then say that it is very good.

When the Jews began to build, the heathen laughed them to scorn. What will these feeble Jews do? Will they revive the stones out of the heaps of the rubbish? If the fox goes up he shall break down this stone wall (*Neh.* 4:2–3). But for all this, the headstone was brought forth with shouting, 'Grace, grace unto it.'

And so shall it be with you, O babe. You shall attain to your perfect stature. So do not look on this small beginning as a thing of no value. God will carry you from repentance to faith, and from faith to obedience, and you shall have food suitable to bring you up. Bless God then that you have learned the first letter of his name, 'The Lord gracious', for so you have tasted him (*1 Pet.* 2:2–3). You have learnt the first lesson in the school of Christ, and till you learn more, consider these things that follow, as well as those that have already been spoken:

(i) Think what a mercy it is that God has put a stop to that fountain of uncleanness which ran over into all your affairs. Consider what you were doing. Were you not committing iniquity with both hands greedily, drinking it down as water, and doing as wickedly as you could? And has God stopped you in your course? Oh, think what mercy it is, how many thousands of actual sins you might have been guilty of, if God had not put this hook into your nostrils, and his bit into your jaws, and so kept you from rushing like the horse into the battle. Had not God hedged your way with these pricking thorns and grieving briars of conviction and repentance, you would have followed your lovers to death and hell; is it nothing that he has prevented you? Bless God, as David did for Abigail's coming, who kept you from sinning this day. You may have been resolved, like Saul (though it was madness in you, as in him) to go on in being injurious, a persecutor and blasphemer; to be as proud, covetous, and unclean as you could, to fully gratify the lust of the eye, the flesh, and the pride of life. But if God has diverted and converted you , bless him for it. It is a great thing to have a stop put to sin, even though it is but newly done, or little else has been done. As the apostle tells the Corinthian babes, Such were some of you, incapable of heaven and fit for hell, but you are washed (*1 Cor.* 6:9–11); and yet the work of grace was still very imperfect in them.

(ii) Consider how many there are yet in the world who have not come so far as repentance from, nor conviction of, their dead works. It may be many of your own relations, your own

flesh and blood, and some that have heard the same gospel and sat in the same pew with you. Yet they are yet dead in sins and trespasses, fast asleep in their security, without any sense of sin or sorrow for it.

Has God awakened you to righteousness? Do not despise the buddings of grace, but bless him that you are so far quickened, that you can eat a little milk, though still only one portion. When so many sit and walk the road to hell in darkness, that your eyes should be opened to see the danger and cry out, 'What shall I do to be saved?' is a mercy not to be undervalued, but to be prized by you, and God to be praised for it. It is great mercy that the foundation is laid, that the work is begun.

(iii) Consider this, that though you are not yet clothed like the sons of nobles and richly dressed like them, the plain cloth, the coarse weave with which you are clothed, will preserve you. It is with God's children as it is with the children of men in this respect: You come to the house of a poor man who has a child newly born, and the child is dressed in very plain cloths. In the rich man's house, the newborn child is dressed up beautifully with fine linen, scarlet robes, and gold lace, and is as fine as hands and money can make it.

God is the Father of all newborn babes, but some he dresses like the children of the poor, and others like the children of rich men. For some, he but covers their nakedness, that it may not be seen. But others he adorns in finery (*Ezek.* 16). When the prodigal came home he put on the best robe and the ring – it was sealing time very early – and the shoes of the preparation of the gospel on his feet, and bread and flesh, strong meat to feed him. With others it may be, though God has compassion on them and takes them into his family and gives them milk to keep them from perishing with hunger, yet they do not have a ring given them all their days, nor anything but milk to eat. And though they are clothed with the same righteousness, it is not so embroidered and pleasant to the eye as the other's is.

The church or spouse's garment is of diverse colours. It is a time of love, but God does not tell them of it as he does some as soon as he has washed the blood from them. The Father loves them, though he does not kiss them yet, as he does some of his other children. Well, however, bless him that he covers your nakedness, though you may not see the riches of his grace laid out upon you, and yet remember that he forgives you.

(iv) *Consider this, that God is better pleased with that little grace than he is displeased with the much corruption which is in you.* Only do not like your corruption the more, but love and praise God the better. Though you are only as gold in the ore, God has more regard for you than to throw away the gold because of the ore. Oh, no, he will lose no gold. The disciples were little better than this, and yet he would not lose one of them nor the least grain of grace that appeared in them, but made much of the willingness of their spirit when the bodily flesh was weak and the corrupt flesh strong. Though they were as bruised reeds and smoking flax, he valued them greatly. Though there might be more smoke than fire, he would not quench but cherish it. Though your grace may be little and your corruption much, he will yet prize you.

(v) *Think of this also, that though you do not have assurance, you have that which will secure you and ensures your soul.* Every grace is assuring in its nature and degree, though you do not have the evidence and comfort of it: Is it nothing to be safe? You are upon the foundation and shall stand and not fall, for you are in a state of blessedness. Eternal life is begun, and there is no falling from eternal life. Even today salvation has come to you, as it did to Zaccheus, and it will never depart from you. This state is blessed, for so are they that mourn, and in due time they shall be comforted (*Matt.* 5:3-4). The beginning of grace, though poor, is blessed.

Poor weeping soul, you little know what joy there is in heaven at your weeping on earth (*Luke* 15:7,10,32). Your sighs make angels sing. The crying of the babe makes the father laugh, as our saying is, and it is true of the heavenly Father; and all this refers to the repentance of babes, their first attainment.

Paul rejoiced that he made the Corinthian babes sorrowful, because they sorrowed to repentance, which was to salvation and never to be repented of (*2 Cor.* 7:9-10). Jesus Christ, seeing the travail of his soul safely delivered, rejoices that a man or woman child is born, though it is not yet any more than newborn. Your sorrow makes him forget his sorrow. Our Saviour, after his resurrection, appeared to Peter before he did to the twelve (*1 Cor.* 15:5), and the angel sent the first tidings of his resurrection to Peter (*Mark* 16:7), for he was repenting and weeping bitterly, which was as another conversion to him, as our Saviour had hinted to him before (*Luke* 22:32). When the incestuous person repented, Paul took care that he might be comforted, lest he should be swallowed up with overmuch sorrow (*2 Cor.* 2:7).

Thus are we given to understand how precious the tears of penitents are, and yet God is not willing that they sorrow overmuch. Though he loves to see them swim in tears, he takes care that they may not be drowned in tears. Though he loves a broken, contrite heart, yet he is not willing that any should break their hearts, or despair and mourn as them that are without hope.

In the Song of Songs 2:14, the spouse was fallen to the ground for grief and sorrow, as I take it, and hid herself in the clefts of the rock and the secret places of the stairs,

[77]

and the little foxes (Satan's temptations and wiles) endeavoured to spoil the vine that had tender grapes. But the bridegroom, seeing her in this disconsolate condition, speaks to her: 'Rise up, my love, my fair one, and come away. Let me see thy countenance and hear thy voice.'

'Lord, alas! I dare not look up, I am so black.' Think also of the poor publican (*Luke* 18:13) who stood afar off and would not lift up his eyes to heaven, but smote upon his breast and said, God be merciful to me a sinner. 'My countenance, O Lord, is not worth looking on,' says this poor soul, 'these wet cheeks of mine and eyes standing full of tears will not allow me to look up.'

'But,' says he, 'let me see thy face, for it is comely. I love it now, the tears run down. I love to see it beset with these diamonds, and silver drops of tears, it is a precious sight in my eyes. And so let me see your face, yes, and let me hear your voice.'

'My voice! O Lord, alas, I can only chatter as the crane and mourn as the dove.'

'Oh, let me hear this voice of yours. Your sighs and groans are music, they make melody in my ears. Let me hear it, for your voice is sweet and your countenance comely. Rise up, my love, my dove, my fair one, and come away. For lo the winter is past, the rain is over and gone, the flowers appear on the earth, the time of singing is come, and the voice of the turtle is heard in our land. The fig tree puts forth her green figs, and the vines with the tender grapes give a good fragrance. I will take the foxes that spoil the vines, and preserve the tender grapes.'

So may the dear and loving Jesus (and oh that he would!) speak to you, poor soul, that after your April of showers, you may have a month of May with all its flowers and be able to conclude as the spouse did (*Song of Sol.* 2:16): 'My beloved is mine, and I am his.'

In the meantime, if you do not hear this joyful sound, if you do not have wine to drink or meat to eat, yet go your way and eat your milk with as merry a heart as you can, for God accepts your work, even your repentance from dead works. Only do not stop here, but go on and believe, too.

And this brings me to address the second attainment of babes, faith towards God, which is another portion of the milk they eat.

THE BABES' FAITH

The second principle of the beginning of Christ, which is called milk (and yet a foundation, too) is faith towards God. The object is God, the act is faith, the manner and power of its working is towards, and only 'towards' God. We see how well our translation has used this word in this case and place, since this word *epi* is hardly used again in all the Scripture, in relation to faith, in the accusative case. It denotes a tendency, and is therefore very well rendered into English, faith 'towards' God.

And so this preposition *epi* is used in Luke 10:9. The kingdom of God is come nigh unto you, or has approached towards you; it is at hand. So this faith is an approach, a coming towards God. It has not attained its perfection and end, but is in motion and tendency. These babes, I speak of the lowest and weakest of babes, are near and at hand, said not so much to have come as to be coming. It denotes a gradual, and only a gradual, attainment. It is not a complete and perfected act, but an act which is begun and is ongoing. Yet it shall be competed in its time, and is accepted for the present, for it is said (*John* 6:37), He that is coming to me (so it says in the Greek), I will in no wise cast out.

The object of this faith is God, the Father, not in

opposition to, yet in distinction from the Son, inasmuch as those judaizing Christians, who were generally babes, kept to the Old Testament spirit. This was a faith towards God, not without respect to the Messiah, for as the Father and the Son act in the soul (no man coming unto the Father but by the Son, or any man coming to the Son unless the Father draw him), so the soul acts towards the Father and the Son, but mostly to the Father. It looks on him to be the person mostly offended and with whom it stands in most need of reconciliation. Therefore as the soul makes its principal address to the Father, yet it is by Christ, or for the Lord's sake, as Daniel says (*Dan.* 9:17).

The distinction is (and it is better known to grown saints) that repentance is towards God, and faith is towards our Lord Jesus Christ, or (*eis*) unto God and unto Christ, as the words are (*Acts* 20:21). But the babes are mostly ignorant of the union between the Father and the Son in this work of grace to salvation, as is hinted to Philip (*John* 14:8–11), and do not consider that they are to honour the Son as they honour the Father (*John* 5:23). Therefore they usually let their faith and its motions to be mostly towards God, without such clear considerations of Christ as the object of faith, as united to and in conjunction with the Father.

The soul is awakened, as I have said, and come to the knowledge that it has displeased God by sin and wronged itself, and therefore is unworthy to be accepted and welcomed upon its own account. It knows further that lacking strength and righteousness, it is unable to make its peace with God; yet if peace is not made, it is undone. The soul then makes addresses to God upon a kind of common faith that he is merciful.

A Jewish babe addresses God as of old, under the notion of a God that must be approached by sacrifices, the types of Christ. A Gentile converted babe makes his addresses in the name of Christ, though too much without the notion of him as the Lord our righteousness. Babes are untrained in that regard, without the proper notion of being found in him, having the righteousness which is by faith. But they make toward him as well as they can.

And therefore, by the way, that act of faith which we call reliance, adherence, and dependence, cannot be the first saving act of babes, though that follows afterwards. But they are convinced by the teaching of God (*John* 6:45) concerning themselves, and they know that unless they believe in Christ Jesus they cannot be saved; that there is salvation to be had by him and no other (*Acts* 4:12); that he came into the world to save sinners (*I Tim.* 1:15); and that whosoever believeth in him shall not perish, but have everlasting life (*John* 3:16). Being convinced of these truths, they do in some measure receive this witness of God, and in like measure, receive Christ Jesus and come to him. It is by these two words, receiving and coming, that the first workings of faith are most usually expressed (*John* 1:12–13; 6:35–37,44,45,47). So this is the beginning of their faith. And in time, this receiving, coming or addressing grows into reliance upon and trusting in him, though still without an assurance that Christ is theirs and they are his. This, I say, is saving faith.

We see therefore that the work of grace is, as experience generally shows, a confused thing. It is a kind of chaos at first with many things jumbled together without distinct considerations, and the babes go stumbling on in the dark. I shall therefore try to show the different workings of grace. These souls may better understand these things by hearing them from another and calling to mind what they have observed, than they will be able to discover them for themselves.

We see, then, that this faith of babes has to do with two persons: God and Christ, though especially God. Let us see now how it acts towards God, and then towards Christ.

(i) How their faith acts towards God

a) Babes believe that God is, and is a rewarder of them that seek him out, for without this it would be impossible to please God and to come to him in a seeking and addressing way (Heb. 11:6). There is a faith called coming, but there is also a faith preceding this coming, which is a believing that God is, for none would look after a nonentity, that which is not or is not believed to be. It is also a belief that he is a rewarder of them that seek him; they shall not seek in vain, if they seek in truth. Now the babe believes this in general, though he cannot yet see that his own coming and seeking shall be welcome and rewarded, as was the case of the woman of Canaan, and the prodigal at first.

b) Babes believe that God can turn them and save them if he pleases; and they believe fully in his power, though not his will, as grown saints do. When Ephraim was bemoaning himself, he said, 'Turn thou me, and I shall be turned'; and God presently says, 'Ephraim is my dear son, a pleasant child. I will surely have mercy on him, saith the Lord' (Jer. 31:18–20). The prodigal, too, believed that his father could yet set him up again, though he had spent all, and that he might be a new-made man. The babe speaks like the leper, 'Lord, if thou wilt, thou canst make me clean,' and it proved so. He believes there is grace and bread enough in God's house, that if he only has the will, he has power enough to pardon. The question is not about his power but about his will. Yet, throughout the Scripture, this is owned and accepted. We read of one poor man that came to Christ distrusting his power, but Christ put him on believing that before he would do anything for him. And when he did, Christ did what he came for (*Mark* 9:22).

c) Babes look further, even to the promises of God. They find many invitations and promises also, and they have recourse to these. But they do not so much look upon Christ, in whom all the promises of God are. They do, as it were, rest upon the ark, but do not come into it, whereas grown saints see Christ Jesus as the foundation and fullness of every promise. Grown saints have little use for the cabinet without the jewel, or for the field without the pearl hidden in it. The promises, indeed, are encouraging means to faith, but they are not the rest of the soul. Forgiveness of sins is not promised where faith in Christ is lacking (*Acts* 26:18), nor eternal life itself (*2 Tim.* 1:1), nor righteousness (*Phil.* 3). Of this, also, the babes have a general notion. And so they make towards Christ not with full sails but with a side wind, as it were.

(ii) How their faith acts towards Christ Jesus

a) One of the things revealed to babes is that Jesus Christ is the Son of the living God, to whom the Father has given and committed all things (Matt. 16:16–17; 11:25–27). When Peter confesses Christ to be the Son of the living God, our Saviour calls him blessed and tells him that it was not flesh and blood but his Father who had revealed it to him. And in the other place he blesses his Father who had hidden this from the wise and prudent, but had revealed it unto babes.

b) Babes believe that God sent his Son into the world to save sinners, and it is a degree of faith that Jesus Christ accepts and commends (John 17:8). Christ tells his Father by way of commendation that his disciples, as yet but babes, had believed that he had sent him to be the Messiah to restore and redeem Israel. Though some of them had understood for a while but carnally, it seems they now

[83]

had a better notion of it. And he tells his disciples that his Father loved them (*John* 16:27) because they loved Christ and believed that he came out from God to save the world. The babes do not have such clear notions of the priesthood of Christ, or of his becoming sin for them that they might be made the righteousness of God in him, both of which are by imputation. Still this general faith carries them towards Christ Jesus; this assent leads them to an addressing faith.

(iii) How their faith acts towards God and Christ

a) This faith which they have towards both God and Christ expresses itself in resolutions to go to God – this, though it might be only on a probability or possibility, such as that of the lepers (2 Kings 7). Uncertain hope is preferred to certain danger and death. The prodigal believed that in his father's house there was bread enough, and for this very reason he decided to go rather than perish with hunger, though he did not know how he would fare. And this was at first only a resolution, I will arise and go.

'Well,' says the soul, 'I see this: If I live in my sins I must die; sin and death keep company. But there is mercy with the Lord, he can forgive me if it pleases him. And it is a faithful saying, and worthy to be received that Jesus Christ came into the world to save sinners. Though I cannot say God will be merciful to me, still I will arise and go, I will take a chance and see what he will do with my poor soul.' And truly God takes this kindly, as it was said of David about building the temple, that it was in his heart to arise and go. These first motions are very acceptable to God.

b) The faith of babes toward God and Christ expresses itself in prayers. The babe not only breathes but cries, as it is said of Paul, Behold, he prayeth (*Acts* 9:11). This faith goes with a petition in its mouth, as the prodigal did: I will not only arise and go, but I will confess my sin, beg pardon, and gain a place in the house, though only of a servant. So, too, the poor publican (yet afar off, as the prodigal was): Lord, be merciful to me a sinner. He begged pardon upon the general account of mercy (for hitherto, said Christ of his babes, ye have asked little or nothing in my name) and he went home justified. This faith puts resolutions into prayers, and prayers into practice. The prodigal arose and came, and was welcome.

c) Therefore this faith expresses itself in obedience and in submitting to ordinances, as baptism, etc. As soon as any were newborn (I speak of adults), and believed in Christ, they were initiated by baptism into the mysteries of the Christian religion. Submission to this was a proof to men of their faith. That this was the constant practice, we see not only by examples but by the apostles' joining of the doctrine of faith with that of baptism. Thus by degrees the faith of babes creeps and moves towards God *and* Christ.

But there are yet more inward things which some of these souls find in themselves, though they can hardly express them distinctly or tell what to make of them.

Some of them are full of ifs and buts, fearing that they are only hypocrites, or there is no true work in them. They say, If there are any true works in us, it is of God; we are wholly beholden to him for it. We cannot attribute our repentance and faith to our own goodness, but if there are any such things, they are worked by God himself, for we are not sufficient of ourselves to think one good thought, in us there dwells no good thing. If we are accepted, surely it is of grace in the beloved. From their prayers for mercy, I conclude that they attribute all to mercy and say, Thanks be to God through Jesus Christ, as Paul did (*Rom.* 7:25). It is, says the poor soul, the

[85]

Lord's mercy that I am not in hell, and if ever I go to heaven I will admire grace and mercy.

They also have a great value for Christ Jesus, though they cannot say that he is theirs, or that they are his. They think him the chiefest of ten thousand, and worthy to be beloved and believed in, though they have not attained him so as to lie in his bosom, as John did and many others do. If they had ten thousand worlds, they would give them for him, for they are more inclined to buy and purchase than to believe . If he would but smile upon them and kiss them, oh how they would love him!

Higher Christians are rich in experiences, but these are rich only in wishes, desires, and yearnings. They so long after him that they would be content to be even as hired servants, anything, in any condition, if he will just receive them; indeed, if they may but gather the crumbs that fall under his table, though they should not have the children's bread bestowed upon them. If he would only let them know that they shall come to Canaan at last, or but open a door of hope for them, they would willingly go through the wilderness and the valley of Achor, too, and lay their mouth in the dust, if there may be but hope. If they may not have a full meal of joy in the Holy Ghost, nor rejoice with joy unspeakable and full of glory, yet they will be thankful for some crumbs of comfort and good hope through grace.

Yet, even if these longings of theirs may not be satisfied, they have this fixed and rooted in them: They would walk in this darkness and pain all their days rather than go back again to their old condition of living in sin. They will wait and beg at God's doors until death rather than dwell in the tents or the most pleasant courts of wickedness. They would rather be God's hired servants than the devil's children, and live with the swine of this world that wallow in the mire and filth of sin and iniquity, as you may read of the returning prodigal. No, they will not go back to drunkenness and uncleanness, to impenitence and hardness of heart. But if they must perish, they will perish repenting and praying. If they must starve, so be it. At God's door they will lie and beg, come of them what will, they will not go anywhere else for salvation. Though he kill them, they will trust in him and rely upon him.

Besides all this, you will find that these babes will confess that now and then they have some private soul-supporting sustenance. But they say, 'We do not know what to make of them, or where they come from, for they quickly depart again, and then our fears return upon us.' Sometimes a word has come and greeted them, but it passed by and went away. They will tell you that they had such a whisper in their souls: My grace is sufficient for thee, or, I have prayed that your faith fail not, etc. Where it came from or where it went they cannot tell, but alas they can tell that it vanished like an echo.

The disciples had many a support at times, yet ever were fearing and doubting again, like them of little faith. So these poor souls, though they have now and then a secret cordial given them, it just keeps them alive. They are hungry, weak, and faint still. Many such things are true of them, and to a grown and knowing saint who has gone through them, they are very promising things concerning the future well-being of these babes. But they themselves scarcely gather any hope from them.

I have shown how the faith of babes acts, and how some of them, the lowest and weakest babes, eat this second portion of milk, faith towards God. Before I show the rest, I think it necessary to say something by way of application.

Application

a) To those who are not babes and do not have faith towards God:

Without breach of charity, I fear that there are still many who, though they profess faith, do not believe even like this. As the bleating of the sheep and lowing of the oxen, to speak in Samuel's language to Saul, their living in sins witnesses against them. The person who can believe unsanctified persons to be believers, when the very natural operation and effect of faith is sanctification (*Acts* 26:18), must surely be very reckless in his faith and have a creed contradictory to that of the apostles. To those, then, I would speak in Christ's own words: Repent and believe the gospel. Take in this milk of the word, that you may live and grow by it.

(i) Consider, I beg you, that not believing shows that you are not yet convinced of the sinfulness of sin. You are not yet awakened out of that dead sleep, nor come to yourself. For if you were, undoubtedly you would resolve with the prodigal to arise and go by faith towards God and confess your sin and beg as the publican, Lord be merciful to me a sinner. If you can sin and sleep in sin, if you can lie contentedly in a perishing and damnable condition and not cry out for salvation, surely you are in a most dangerous position, notwithstanding your name of Christian. For what will it help you to have a name with the living, if you are dead?

If you tell me you have repented from dead works, I can answer you that it cannot be so while you are dead in sins and walk in them, for they are dead in sin who live in it (*Eph.* 2:1–3). But if it were indeed true that you had repented, yet know this, that righteousness is not by repentance but by faith. So that if you repent and do not believe, though you are not far from the kingdom of heaven, nonetheless you are no nearer, for the one thing necessary is wanting. And though you seem too good to go to hell, yet you are not good enough to go to heaven.

(ii) Consider, too, that you have long had the means of faith: the preaching and hearing of the gospel by which faith comes. Now what a sad thing it is when the gospel comes to you, and you do not come to God! when it comes in word and not in power! It would have been better for you never to hear, than to hear and not believe. Better that you had never known the way of righteousness than knowing it, not to walk in it. It will be easier for the heathen than for you, as it will be for Sodom and Gomorrah than for Capernaum in the day of judgement, as our Saviour says (*Matt.* 11:20). These things are said, as the gospel is written, that you may believe that Jesus is the Son of God, and that believing you might have life through his name (*John* 20:31). And truly if you do not believe the gospel, neither would you believe if one should come back from the dead. The more means of faith, the greater the condemnation if men do not believe, and God has appointed no greater means than that.

(iii) Consider that Christ may take his gospel and be gone, that you may die in your sins and be damned forever. To-day, therefore, while it is called today (now, or it may never be), hear his voice who calls you to repent and believe the gospel that you may be saved. If you do not, the same gospel says, He that believeth not shall be damned. Can you quietly think of going to hell? If not, believe. It would be better if you had never been born than to die without being newborn. It is sad to be dead in sins, but to die in sin – Oh, who but those in hell can tell how sad it is! Hear then and believe, that your soul may live.

b) To those that are babes and have faith towards God, but are discouraged:

I say to you as I have said before: Do not despise the day of small things. Who knows to how great a tree this grain of mustard seed may grow? or how great a fire this little spark may kindle? or how tall a poor babe may someday become? Though you can eat only milk, you may grow by it. You have got down one portion of milk more already. Not only have you repented from dead works, but you also have faith towards God. Though you have no wine to make your heart glad, or oil to make your face shine, or bread to strengthen your heart, yet bless God that you are alive and have milk to eat.

(i) Consider that you have gone farther than you are aware of, you are nearer heaven than you think. For in having faith towards God, though you are a great way off, you are within your Father's view. When the prodigal was yet afar off, but still coming, his father saw him and had compassion on him. The father saw him before he saw the father, and his coming was looked on as if he had already arrived. Abraham is said to offer his son in that he intended to and was about to do it; so the prodigal and the babe are said to have already come. It is something to be on your feet, your journey begun. Your Father sees it and has compassion on you. And as to Christ Jesus, he will never cast you off, no, by no means (*John* 6:37–39).

(ii) If you should go no further than to be a babe all your days, remember that you have gone far enough to be saved. By faith we are saved, as safe as if we were saved already. There is a blessing for this faith (*Matt.* 16:17) and justification for this faith (*Luke* 18:14), and God loves such believers (*John* 16:27). It is not a little remarkable, that blessedness comes to the lowest as well

as to the highest form in the school of Christ, as in the Beatitudes (*Matt.* 5). To the Hebrew babes the apostle says, Though you are but babes, I hope better things of you than of some that had once been enlightened, and things that accompany salvation (*Heb.* 6:9–10). Salvation is not connected with degrees but with the reality of grace, even in the lowest degree (*John* 6:37).

(iii) As weak as your faith is, the gates of hell shall not prevail against it. You shall be kept through this faith by the power of God unto salvation (*1 Pet.* 1:5). A poor babe is apt to falter and say, 'Alas, my faith is small, if any, and I fear what will become of me in an hour of temptation; my strength is so small that I shall falter in the day of affliction.' But the Lord says to you, 'Fear not, for though you have but a little strength, but because you do not deny his name, God will keep you from the hour of temptation, or from the temptation of the hour, as it may be' (*Rev.* 3:8–10).

Though Saul might pursue you and hunt you, the house of Saul shall grow weaker and weaker, and the house of David shall grow stronger and stronger. And the weak shall be like David, who notwithstanding his fear, did not perish by the hand of Saul. Though your enemies be strong and your grace weak, your weak grace shall be too strong for your strongest enemies. Though the sons of Zeruiah be strong, and in your eyes too strong for you, yet you shall die in peace. Notwithstanding all the malice and power of Satan, the gates of hell shall not prevail against you, as Christ promised Peter, who believed as you do, that Christ is the Son of the living God. Nor did it fail when Satan sifted him, for though he denied that he knew the man, he still believed that Christ was the Son of God, which was the faith that Christ prayed might not fail.

Let the rain descend, the floods come, and the winds

blow and beat altogether upon you. Your house shall stand, for it is founded, like Mount Zion, on a rock that cannot be moved (*Matt.* 7:24–25). Indeed, if any faith alone were to battle with Satan, it would be an unequal match. But you are kept by the power of God and the prayer of Christ. So there is more power for you than there is against you, though it be all the power of hell.

(iv) These present experiences of yours can never be had by any but a true saint. The most exquisite hypocrite that ever was, never attained to what you have: to be newborn and to be a babe in Christ. To which of the saints will you turn? Ask them one by one whether any that cast themselves upon the grace of God in Christ Jesus, as you do, ever perished or had their hope ashamed. No, the hypocrite's hope shall perish, though he might gain a great name and reputation. But yours shall not, though you be poor in Israel and one of the least of many thousands.

If you hold fast the workings of faith – and I know you can if you are in Christ Jesus, though but a babe in him – then that is more than the most exact, most studied and polished hypocrite ever did or can attain to. A hypocrite may be gilded over, but you are gold. He may be enlightened, but you are light in the Lord. He may grow up as the grass, but you are as a tree planted and rooted in Christ Jesus. He may seem to be, but you are a Christian. Whatever may be counterfeited, the new birth cannot be counterfeited. When the conceitedly rich Laodiceans shall be found poor, you who are as Smyrna, poor in your own eyes, will be counted rich by God himself (*Rev.* 2:9).

Blessed are the poor in spirit, for theirs is the kingdom of heaven (*Matt.* 5:3). It was the first blessing that Christ ever pronounced with his mouth that we read of, and it was spoken of such as you.

(v) Whatever you think of it, it is a joy to good men and ministers, as it was to John, the bridegroom's friend, that you hear the bridegroom's voice and come unto him (John 3:26–30). Your Saviour rejoiced in spirit and thanked his Father that such things were revealed to babes (*Luke* 10:21). There is joy in heaven at the return of the prodigal, though but newly come home, just alive, just found and no more, yet see what joy there is at his coming (*Luke* 15). The joy is not delayed and put off till he is grown up, but there is a feast for his birth and joy that the man-child is born. His father's heart leapt for joy when he still had neither the robe nor the ring put on. Do not, then, reckon as small that which God makes much of.

(vi) To make you almost as happy as angels, you lack only the knowledge of your happy state. You are a son, and if you only knew it, you would be almost in heaven. In Christ you live, move, and have your being, and if you only knew this, what well-being would you enjoy. Paul, speaking of babes (*Gal.* 4:9), says, they are rather known of God than know God. Indeed, what God is now doing they do not know, but they shall know hereafter, as Christ told Peter (*John* 13:7). And when you shall come to know as you are known, you will be filled with admiration and delight. Meanwhile, wait with patience.

(vii) Remember to press forward, that you may apprehend that for which you are apprehended of Christ Jesus (*Phil.* 3:12). Seeing you are in the way, keep up your pace. Do not be slothful, as the apostle tells the Hebrew babes, but be followers of them whose conversation is in heaven (*Phil.* 3:17,20), who through faith and patience inherit the promises (*Heb.* 6:12). Grow in grace, not only by adding new acts of the same kind, and so persevering to the end; but add faith to faith, for the righteousness of

God is revealed from faith to faith (*Rom.* 1:17). Go on, then, from a faith of address to a faith of reliance, and so on to the full assurance of faith and hope, as the apostle desires his babes to do (*Heb.* 6:11).

You believe in God, believe in me also, says our Saviour (*John* 14:1). If you will grow in grace, it must be by growing in the knowledge of our Lord and Saviour Jesus Christ, as Peter tells his newborn babes (*2 Pet.* 3:18). Grow by being skilful in the word of righteousness and having your senses practised to discern not only between good and evil, but between good and better. Focus on Christ more immediately and perfectly, and not only through the intervention and mediation of your own graces. Keep your eyes not so much on his attendants as on the King of Glory himself. In your graces you may see something of him by reflection, but in him you will see perfect beauty, righteousness and strength.

Till you come to this, or if you should never come to it, then know for your comfort that it is no small thing to be known and accepted of God. 'You have I known above all people' is the way God expressed the privileges of the old Israel. God's knowledge is not like ours. We know this or that man, but he is little the better for it, it does not change him. But God's knowledge is operative and efficacious.

It was Job's consolation that though he could not know the way of God, yet God knew the way, and when God had thoroughly tried him he should come out like gold (*Job* 23:9–10). This world is your furnace and purgatory, and though you do not know what God is doing, he knows that he is now purifying you from your dross that you may be pure and fine gold. Though you will lie down in the dust of the grave, he will raise you up in glory; and when you awaken you shall be filled with his image. If, in the meantime, you do not know what to do, let your eyes be to him. He is never at a loss or distracted from his way, but is still carrying on his work to perfection, though it may be in the dark to you.

THEIR SUBMISSION TO BAPTISM AND OTHER ORDINANCES

Of the six principles mentioned above, the two following show not only the doctrine which was taught to babes, but also their submission to it, which are proofs before men of their conversion.

As to baptism and laying on of hands, there is some controversy among interpreters. Of the doctrine of baptism (Greek *baptisms*) some say that it refers to the several washings used by the Jews, one of which was with reference to the admission of proselytes, to which baptism succeeded. Others say that it refers to both the outward and the inward baptism, one of water and one of the Spirit.

Of the doctrine of laying on of hands, some say that it refers to confirmation; others, to absolution; others, to ordination. It seems to have been the practice of Christ's apostles, after they had baptized persons, sooner or later to lay hands on them, by which practice gifts were conferred (*Acts* 8:17; 19:4–6).

Now, whether the doctrine of baptisms may not refer to the baptizing of Gentiles as well as Jews, and laying on of hands also refer to both, a thing which the Jews could hardly bear, I leave to the consideration of others. For our present purpose (not to meddle with controversies), I shall not go beyond observing that in general babes submit to the obedience of such institutions.

They submit to such ordinances and duties as they are capable and convinced of; the ordinances are not required of them till they are able to submit. Whatever doctrine comes under the name of strong meat, they cannot bear.

Our Saviour would not put meat into babes' mouths any more than men would put new wine into old bottles. Therefore they were not required to fast, and due partly to its lack they could not cast out one kind of demon (*Matt.* 17:19–21), till Christ's departure and the descent of the Spirit (*Matt.* 9:14–17). This duty of fasting, however formally used by the Pharisees, is a duty too strong to be expected of babes.

Our Saviour had many more things to say, which they could not bear till the Spirit came upon them (*John* 16:12–13). They could hardly endure the doctrine of Christ's death (*Matt.* 16:21–22). They did not understand either that (*Luke* 9:44–45), or the doctrine of his resurrection (*Mark* 9:9–10), or that of his ascension to the Father and intercession for them (*John* 16:16–18). These are the strong meat that grown believers feed upon (*Rom.* 8:34), as the disciples also did afterwards. They were, while babes, exceedingly sorry at these things (*Matt.* 17:22–23), which were to turn to their greatest joy after they came to a riper understanding of his love and design, as Christ told them they would (*John* 16:19–28), and strong believers do (*Rom.* 8:34–39).

He had also some commands for them, that they should go and preach to the Gentiles, and baptize and lay hands on them, which as yet they could not bear. And while under this weakness, their first commission was only for the cities of Judea. Even after Christ's ascension, Peter himself needed a vision to be convinced to go to the Gentiles. And it was a matter of great wonder to the Jewish converts, who generally were but babes, that God had granted the Gentiles repentance to life (*Acts* 11:18).

They were babes in point of gifts, too, for they were to

do greater things after Christ's ascension than they could before (*John* 14:12), which we can read of (*Mark* 16:15–20). These went much beyond the first commission, both as to persons to be preached to, and things to be done (*Matt.* 10:1).

And in grace also they were babes. They were but of little faith (*Matt.* 6:30) and very carnal in their apprehensions of Christ's kingdom, as if it had been of this world. There was much strife and envy among them, and a wrathful spirit calling for fire from heaven. They were eager to promise but not so to perform, for they could not watch with him one hour. By this it appears they were as carnal and but babes, not capable of strong meat for doctrine or for duty.

What babes are and are not capable of, or able to bear, I shall not try to determine. But this I am sure of, that they are not to be received to doubtful disputations, if that is the meaning of Romans 14:1. But what they are capable of and convinced of, they submit to and act accordingly (*Acts* 19). There were disciples that had not heard whether there was a Holy Ghost or not, but as soon as they were convinced, they submitted.

The disciples were convinced of the Messiah's offices only as a general notion, without a clear understanding of the manner and way in which the world would be restored. Therefore, till after his ascension, which proved theirs too, they had asked nothing in his name (*John* 16:24–26). Christ indeed had declared his Father's name, 'The Lord gracious' (*Exod.* 34:6), and taught them to pray, 'Our Father', and tells God that they had kept his Word and believed that he came out from him, as sent by him (*John* 17:6–8). But a more specific faith in him and praying in his name were to be taught by the Spirit; these were things they were not yet convinced of.

i) How babes follow ordinances

Now, these babes follow ordinances to do their duties, alas, in a very poor, low way; but God overlooks the weaknesses and accepts their will for the deed, and many times, is better to them than that.

a) They use ordinances much, but make little use of them, and if I may so speak, are very full of duties, but little dutiful. Very little comes of all their attendance upon and addresses to God. They are in the same place still, making little headway, God knows. They do a great deal of hearing and praying, hear precept upon precept and line upon line, heap duty upon duty, but are bunglers at it, and afterward have not profited.

Like young children that take many meals, eat all the day long and spoil as much as they eat, they mangle and crumble what is set before them, and dwindle away their time without feeding. Thus it was with the Hebrew babes. They ate and ate, yet were always in need of milk. They do not, cannot, walk in the strength of their meat, as the prophet did, but are soon hungry again. The Word profits them little because it is not mixed with faith. They have bad digestion, and though they eat much, they are lean from day to day.

The disciples who heard Christ Jesus preach so often were yet, like the Hebrews, dull of hearing. Every now and then they were to know the meaning of this and that very plain and easy similitude and parable with which Christ taught them, but did not understand other sayings. They were so unacquainted with praying that they must have a Form of Prayer or a Directory set before them.

Though the Jews fasted often, it was not to God at all, or very little. Babes abound in performing and keep on the road and round of duties, yet accomplish little. There is little faith in their believing, little love in their loving, little obedience in their obeying. There is much of quantity but little of quality. There is a great bulk of duties, but little of Spirit and life in them; their much is little.

b) They are very apt to confine religion to some certain duties. They say, It is good to be here, as Peter did, not knowing what they say. They are apt to think that there are no duties (and that they must hardly do anything else) but to hear and pray. If I may allude to what is said of the Pharisees (*Matt.* 23:23), they are exact and punctual at positives, but defective in morals; they neglect too much the weightier things, such as faith and love.

A grown Christian sees that the great part of his duty is in faithfully discharging his particular occupation, in buying and selling, eating and drinking, and doing all he does, from the highest to the lowest duty, to the glory of God. The babes are, as I may say, hearing and praying Christians. So are the grown Christians, but along with that, they are doing and practising Christians, which the babes are little acquainted with.

When Jesus Christ had cast a demon out of a man, he that had been possessed prayed that he might be with him, but Christ had other work for him to do (*Mark* 5:18–19). So these babes cry to 'be with him', for so they call being at sermons and prayers, little considering that they may serve him better in being elsewhere many times. These things you ought to do, and not to leave the other undone, say I to the babes, as Christ did to the Pharisees. Constant walking with God, and finishing the work he has given us to do, is the best 'being with him', and that properly is our communion with him. Hearing and praying is but relative, as means and helps to such an end (*1 John* 1:6–7). Oh, that babes would learn this.

Young beginners think they must lay almost all aside

in favour of hearing and praying, as if following their occupations and doing the work assigned to them were nothing to this. The excellence of a grown saint lies much in this, that he divides his work rightly, and gives every one its portion in due season, for then it is beautiful; and so he is, in this sense, approved of God, a workman that needeth not to be ashamed (*2 Tim.* 2:15).

c) They are apt to place more in ordinances and duties, and to look for more from them than God has placed and put in them. They go to them as Rachel to Jacob: Give me children or I die. But they may answer, as he did her, Am I in God's stead? if God shut, who can open?

Poor babes, if they do not have what they want, they are sullen and discontented; what should I hear, pray, and wait for? They looked for joy, but none came; they went to hear the joyful sound, but did not hear it; they went to the Lord's feast as to a sealing ordinance, but found no impressions of its seal. So they are apt to complain, Why should I go any more? But let me tell you, this is your babyishness, as that king said to the woman who came to him for help. So may ordinances say to you, How can we help if God does not help?

God has not called ordinances and duties your comforters, but his Holy Spirit is the comforter. The partaking of the Lord's feast does not seal; that is the Spirit's office. God never intended that you should make gods and saviours of his ordinances, but that you should look through them and above them while you use them.

Grown saints do so, they go to (and also go from) a duty and ordinance to God himself. They know it is not the man that speaks the word, nor the word that man speaks, but God that works. They go to them as to God's wells and pipes, which they know have no water but from the fountain, in whom all their fresh springs are and from whom all their fruit and increase is (*1 Cor.* 3:6–7). Paul's planting, and Apollos' watering comes to nothing if God does not give the increase by his blessing.

d) Some babes are too prone to think that they deserve something at God's hand by what they do. Being yet under the bondage of hired servants and an Old Testament legal framework, they do not so much work righteousness as much as they work *for* righteousness. They think they can pray and weep themselves into the love of God, and are as carnal men, who think to be heard for their much and long speaking. They make vows and covenants, setting tasks on themselves, so many chapters, and so long at prayers. But if they fail in their expectations, then they are apt to say, What profit is there if we keep his ordinances? and what gain if we draw nigh unto him, and have hands laid on us? and why have we afflicted our souls, like them in Isaiah 43:2–3?

If they do anything bigger and, as they think, better than ordinary, they conclude, as Leah did (*Gen.* 30:20), God has endowed me with a good dowry, now will he dwell with me, for I have borne him six sons. And they call their duties Zebuluns, or dwellings. If they attend to their duties well and plentifully, they say, Shall we have something from heaven today? a smile, or a token for good? We have prayed with sighs and tears as well as groans today, and attended upon ordinances with longing; now we shall be God's darlings, surely he will make much of us. Being ignorant of God's word of righteousness, they go about to establish their own, looking for acceptance and manifestations of love from their humiliations and prayers, which are to be had in, by, and through Christ only.

And so they do not attain them, because they seek them not by faith, but as it were, by the works of the law (*Rom.* 9:31–32; 10:2–4). Their hopes of heaven and thoughts of God's love flow and ebb, are higher or lower, according to the workings of their heart in their duties. They rejoice in these things as the disciples did at the subjection of demons, more than (as grown saints do) that their names are written in heaven (*Luke* 10:17-20).

They promise themselves great things from their performances and submission to ordinances, as if the work done deserved something. My beloved, I do not say these things to shame you, but, as Paul did to his Corinthian babes, as by beloved ones, to warn and instruct you (*1 Cor.* 4:14).

To make this a little more clear, I ask you to observe that when Christ had told the young man that if he would leave all and follow him, he should have treasure in heaven (*Matt.* 19:21), almost immediately Peter said to him (19:27), 'Behold, we have left all and followed thee, what shall we have therefore?' This was a babyish response, as if they had deserved something great. Pray, what was this 'all' he talks of? It was a great 'all' indeed: a poor little fishing boat and an old net. And was this not worthy to be ushered in with a 'Behold'? and concluded with a 'What shall we have therefore'?

Alas, poor babes, they thought themselves very profitable servants, as our Saviour intimates to them (*Luke* 17:7). To what purpose does Christ tell them this story, but to let them know that he owes them no thanks, that they are servants to whom he is not beholden, for they had done only what was (and not all that was) their duty to do? And therefore he makes the application (*Luke* 17:10). So likewise ye, when you have done all things commanded you, sit down and write at the end of your accounts, We are unprofitable servants. Thus, he reproved them for expecting a reward as due. Christ will reward them, not as a debt, but by the gift of grace.

Take now a grown saint. He looks upon his all to be so

little, and his best so bad that he knows himself in debt to God, and not God in debt to him. He gives God but his own, what he first received and which is still God's due, and never thinks that he merits anything by paying his debts and doing what is his duty to do. When such a saint has done anything for God, he is so far from demanding a reward by way of due that he looks for it only as a gift, as Paul did (*2 Tim.* 4:7–8), and does not attribute only the reward to gift and grace, but even all the duty and work which he has done, and thanks God for that, too (*1 Cor.* 15:10). He looks on himself as needing Christ Jesus for his acceptance not only after his ill doing, but after his well doing, and would not for all the world be found in any righteousness but that which is by faith (*Phil.* 3:9). When he has done all his duty, he looks upon himself as an unprofitable servant, just as he does when he falls short of doing all his duty, or as if he had not done anything at all (*Matt.* 25:37).

e) They too often value ordinances according to the dispenser and administrator of them. Some of the Corinthian babes gloried that they were baptized by Paul, others that it was by Apollos, others that it was by Cephas (*1 Cor.* 1:12–16). And so with preaching. They are apt to confine God to such a man or such a sort of man; they like the same truth better if one man deliver it than another. And they would rather receive the sacrament from this man than from that. Thus babyishly partial are these poor babes.

It is true indeed, God may make one man's ministry more useful than another's, and that greatly endears the man and his ministry to those persons as have sat under it and felt it. But when people are divided by this and puffed up for one against another, it is then as carnal, as I shall show, and the apostle chides them for it as being babyish (*1 Cor.* 3:4; 4:6). When men are taken in with the ordinance not as God's but as man's, it is babyish. As it is noble indeed to receive the word not as man's, but God's (*1 Thess.* 2:13). To overvalue one and undervalue another, or to value the word of God for man's sake, is a foolish and babyish thing.

Take a grown spiritual Christian who is built up in the holy faith and taught the way of God more perfectly; whether Paul teaches him, or Apollos, or Cephas, it is all one to him, even Aquila and Priscilla (*Acts* 18:24–26). Babes, though, must hear their Paul, Apollos, Cephas, or nobody. It is the same if they are to join in prayer. They are dull and dead if this or that one does not pray and be their mouth to God, whereas an intelligent saint, it may be, finds much more of God's Spirit breathing in one that these babes cannot have the patience to hear. Many more such things are with you, poor babes, but as yet I spare you.

f) These babes sometimes sense their weakness and inability as to outward performances, but do not so much observe and sense their inward defects, as secret pride and confidence in what they seem to do well. They say, as the disciples, Why could we not cast him out? (*Matt.* 17:19). They were aware that there was a defect of power, for they attempted to do it, but could not. Yet at other times, when the demons were subject to them, there was a taste of pride in their rejoicing (*Luke* 10:17–21). And though Christ thanked his Father for what they had received, he calls them babes.

This word 'us' (the demons are subject to 'us') seems to take away a share from Christ, though they do add 'through thy name'. But you shall find that after they had received the Spirit and were spiritually more grown, they wholly laid the 'us' aside and gave all the glory to God in Christ (*Acts* 3:12–13). 'Why gaze ye on us, as if we by our power had made this man walk? God hath glorified his Son Jesus.' Now, you see the 'us' is laid aside, and they do not take a share from Christ as they did before.

So it is with babes as to ordinances and duties. They find a weakness, they cannot do what they endeavour to do. They are willing but do not have the power to do as they will, and this they are aware of. But then, when they meet with any power and do something well, they are apt to be lifted up, and if not to rest in it, then to divide the glory between God and themselves. So it is until they grow up, and then they will say, 'Not I but Christ; not I but the grace of God; and not to us, not to us, but to thy name be all the glory.'

Application

a) Words of exhortation for babes:

These things being so, which you cannot well deny, poor babes, let me speak to you and exhort you.

(i) Consider not only what you ought to do, but how you ought to do it, not only the matter but the manner of all duties. Measure your obedience more by the quality than the quantity, by weight more than by number, together with what ends you have in it. It is not the size or juiciness of the fruit, but the relish that gives the commendation, and that is the end you have in doing your duties. If your obedience does not have a good taste, though your duties be ever so many and well coloured and seem full of devotion, they are not acceptable to God or a sweet-smelling savour to him.

The usual question that babes ask is about the 'what' of duty. What shall we do? they say. What must I do? saith the jailer. Lord, what wilt thou have me to do? saith Paul. They mind the matter of duty and ask often about the 'what'. But as we should mind *what* to hear and do, so we should mind *how* to hear and do. We should not only receive the Lord's Supper, but so as to discern the Lord's body; not only pray, but pray according to his will; not only submit to baptism, but mind the how and why (*Rom.* 6:3-5, *Col.* 2:11-13).

God does not look so much to the hand as to the heart, to the action as to the spirit of it, and the end for which it is done. The rich man threw in much more for quantity than the widow, yet her mite was more than their abundance. There may be more of prayer in a short utterance than in a long prayer of many words. God is taken more with a little well done than with much good done. Adverbs describe God best, as all that he did was good exceedingly, and Jesus Christ is not only true but truly bread. So adverbs describe our best, when we do what we do, truly, sincerely, faithfully, for these express the spirit and end of duties.

A little gold refined has more worth than much in the ore, and one diamond has more value than a heap of common stones. A short prayer may have more in it than a long one – not that I speak against any person's great devotion in duty, for if God opens, who can shut? But no one should consider the excellence of a duty by length or merely fervency, for many things may occasion it. It may not be fervency of spirit originating with the Spirit of God.

It is not how much but how well, not how emotional but how spiritual, that God takes into account. Many lads when they begin to write strive to write much, but their masters say, Write me two lines well and I will take it better than if you scribble and scrawl on a side of paper. It is not worshipping at Jerusalem but in spirit and truth that God wants. And as to place, so it is to amount. To what purpose are your many sacrifices? It is a broken heart that I will not despise. The apostle takes care not only to pray or sing but to do it with understanding and his spirit also (*1 Cor.* 14:15). Spiritual things should be done spiritually; we should not only do the things which are pleasing to God, but do them so that the doing of them may be pleasing to him, his will according to his will.

(*ii*) *Consider the true design of ordinances and duties.* They are not your food, but the dishes in which your food is set before you; not the water of life, but the pipes through which is it conveyed to you. It is not ordinances and duties that you should make your end; no, they are but means to an and. Would you eat well and take up sport without health? Why then attend ordinances without the power, blessing, and effects of them? I do not say this to put you off ordinances and duties, but so that you do not look there for what God has not placed there, nor have that value for them and trust in them which is only to the God of ordinances. Do not live without ordinances, but live above them while you use them.

(*iii*) *Be more universal in your obedience, and do not confine religion to certain days and duties.* God is the universal good, and we are most like him when we are universally so. We shall not be ashamed when we have respect to all his commandments (*Psa.* 119:6). It was the great commendation of Zacharias and Elizabeth that they walked in all the commandments and ordinances of God without blame. They did not pick and choose some, make 'ifs' and 'ands' as to others, but were indeed lovers of all. And here is love, that we keep his commands, all of them, and find none of them are grievous (*1 John* 5:3). Every creature is good in one respect or another; they have particular goods, this or that. But God is all good and does good to all. All his commands also are holy, just and good, and we should study to know and do all the good and acceptable and perfect will of God (*Rom.* 12:2), to be as like God, and to do all that God likes, as much as possible.

(iv) Observe the proper season of ordinances and duties, of hearing and praying, and so on. Everything is beautiful in its season. It is the glory of the tree planted by preaching, watered by baptism, blessed with the laying on of hands, to bring forth fruit in season. For the earth, which drinketh in the rain that cometh oft upon it (precept on precept and line on line), to bring forth herbs suitable and seasonable for them by whom it is dressed, receiveth blessing from God (*Heb.* 6:7). This refers to the parable of the good-ground hearers, as the next verse refers to the thorny ground.

There is a time for all things, and because man does not know his time, his sorrows are great. It is unseemly for a man to mourn in a time of joy, as it is to rejoice in a time of mourning. But, to speak particularly to babes: to be praying in a time that calls for another duty, or to be hearing when some duty in your occupation or family calls upon you to be then and there to attend to that, is not beautiful because it not seasonable. Babes are too apt to rob Peter to clothe Paul, to take from one duty and give to another.

(v) Do what you do more out of love than fear, and more out of thankfulness and gratitude than custom or restraint. Many carnal ones come as the people cometh (*Ezek.* 33:31). Company, custom, and the bell, more than conscience, tolls them to ordinances. And too often babes in Christ are as carnal in this matter, sometimes not properly coming but being driven and forced to ordinances and duties.

There is a thing called conscience which, when it is awakened, makes a great deal of noise, and when men are convinced of sin they will do almost anything for the sake of ease and quiet. When they have been used to hearing and praying and have found some relief by it, they are under a kind of bondage and dare not omit it, even though perhaps it is not the proper time. But they fear conscience shall fly in their face, will chide and whip them. And to prevent this, they resolve to hear and pray.

But if you will do anything well, do it from a better nature, from love and a childlike spirit. Be as one who knows his obligations to be dutiful and not to sin, apart from any threats or terrors attending the omission of good or commission of evil.

(vi) Go on to address God in the way of his ordinances and your duties, though you should not meet with all the encouragement which you long for. Commit yourselves to God in all ways of well doing, though you may not have such joys and raptures as some have and you desire. Do not serve God merely for benefits. Be more generous and noble, and think what a great honour it is that you can serve him and do your duty. It is true, God has made all our duties privileges, and in keeping his commands, as well as afterward, there is great reward. His service is not only a means but a part of our happiness. Yet we serve him best when we do our duty as it refers to God rather than as privilege which refers to us. A generous soul will serve God and thank him that it may, though it gets not a penny for its pains and labour and bears the burden and heat of the day. It is not an affectionate child that will not be obedient longer than it is lured and bribed by fine things.

It is a greater honour to us that we serve God, than it is to God that we serve him, as it was to Solomon's servants more an honour that they waited on him than it was to him to be waited on by them. Blessed are thy servants, saith the queen of Sheba. It is a blessing to be dutiful, beside the blessing that is to come after we have been dutiful. Take care about your duty, and God will take care about your comfort. Only (mark this) let your way of life be as becomes the gospel; take care for nothing but that (*Phil.* 1:27). It is said of Christ (*Isa.* 49:3–5), Thou art my servant, O Israel, by whom I will be glorified. Now, though much of his labour was in vain as to the Jews, his judgement, work, and reward was with the Lord. The apostles also were a sweet savour unto God, though some perished (*2 Cor.* 2:15).

If you receive no other comfort, comfort yourself that you are doing your duty, the work that God has given you to do. You have been often at ordinances and duties, and you have said, Oh that I might see God as well as seek him, and yet he has not lifted up the light of his countenance upon you. Well, yet be glad that he has kept you in the way of duty. You need more patience, yet after you have done the will of God you may enjoy the promise. However, do go on to serve him, and take care you do it not out of constraint or for lucre's sake, but of a ready and generous mind (*1 Pet.* 5:2). If you find any duty too hard for you, pray as the disciples did when Christ bid them forgive seven times, a hard duty, Lord, increase my faith (*Luke* 17:5). Much and great faith will help you to do much and great work.

(vii) And lastly, look to Jesus Christ and cast yourself on him even if you do all things well. We need a Christ not only for the doing of duty, without whom we can do nothing (*John* 15:5) and through whom we can do all things (*Phil.* 4:13), but we need a Christ for the acceptance of what we do. Even our fruits of righteousness are not acceptable except through him in whom we are accepted. Our most spiritual sacrifices must be offered on this altar and by it be sanctified (*1 Pet.* 2:5, *Rom.* 8:3). We need a Christ not only to bring us to God at first, but always and forever. As our sin is pardoned, so our duties are accepted for Christ's sake. Christ is all and in all. Do

all you can as if there were no Christ, and after that rely on Christ as if you had done nothing, as you trusted him at first when indeed you had done nothing. It is with him and what is in him that God is well pleased.

b) Words of consolation for babes:

Though I have shown your weakness, I have a few words of consolation for you.

(i) *God will separate the precious from the vile, and gold from the dross; he will pick out the best and make much of it, be it only a little.* And for what you judge yourself, you shall not be judged by the Lord, as the apostle tells his babes in relation to their ill way of attending upon that great ordinance of the Lord's Supper (*1 Cor.* 11:31). He will put your tears into his bottle, he will remember your thinking on his name when others said, It is in vain to serve God, and what profit is there that we have kept his ordinances? (*Mal.* 3:14–18). You have toiled all day and caught nothing, yet at his command you have cast in your net again and have caught a great catch. Some are good and some are bad; but God will separate the good from the bad. He will gather the good into his vessels and cast the bad away (*Matt.* 13:47–48).

In the story of Sarah (*Gen.* 18:12–15), what grace could you find there? And yet God does, and it is recorded (*1 Pet.* 3:6) that Sarah called her husband Lord, which she did at that time, when the angel chided her for unbelief and for telling a lie, too. When the disciples failed in their duty and promise to Christ, he yet picks out this, that their spirit was willing (*Matt.* 26:41). He takes it ill that they do not watch, but takes it well that it was in their heart and they were willing to watch. And though they had often failed, our Saviour puts a better interpretation upon them than they or anybody else could, and tells his Father, They have kept thy word (*John* 17:6).

When David prays to God to hear his voice, he brings in what at first view seems a strange argument (*Psa.* 130:2–3): If thou shouldst mark iniquities, who shall stand? He tells God of his iniquities which might stand as a cloud between God and him. It is an excellent way to confess our sins when we pray, and then they shall not hinder good things from us, because God will not mark them when we do. For there is forgiveness with him that he may be feared (130:4). And for this reason and in this way, David exhorts Israel also to hope in God, for with him is mercy, plenty of it (130:7). And so he also says in Psalm 103 and infers that God will not always chide (103:8–9). As a father pitieth his poor, weak, and defective children, so the Lord pitieth them that fear him, for he knows their frame as well as their frailty (103:13–14).

(ii) I tell you this for your comfort, that though you sin in falling so short of righteousness, yet you have an advocate with the Father, Jesus Christ the righteous, who is the propitiation for your sin (*1 John* 2:1–2). I write this that you may not sin. But if any one of you that are called sons, though but a babe, if any of you sin, we, from the highest to the lowest, have an advocate, who is the Lord our righteousness, and by whose righteousness our sins shall be taken away. For he will never stop making intercession till he has saved to the utmost, which he is able to do, because he ever lives to make intercession for all that come to God by him. And therefore, when the apostle has said (*Rom.* 8:34), Who shall condemn? he does not only say, It is Christ that died, or rather that is risen again, or even that he sits at the right hand of God; but he says also that he maketh intercession for us. This secures all the rest. It is the utmost completing act of our high priest, and the way he saves to all intents and purposes, perfectly.

(iii) Take this word of consolation also: There is a resurrection and eternal judgement to come. After that, though you shall not rest day or night from serving God in praise (*Rev.* 4:8), you shall rest from your labour and serve him no more in a way of toil as you do now (*Rev.* 14:13). In the meantime, though your soul may lie under the altar (not sleeping, though at rest), it shall be clad with white and glorious robes (*Rev.* 6:9–11). And after the sufferings of the brotherhood shall be accomplished, the same God of all grace, who has called you into his eternal glory by Christ Jesus, will bring you into that glory and perfect all that concerns you (*1 Pet.* 5:9–10). Then you shall keep an everlasting Sabbath or rest with God without interruption or distraction, and sing songs with Moses and the Lamb forever. Comfort yourselves and one another with these words (*1 Thess.* 4:18). The resurrection and eternal judgement shall come and will not tarry. And this brings me to the next things mentioned as foundation doctrine, and some of the milk which babes take in.

THEIR BELIEF IN THE RESURRECTION OF THE DEAD AND
ETERNAL JUDGEMENT

I do not intend any long discourse about the resurrection and judgement to come, but only as much as serves our present purpose, to show the attainment of babes.

Babes not only submit to ordinances for a time, the time of their life, but they believe in another life after this is over. Time is but a forerunner of and prophet for eternity. They believe this with an operative faith which influences their practice and way of life, and so denotes a further attainment of theirs.

Faith is for eternity: The belief of a resurrection supposes dying, and eternal judgement supposes that man is to be accountable for his living here in time, and that as he sows he shall reap. He that does not believe in an after and eternal state, believes and is baptized to no purpose, as the apostle concludes (*1 Cor.* 15). So then the babes in Christ not only repent from dead works, act faith towards God, submit to ordinances and do duties; but they also believe in the resurrection of the dead and eternal judgement. Those who do not believe this are not newborn and cannot be called babes in Christ. Faith in Jesus is for eternity, and not only for this life, for otherwise true Christians would of all men be most miserable, as the apostle says.

(i) *Which resurrection is here meant*

We may in the first place here understand the resurrection of Christ from the dead, by which we are begotten again to a hope of life (*1 Pet.* 1:3). When the apostle mentions our freedom from condemnation as grounds for our rejoicing in Christ Jesus, he puts a 'rather' upon Christ's resurrection (*Rom.* 8:34). And when he writes to the Corinthian babes about the resurrection, he begins with this as the foundation of all, that Christ died and rose again, and from there proves the general resurrection (*1 Cor.* 15:3–4,12).

Corresponding to this, we may understand that the judgement concerning men's eternal condition is committed to Christ; that he, who is raised and is the resurrection, will raise the dead and judge the dead to their eternal states (*Acts* 10:41–42; 17:31, *2 Tim.* 4:1). But for fear, and indeed I do fear, that babes may not have so distinct and exact a knowledge of this as other saints have, I shall fix upon another sense.

Babes, in general, believe that there shall be a resurrection of all persons unto judgement, and a judgement of all persons to an eternal good or evil state;

therefore it is called an eternal judgement (*John* 5:28–29). The time is coming in the which all that are in the graves shall hear his (the Son of Man's) voice, and shall come forth; they that have done good, to the resurrection of life, and they that have done evil unto the resurrection of damnation (*Matt.* 25:31,46, *Rom.* 2:6,16, *2 Cor.* 5:10). There are many special things about the resurrection of which the babes have little knowledge, and of which I shall say nothing now. But they do believe in general that such a thing there will infallibly be, as a future eternal state of happiness or misery to men according to what they have done in this life. Those who do not believe this are but falsely called Christians. A saint who does not believe in a life to come is not less than a contradiction in terms.

Perhaps it will be objected that a man may be in Christ, though but a babe and as carnal, and yet not believe this doctrine of the resurrection, for among these Corinthian babes it seems some did not own it (*1 Cor.* 15:12). To this I answer that the 'some among you' may not refer to the Corinthians themselves, for it is not said 'some of you'. But false teachers came among them, perhaps worse infidels than Hymenaeus and Philetus, who said the resurrection was past already (*2 Tim.* 2:18); for these said there was none at all. This, indeed, was to deny Christ to be risen, and he that does so cannot be a Christian, cannot be a babe in Christ. But in the faith that Christ was risen the Corinthians stood (*1 Cor.* 15:1–4). Therefore I suggest they were some 'among them', but not 'of them' (as in *1 John* 2:19).

However, the foundation of God stands sure, and the apostle does not speak this so much by way of charge as of caution, less of accusation than of warning (*1 Cor.* 5:34). I speak this to your warning, that you may fear and beware of such Sadducees who have not the knowledge of God nor Scripture (*Matt.* 22:29), and whose evil words and Epicurean language are apt to beget evil conduct.

So notwithstanding this objection, it is clear enough that he cannot be a true Christian, no, not of the lowest form, who does not believe in the resurrection of the dead and eternal judgement.

(ii) What attainment results from this belief

What babes gain from this belief is that they tremble at this word of God, which is a blessed frame of mind (*Isa.* 66:2). If hearing it makes wicked men tremble, as it did Felix (*Acts* 24:25); if the sense of an after-state makes men pray, as Balaam did, 'Let me die the death of the righteous, and let my "afterward" (so in Hebrew) be as theirs' (*Num.* 23:10); how much better influence has it on babes in Christ! This trembling of theirs is of great use in working out their salvation (*Phil.* 2:12). It makes them wary and cautious not to run with others to the same excess of riot (*1 Pet.* 4:3–5). Besides dissuading them from sin, it helps persuade them to duty. Knowing the terror of the Lord, with reference to judgement, we persuade men (*2 Cor.* 5:10–11).

The consideration of a future judgement awes the most eminent saints, as it did Job (*Job* 31:14,23) and David (*Psa.* 119:120), but it makes babes especially to tremble, because they are yet without assurance of eternal welfare. Perfect love casteth out fear and hath boldness in the day of judgement (*1 John* 4:17–18), but poor babes are all their life long subject to more or less bondage by the fear of death and judgement (*Heb.* 2:14–15). Though Christ has died, they fail to apply his death particularly to themselves. Grown saints have attained to this and can therefore challenge and brave death itself, as Paul did (*Rom.* 8:34–39, *1 Cor.* 15:55–57),

[116]

and can desire rather than fear to die (*Phil.* 1:23, *Heb.* 11:35, *2 Cor.* 4:16–18).

Babes are fearful, yet God makes many and great uses of this fear and trembling for their good and his glory. Fear lays great restraint upon them as to sin and (as love does others) it constrains them to obedience. Therefore our Saviour speaks to their own concern: Fear him that can destroy both body and soul in hell (*Matt.* 10:28). And Paul says (*2 Cor.* 5:10–11), We persuade men, even poor babes who walk as men, and are only a little beyond natural man. Terror persuades with natural men; put them in fear, that they may know they are but men (*Psa.* 9:16,20). They hardly know God or acknowledge him, except by the judgements which he executes.

It is worth noting how many ways this theme of judgement to come and the terror of the Lord is used to persuade men and babes, who are as carnal and walk as men:

This idea of a judgement day provokes to repentance (*Acts* 17:30–31), and this is babes' milk.

It is an argument for faith and baptism, too (*Mark* 16:16). He that believeth and is baptized shall be saved, but he that believeth not shall be damned. The fear of this dreadful damnation drives many into faith and baptism.

It persuades men to fear God and keep his commands (*Eccles.* 12:13) and to be moderate in the use of worldly enjoyments which belong to life below (*Eccles.* 11:9–10, *Luke* 21:34–36).

It persuades men to embrace and make full use of gospel opportunities and the means of grace, as our Saviour hints (*Matt.* 11:20–24).

It persuades men not to censure, judge, despise and revile one another, which babes are apt to do (*1 Cor.* 3:3, *1 Pet.* 2:1–2). I say it persuades them not to do such things (*James* 4:11–12, *Rom.* 14:10, *1 Cor.* 4:3–5, *1 Pet.* 4:4–5, *Jude* 15).

It persuades them to patience (*James* 5:8); to abide in Christ Jesus and not apostatize (*1 John* 2:28); and to watch and be ready (*Matt.* 24, *1 Thess.* 5:1–7).

In a word, judgement is a very powerful argument to spur to every duty and to serve God acceptably (*2 Cor.* 5:9–10, *2 Tim.* 4:1–2, *Heb.* 12:28–29).

Thus we see the great value of believing the doctrine of the resurrection and eternal judgement, as babes do, and with fear. It is true indeed that love, which moves the more grown saints, is the more generous and noble principle. But fear is of great use too, for the fear of the Lord is the beginning of wisdom, as love is the fulfilling of the law. Under the Old Testament, when men were generally babes, religion was expressed by fear as much as it is expressed under the New Testament by faith and love. And while babes are not wholly destitute of faith and love, they act mostly upon fear. The babes' faith is a fearful faith, which argues its imperfection; but the grown saint's fear is full of faith, which is an argument of its perfection. For it loves to please the God it fears, and fears to offend the God it loves. Self-preservation is natural to men, and fear causes men to avoid what will hurt them, as much as love causes them to do what will preserve them. It is true, fear has torment, which perfect love casts out. But yet it leads to escaping a greater torment, and is therefore useful to the state of babes.

But lest they should fear and tremble more than need, I shall speak to them a little by way of application.

Application: Encouragement to babes concerning the judgement
Come, poor babes, you that tremble at the word of God and serve him, though with fear. Hear this for your

consolation: The high and lofty one who dwelleth in the high and holy place does not despise such a trembling soul, but will dwell with it (*Isa.* 57:15). Do not be afraid of the resurrection or of judgement, it will be a happy day for you. Read yourself what is said in 1 Thessalonians 4:13-18; 5:1-11.

You have a friend in the court of heaven, Jesus Christ your advocate, and he it is that shall be your judge. To be sure, he will not condemn any that are in him, although they may be but babes. He will remember your labour of little love (*Heb.* 6:9-10). You may see him telling you beforehand, in what he says about a cup of cold water and so on (*Matt.* 25:34-37), that he remembers what you have forgotten, and regards that which you may have feared was worth nothing. He is so gracious that he will remember your sins no more, but he is so righteous that he will not forget your labour of love, no, nor your fear. For he has a book of remembrance written for them that feared the Lord and thought, and perhaps could do little more than think, upon his name (*Mal.* 3:16).

Well, then, as the wicked should rejoice with trembling (*Psa.* 2), you should tremble with rejoicing. Abide in him, keep close to him whom you have chosen for your Saviour, and you shall not be ashamed before him at his coming (*1 John* 2:28). Be steadfast and immovable, abound always in the work of the Lord, for your labour shall not be in vain at the resurrection (*1 Cor.* 15:58). Live as one that looks for and hastens to the coming of the Lord (*2 Pet.* 3:11-12). And he will come, without sin, a Saviour, and change your corrupt body and make it like his most glorious body.

So let not only your affection but conversation be in heaven (*Col.* 3:1-4, *Phil.* 3:20-21), which no one can do who does not believe in the resurrection and eternal judgement. Be glad and bless God, who has given you this milk and taught you to take it in, for without it you would still have been without God in the world, and in the world to come. That shall be a world of happiness to you and all saints, who do not have their portion of good in this life, as the wicked have, but who have good reserved to be theirs at the resurrection and eternal judgement.

THEIR TASTING THAT THE LORD IS GRACIOUS, AND
THEIR DESIRING THE SINCERE MILK OF THE WORD
(FROM I PETER 2:1–3)

The Apostle Peter, as well as Paul, had to do with babes, for such were the Jewish converts, generally. Having told them (*1 Pet.* 1:23) that they were born again, he exhorts them in this text to lay aside all malice, and all guile, and hypocrisies, and envies, and all evil speaking, to which they, being yet as carnal, were too prone; and as newborn babes to desire the sincere milk of the word, that they may grow thereby, if so be (or seeing and because) they have tasted that the Lord is gracious.

This tasting is their coming to Christ and believing in him as the chief corner stone, and their growth is their being built upon him a spiritual house (*1 Pet.* 2:4–6). These denote both the nature and inclination of these babes – to come to and believe in Christ, and then to grow up in and to be built on him. As he is precious or an honour to them, so they may be precious or an honour to him and show forth the virtues, and thereby the praises, of him who has called them out of their darkness into his marvellous light (*1 Pet.* 2:7–9).

But having spoken before of their faith, I shall now speak of some of their experience, which I believe is expressed in this word of 'tasting'. The mature Christian has many active senses and is full of many and rich experiences (*Heb.* 5:14). But the babe has the use of this one sense, tasting, which produces in him a desire and longing after the Word for growth, that he may suck and be satisfied with consolations, that he may draw milk and be satisfied with the abundance of glory (*Isa.* 66:11).

The babe has a taste as soon as he is born and has milk given him to eat, in which he tastes a sweetness and from which he finds the nourishment and strength to keep him alive. If he were not alive he could not taste, and if he did not taste he could not live. Experience is often expressed by tasting, which is beyond hearing and is joined with seeing. Oh, taste and see that the Lord is good (*Psa.* 34:8). Now, as seeing, so tasting affects the heart and whets the appetite; therefore, says Peter, desire the milk. This expresses not only the duty, but the nature and inclination of babes, and that is grounded on tasting, seeing or because they have tasted that the Lord is gracious. They have had several experiences, or tastes, of this:

1. That the Lord will admit them to repentance is of his grace. When man had sinned the law was strict, a man's repentance could find no place for re-acceptance, though it might be sought with tears. God might have chosen whether he would have admitted man to repent. But now that he has, it savours of grace, and by this the babes taste that he is gracious.

2. They taste that the Lord is gracious in that he has provided a new and living way to come to him, that they may be saved at another's cost and charges; that he sent his Son into the world to save sinners, and that through him they might believe in God and have hope in him (*1 Pet.* 1:21).

3. They taste grace in this, that God calls for no greater things at their hand than to eat milk and to repent and

believe the gospel. He does not put them to do penance in hell for thousands of years, or do some extraordinary tasks of duty in this world, to weep out their eyes or wear out their knees.

4. They taste his grace in that he not only commands, but invites and entreats them to come, to repent and believe, that they may live. That God should condescend so far as to beseech and go begging to them, as the word is, that they would be reconciled, gives them a taste that the Lord is gracious (2 Cor. 5:19–20).

5. They also taste it in that God encourages them to come by many great and precious promises (Isa. 55:1–3, Matt. 11:28–30). Indeed, he swears to them that as he lives he takes no delight in the death of a sinner, but that he should return and live.

6. God has knocked often and waited long to lead them by his goodness, patience, and long-suffering to repentance. Though they have answered only in a surly and sinful way, though they have tried his patience, that he should still knock and wait, this gives them a further taste that the Lord is gracious.

7. It is of grace that they have at last been convinced of the necessity of repentance toward God and faith in our Lord Jesus Christ, that they are come to themselves to see their dead, lost and undone condition. For who could have or would have opened their eyes and worked in their hearts but a gracious God? In this they taste his grace.

8. That they have been enabled, with the prodigal, to act on this conviction, to arise and go, to repent from dead works and to make toward God by faith, they taste his grace in it, for repentance and faith are both gifts to them of a gracious God (Acts 5:31, Eph. 2:1–8).

9. They taste that the Lord is gracious in giving them a spirit of prayer and supplications, that they can bow their

knees and beg not only the pardon of their sins but the sanctifying of their souls. In this they taste his grace.

10. They have a taste of his being gracious in that they are welcomed when they come, and that not only his saints receive them freely into the brotherhood and fellowship, but that now and then God smiles on them, too, and is pleased to kiss them and to grant them some fellowship with himself.

11. They taste that the Lord is gracious in that he sits on a throne of grace and gives them leave to come with boldness for more mercy and grace for their relief, and that he allows them sincere milk to grow thereby.

12. They taste his grace in this also, that they can discern the difference between their former and present state, how desperate and damnable that was, but how hopeful this is, that they would rather die than be dead in sins again.

13. What present peace they have and whatever hopes of more, even to everlasting consolation, it is from the grace of God, and in it they taste that he is gracious (*2 Thess.* 2:16).

These are some, among others, of the experiences that babes have, or tastes of the Lord being gracious. I have not enlarged upon them, because I would give them to you as they have them, for tastes. And though they are only tastes, these tastes beget desires and longings after the sincere milk that they may grow thereby. By this taste of theirs they can begin to distinguish between sincere and falsified milk, between pure and impure milk, between good and evil doctrine, though not so well as grown saints. Their ear tries words, whether they are sound, and their taste tries milk-meat, whether it is wholesome and nourishing or not (*Job* 12:11; 34:3). So though they are full of appetite and desire, it is only for sincere milk, for they cannot thrive or live by any other.

Now though their desire after high attainments is at present almost their highest attainment, desires are not worthless things, but of value. The desire of a man is his kindness, and a poor man is better than a liar (*Prov.* 19:22). Though poor as to attainments, they are rich in desires, and God takes this kindly at their hands, as it is in their hearts to do greater things and to grow. This poor man is better than a liar, better than a hypocrite that pretends, makes professions and promises great things without kindness or a real desire to the things which he makes a great show of.

If there is first a willing mind, it is accepted according to what a man has, and not according to what he has not (*2 Cor.* 8:12). It is not a little to be able to say, as Nehemiah did (*Neh.* 1:11), Oh Lord, I beseech thee, let now thine ear be attentive to the prayer of thy servants, and to the prayer of thy servants who desire to fear thy name; and as the author of the epistle to the Hebrews (13:18): Pray for us, for we trust that we have a good conscience in all things willing to live honestly. This babe is a man of desires in both senses. He is loving and beloved, he is desiring and desired (S*ong of Sol.* 7:10, *Isa.* 26:8–9, *2 Cor.* 7:7).

Thus you have seen the tastes and desires of babes to grow, which is an attainment not to be undervalued by them or by others. And finally, to all their former attainments and characters I shall add one more, which is much taken notice of in Scripture.

THEIR LOVE TO THE BRETHREN

One thing more I shall note in relation to babes' attainments, and that is their love to the brethren. In this they act like members of the body of Christ, whose office it is to have the same care one for another (*1 Cor.*

12:25) and not to be like this world, every man for himself, or say like Cain, 'Am I my brother's keeper?' Peter attests that they do love the brethren fervently as well as truly. Writing to babes, he says, Seeing ye have purified your hearts in obeying the truth by the Spirit unto unfeigned love of the brethren, see that ye continue to love one another, with a pure heart fervently (*1 Pet.* 1:22). He exhorts them to do fully what they already do in part (*1 Thess.* 5:11): Comfort yourselves together, and edify one another, as ye also do.

It is the great character of Christ's disciples that they love one another (*John* 13:35). By this they are known to have passed from death to life, because they love the brethren (*1 John* 3:15). Allow me to mark that in the first epistle of John, the great duty urged, spoken to and of all the children of God, is to love one another. And the sin so much declaimed against is hating or not loving one another. When he says (*1 John* 3:8), He that sinneth is of the devil, he means this sin in special, for he says (3:9), Whosoever is born of God does not commit sin, this sin, because the seed of God, of whom he is born, remaineth in him. That is the same reason given by Peter pressing to the same duty (*1 Pet.* 1:22–23). And in verse 10 John distinguishes the children of God from those of the devil by this very thing. He then takes Cain as example, who was of the wicked one, breaking this command of loving his brother. And perhaps the sin unto death spoken of (*1 John* 5:16–19) refers to this sin, for such a person abides in death (*1 John* 3:14; 3:7–16), and this seems to be very clear.

As to babes' love for the brethren, it is clearly manifested in that (among other things) they are ready to minister to their necessities as occasion, opportunity, and ability allow. The apostle boasts of his Corinthian babes' readiness of mind (*2 Cor.* 9:1–2). And the author of the epistle to the Hebrew babes tells them that God was not unrighteous to forget their labour of love, which they had shown to his name in ministering to the saints. It is upon this score he is persuaded such good things of them as accompanied and contained salvation (*Heb.* 6:9–10), of so great an esteem is this grace of love, demonstrated by ministering to the saints. And indeed, it is the great thing for which Jesus Christ says, Come, ye blessed of my Father, inherit the kingdom prepared for you. Why, Lord? For I was hungry, and you ministered to me. In doing it to mine, you did it to me (*Matt.* 25:34–40). This labour of love is not in vain in the Lord.

SUMMING UP THE ATTAINMENTS AND CHARACTERS OF BABES

And now that babes may see themselves in this glass, I shall sum up their attainments and characters:

They have the foundation laid, they are newborn, and they eat milk in obeying the principles of the doctrine of Christ. They have all things necessary to being a saint, those things which accompany or contain salvation. But they do not have enough to prosper here, or to gain a great reward in heaven, as other saints have.

They have all essential graces as repentance, faith, and love, though not in as high a degree as the other classes have. After their manner, they press forward, desiring to grow.

Though they cannot run the race, they walk in the way of God's commandments. They press after to follow the other saints, but slowly and unable to keep pace.

This is their picture, a sketch of their attainment.

I shall now show their defectiveness in comparison of other saints, and how they are as carnal, that I may provoke them to jealousy and emulation, and by these to perfection.

THEIR DEFECTIVENESS AND FALLING SHORT COMPARED WITH OTHER SAINTS

It is obvious and easily granted that babes fall short of fathers and young men, who are strong saints. But they also fall short of the little children.

The character of little children is that they know the Father to be their Father (*1 John* 2:13). But the babe-child, the infant of attainments as well as days, the sucking child fed only with milk, though he has a Father that provides for him, does not know him to be his Father.

Most people in the Old Testament were but babes, and their usual way to address God was as the God that made heaven and earth, the Creator, and sometimes as the God of Abraham, Isaac, and Jacob, the Promiser. But as a collective body, seldom – not more than twice – did they address God as their Father. The places where they did are Isaiah 63:16, and 64:8. Both of these are prophecies of what they should do hereafter, rather than assertions of what they then did, as some believe. And in this latter, they address him as a Father, a Maker and Sovereign, as it appears by calling themselves the clay and God the Potter, and telling him that they are the works of his hand.

An objection may be made that the prodigal at first addressed God as his Father ('I will go to my Father', and 'in my Father's house'). But this might be in the sense of a Creator, as in Deuteronomy 32:6. Besides, I may say that he seems to represent a returning back-slider, rather than a convert. And though returning also is a conversion and works much like conversion at the very first does, the story of the prodigal has respect to a former relation which was not wholly cut off, as was the case of returning Israel (*Hos.* 1:7, *Jer.* 3:1–5). They spoke of him as theirs, though they had been called by him *Lo-ammi*, Not My People, and almost divorced by him, which they deserved to be.

So for a while at the beginning of the gospel, the disciples were as babes, for they did not know the Father (*John* 14:6–11). And though Christ had taught them to pray, Our Father, it was a long time before they learned to ask of the Father in the name of Christ (*John* 16:23–24), or to know their union with the Father and the Son.

That is why our Saviour told them so often that they would know and enjoy more at that day. What day? When he was ascended to the Father, for then it was 'my Father and your Father, my God and your God' (*John* 20:17). And the Spirit descended from the Father, the Holy Ghost not being given till Christ was glorified (*John* 7:39). Christ said, At that day you shall know that I am in my Father, and you in me, and I in you, which yet you know not, though it is so (*John* 14:20). In that day you shall ask me nothing; verily, verily, I say unto you, whatsoever you shall ask the Father in my name, he will give it you. The time cometh (that day) when I shall no more speak to you in parables, but show you plainly of the Father. And, In that day you shall ask in my name (*John* 16:23–26).

And accordingly, after Christ's ascension and the receiving of the Holy Ghost, they did usually cry Abba, Father (*Rom.* 8:15–16, *Gal.* 4:6). They addressed God as the Father of our Lord Jesus Christ, and God our Father, as may be seen in verses too many to be quoted here. They had more knowledge and assurance of their interest in the Father and the Son, and of communion and fellowship with the Father and the Son (*1 John* 1:3), which for a great while they had been unacquainted with.

These then are the conclusions which I draw from these premises:

(i) Though the babe-saints have interest in and communion with God and Christ, it is much in the dark to them.

They do not have the assurance of it, as the little children and other saints have. I may say of these as God did of Israel in their infant age (*Hos.* 11:1–3), When Israel was a child, a babe, I loved him; I taught Ephraim also to go, but they knew not that I healed them. The babes are said to be known of God rather than said to know him (*Gal.* 4:9).

Babes have a measure of life and light and power. There are influences from God to them and a private communication between God and them, which now they apprehend and discern only a little. They are not sure whether this is God that comes down, or grace that goes up. It may be said of them as Jacob said, Surely the Lord is in this place, and I knew it not (*Gen.* 26:16).

The best of saints see but darkly and through a glass; they know only in part what shall one day be fully known. Babes see even more darkly and know even less. Being babes, their understanding is insignificant in comparison with that of men (*1 Cor.* 14:20). They see as the poor man did at first in a confused way, men as trees, yet walking. Other saints see them as they are, men clearly, as that man did after the second touch of Christ's hand (*Mark* 8:24–25).

These poor babes act by grace, but can hardly say it is grace. They walk and follow, as Peter did the angel out of prison but did not know that it had truly been done (*Acts* 12:9). They hear God and answer to his call as little Samuel did when he did not yet know the Lord (*1 Sam.*

3:7). They have attained to more things than they have attained to the knowledge of, which is the advance of other saints. Their eyes are in great measure held, as the disciples' were, so though Jesus draws near and talks with them, they do not know him (*Luke* 24:15–16). He tells them this and that, and they feel its working but do not know what to make of it and are afraid to ask him (*Luke* 9:45). Mary saw and talked with Jesus, yet took him for the gardener and did not know him till a while after (*John* 20:14–17).

So it is with these poor souls. Though God knows them, works in them, and talks to them, they do not yet know what he is doing, as Christ said to Peter (*John* 13:7). If they are in the Mount and see any glory, they are more afraid than transported. They say, It is good to be here, not knowing what they say (*Luke* 9:33). While Christ talks to them their hearts burn within them, they feel some heat and warmings, but they do not know him (*Luke* 24:16,32). They are troubled, and thoughts arise in their hearts, though he says, Peace be to you. They do not believe what could make them joyful (*Luke* 24:36–41). That which would promote another's faith seems to obstruct and put a stop to theirs.

This is their first defect in comparison of others, and how they fall short: Though they are, and act to some degree like God's people, they still do not know it and cannot yet discern clearly the work of grace. They cannot yet say, I am my beloved's, and he is mine.

(ii) They are defective and far short of other saints in that, being babes, they are unskilful in the word of righteousness (Heb. *5:13*).

The word of righteousness is the gospel, or Christ Jesus, who is the whole of the gospel. To preach the gospel and to preach Christ is all the same; and a minister of Christ and the gospel, or the word, is all the same. Christ Jesus is called the word (*John* 1:1), the word of salvation (*Acts* 13:26), the word of God's grace (*Acts* 20:32), the word of life (*Phil.* 2:16), and here (*Heb.* 5:13) the word of righteousness, in which these babes were unskilful (*apeiros*). The word does not exclude all knowledge, but excludes full knowledge and skill. They were inexpert or unskilful in discerning and knowing Christ (as they should) as the root of righteousness, for justification and sanctification, and to be made of God to us righteousness both by imputation and operation.

a) For justification: They were unskilful in the word of righteousness for justification. These Jewish or Hebrew babes could not easily put off the legal man, who seeks righteousness by, or at least as it were, by the works of the law (*Rom.* 9:32; 10:2). He cannot understand the word of the gospel which teaches the true righteousness, and that is justification by faith and not by the works of the law. This babe knows the elements, the letters of the gospel, but is not yet able to spell and read the whole word of righteousness.

Though Jesus Christ was made of God righteousness to the Corinthian babes (*1 Cor.* 1:30), they were ignorant of how: namely, that he became sin and a curse for us that we might be the righteousness of God in him (*2 Cor.* 5:1). Therefore the apostle resolved to make known nothing among them but Christ and him crucified (*1 Cor.* 2:2), as dying for our sins (for he knew none of his own) and rising again for our justification (*Rom.* 4:25). This was what he preached to the Corinthians at first, but doubted a little whether they firmly believed it (*1 Cor.* 15:1–5). For this, as well as for other things (*1 Cor.* 3), the Corinthians were but babes.

That this is the apostle's meaning to the Hebrew babes is clear from the context and scope of the whole epistle, which shows the excellence of Christ the high priest after the order of Melchisedek, the Lord our righteousness, beyond that of the law which made no one perfect nor righteous. He begins (*Heb.* 5:10–11) with this high priest after the order of Melchisedek, which is the word of righteousness, and strong meat, and the sum of all he had to say, as he says in 8:1. There he resumes his discourse, telling them that this is more excellent and better. He uses this word 'better' at least thirteen times in speaking of Christ and the gospel dispensation. But their weak stomachs could not digest this, and therefore he calls them babes. He who thinks he needs the ceremonial types and makes them his meat cannot take in the word of righteousness, the evangelical covenant, for he is a worse babe than those of old.

The Galatians also were guilty of this babyishness and were not past the spoon. They were receding, going back again to the law for righteousness, or at least blending and mixing it with faith. Paul calls them foolish for this, the same as babes and unskilful, as the whole epistle indicates. Indeed, he travails again for them, to bring them out from the law to a more perfect knowledge and image of Christ (*Gal.* 4:19).

So then, the babe's defect is that he is unskilful in the word of righteousness, in not knowing that Christ is our righteousness, and how. Many of the Christian Jews were but Jewish Christians. They were not easily persuaded to lay Moses and his law aside. The Christian Gentiles were too much Gentile Christians, who could hardly part with the law of nature and works. Few could do as Paul taught, to rest only in Christ Jesus, to reckon all ceremonies, privileges, tears, prayers, humiliations, and all that may be called our own righteousness, as loss and rubbish as concerns justification, though they might be blameless as touching the law.

Few could come to the point of being found in him and the righteousness that is of God by faith in him, and having no confidence in the flesh, but rejoicing in Christ Jesus.

Therefore we see that the apostles, whether writing to the Jews or Gentiles, made it their business to bring them away from every law and covenant to that of faith, and to ground and build them upon the only true foundation and corner stone, Christ Jesus, that he, as he deserves, might have the pre-eminence in all things and be all in all (*Col.* 3:11, *Gal.* 6:15–16, *Heb.* 13:7–8, *I Pet.* 2:5–6, *I Cor.* 1:29–31).

b) For sanctification: Babes are also unskilful in the word of righteousness for sanctification, in knowing him experientially as the root of sanctification, and understanding that it is only by and in him that they are to bring forth fruit. We have not only our first but our future grace from Christ. Our fruits of righteousness, even when we are filled with them, are acceptable to God and to his glory and praise only when they are from Christ, in whom all our fresh springs are. In him is our fruit found, from his fullness we receive grace for grace, and without being and abiding in him we can do nothing (*Phil.* 1:11, *I Pet.* 2:5, *Hos.* 14:8, *Psa.* 87:7, *John* 1:16; 15:5).

They that will grow in grace must grow in the knowledge of Christ as the root of that growth (*2 Pet.* 3:18). As they have received him they may walk in him, rooted and built up in him (*Col.* 2:6–7), that he may be not only the foundation but the whole structure, and the adorning may be from him. As it is essential to gospel sanctification to do everything for God as our end, so it is to do everything from and in the strength of Christ, through whom alone we are able to do all things (*Phil.* 4:13). As the glory of God is the final cause, so Christ is the efficient cause of all the fruits of righteousness (*Phil.* 1:11).

Indeed, it is as hard to live beyond ourselves and get everything from another, to say as Paul, It is not I that live, but Christ liveth in me, as it is to live not to ourselves but to another. Babes act and speak as if they lived on their own resources. They boast too often, as the Corinthians did, as if they had not received (*1 Cor.* 4:7). This principle of deriving all sanctification from Christ is not clearly known to all believers. Probably the disciples did not understand it till Christ taught it to them (*John* 15). This indeed is the case with babes, for though to them Christ is made wisdom, righteousness, redemption, and sanctification, they are still unskilful and inexpert in having particular recourse to him for these.

(iii) Babes are defective in that though they love to listen a great deal, they are unable to bear much, especially anything that is beyond milk, and called strong meat.
It would hurt and not help them to feed them with bread and wine, such as Melchisedek presented to Abraham (*Gen.* 14:18). Our Saviour's heart was full of many things to say, but he could not tell his disciples then, for they were not able to bear it (*John* 16:12). Paul told his Corinthian babes that he had fed them with milk and not with strong meat, for hitherto they were not able to bear it nor yet were they able (*1 Cor.* 3:2). The Hebrew babes, too, were dull and thick. It was hard for them to hear the doctrine which he calls strong meat; they could digest only milk (*Heb.* 5:11).

Hearing strong meat makes babes sick. It is like Saul's armour on David, too heavy for him. He had not been used to it or tried it, and therefore could not bear it. He could use only his sling to perform feats. Babes are not yet strong enough to put on all the armour of God. They

cannot wield the sword of the Spirit or use the shield of
faith ably. They are not yet weaned from the milk, and
who can teach them any high and great knowledge of
wisdom? They must have line on line, now and then a
little (*Isa.* 28:9–11). They must have the same things over
and over, as little ones when they go to school take a long
time learning their alphabet and must be shown again
and again which is A and which is B. They must be
taught in childish language that they understand.

Many a young student takes a great deal of pain, is
ever reading, but does not master what he reads. And the
fault lies not so much in the memory or the will as in the
understanding. So it is with these babes. They hear and
read much, and even though they remember it, they
cannot digest and use it. But strong men love to make
their meals of strong meat (*Heb.* 5:14).

*(iv) Babes are defective in that they have not developed the
habits of grown saints.*
There is as much difference between habit and disposition as there is between grown saints and babes (*Heb.*
5:14). Habits develop skill and strength and make the
doing easy, whereas dispositions are faint and weak,
mere efforts and attempts, such as in babes learning to
speak and walk. Like David with the armour, they are
not used to such things and cannot walk in them as
others can who have tried again and again. We easily do
things we are used to doing, but we bungle things for lack
of practice, which is the case with babes. So the
difference between saints is as great as between the
strength of manhood and the weakness of infancy, or
between a developed and practised habit and a mere
disposition or inclination.

(v) Babes are defective in that they do not have their senses developed.

They have the sense of taste, but not all the senses are exercised to discern both good and evil (*Heb.* 5:14). Babes lack what strong men have: discerning faculties and the ability to distinguish things that differ, that they may approve things which are most excellent. This Paul prayed that the Philippians might do (*Phil.* 1:10), and not only hold fast that which is good.

(vi) For want of this discernment, the babes are apt to be tossed to and fro with every fair wind of doctrine.

They can be abused by crafty companions and false teachers who can purposely contrive and use feigned words (*Eph.* 4:14): That we henceforth be no more children (Greek: babes) tossed to and fro and carried about with every wind of doctrine, by the sleight of men and cunning craftiness, whereby they lie in wait to deceive.

Of all those to whom epistles were written, those called babes were in the most danger, as the Corinthians (*1 Cor.* 4:15–21). The apostle cautions them to watch, to stand fast in the faith, to quit themselves like men, and to be strong (*1 Cor.* 16:13). And again he tells them his fears of them lest, as the serpent beguiled Eve in her infancy through his subtlety, so false teachers should corrupt their minds from the simplicity that is in Christ (*2 Cor.* 11:1–5; 12–15). The Hebrews, too, the babe Christian Jews in Judea, were in great danger of being turned aside by false teachers, which is why that epistle was written to them. The dispersed Jews appear to have been in like danger (*2 Pet.* 2:1–3; 3:17), and the Galatian babes also (*Gal.* ch. 6–9). But the little children are more fixed and firm (*1 John* 2:18–27).

(vii) The babes' defectiveness is seen in that they serve God more as servants than as children.

They are, as the prodigal at first wished to be, as hired servants. This is clear from Galatians. The heir, as long as he is a child (Greek: babe) differeth nothing from a servant, but is under tutors and governors, a school-master, the law (*Gal.* 3:24). And while they are children (Greek: babes) they are in bondage under the elements, or rudiments, of the world, which Paul calls beggarly (3:9), and tells them that this is, though they desire it, to be in bondage, opposed to being a son (3:6). But the grown saints stand fast in the liberty by which Christ has made them free, as Paul exhorts (*Gal.* 5:1), and will not be again entangled with this yoke of bondage, but worship God in spirit and in truth.

THEIR BEING AS CARNAL AND WALKING AS MEN

I have shown how babes are defective in comparison with other saints. Now I must show worse things: how they are as carnal.

These poor babes are only a degree above carnal men; though they are not carnal, they are *as* carnal. This is true for many of them, but as I have already mentioned, they are not all alike. Some are less defective and less carnal than others. The apostle said of the Corinthians not only that they were babes and not spiritual, but that they were *as* carnal, and walked *as* men. There was little difference, in many ways, between them and mere carnal men, who walk in and after the flesh (*1 Cor.* 3:1–3). This appears alas! in far too many instances.

(i) They were as carnal in that there was among them envy, strife, and division or faction (1 Cor. 3:3).

Because of this the apostle appeals to them to judge for

themselves whether they were not carnal and walked as men, in the flesh, or according to man and not according to God: Are you not carnal? You cannot deny that you are envious and divided. It is obvious to yourselves and is witnessed by others, and therefore you cannot deny that you are carnal, for such things are the works of the flesh (*Gal.* 5:19–21). They are not only from the earth and men, but from hell and the devil, who works these things in the children of disobedience, and in you, who in doing this are disobedient children. If you have bitter envying and strife in your hearts, glory not, and lie not against the truth, for this wisdom descends not from above, but is sensual, earthly, and devilish (*James* 3:14–15). A spiritually and heavenly wise man would be ashamed of such things.

What marks the Corinthians as babes and as carnal will also mark any and all others, however high or great their names may be, wherever it is found. Only note this: This is not ascribed to them from any particular act, but it is from a kind of habitual frequency and continuance, for that is the full meaning of the word 'walking'. A Christian should excel the best of men in all morality and candour. To be like the worst of men, envious ones, the devil's image, is very carnal indeed. But let us enquire a little into the occasion and cause of this.

The occasion was taken (not given!) from Paul and Apollos, who planted and watered them. From there the Corinthians became more than appreciative, more than loyal. They were envious for the glory of their teachers over against one another. One was for Paul and another for Apollos, as being of them, and this was their carnality (*I Cor.* 3:4; 4:6). But how was this carnal? Were they more carnal in saying, I am one of Paul's children, or one of Paul's hearers, than Paul was in calling himself their father and teacher? Surely not; the carnality did not lie in this. Paul calls Timothy and Titus his sons, and says of these Corinthians (*1 Cor.* 4:14–15) that they were his sons, that he had begotten them, that they were of him. And so in that similar sense they might without carnality call him father, and say they were of him. But the carnality lay in such things as the following four points:

a) They were more taken with the gifts and attributes of either teacher than with their office and graces.

People have, as I may say, various characters and moods, and they take a liking to different sorts. So some that were for utter plainness took Paul's part. Others that were more discriminating were taken with Apollos' eloquence. For Paul came not with oratory (*1 Cor.* 2:1–4) but with plainness of speech (*2 Cor.* 3:12), and Apollos was an eloquent man (*Acts* 18:24). In all this the Corinthians were babes and as carnal. For rather than admiring the men themselves and their attributes, they should honour the man of God for the work's sake. Instead, they seem to honour each for their own word's sake, and not for the sake of God's word, which came to them.

And alas! how many such babes are there among us also? Some are all for a bold preacher that comes with blows, or for one who speaks plainly; others with finer tastes must have the dish garnished, the cloth laced and trimmed and do not care for plain decor. This is all babyish and carnal, to look after what suits our taste and not after edification and increase.

b) These babyish and carnal Corinthians, it seems, confined not only themselves but God, too, to a particular man's ministry.

Some of them looked for no increase unless Paul preached, and others, unless Apollos preached, as if their faith and the blessing had come from the man (*1 Cor.* 3:5–7; 1:13–14). If Paul baptized, preached, and administered the Lord's Supper, then they expected great things, as others did from Apollos, as if the success had been from men and not from God. Poor babes, that will let no one feed them but this nurse, or that servant. As if the milk would do them most good when this or that person puts it into their mouth.

How many of these there are to this day, that do not care to listen unless such a man preach. 'Tush,' they say, 'this is not the man I came to hear,' and away they go. 'My heart will never be beaten down and broken,' says one, 'unless Paul preaches.' 'Nor mine lifted and raised up,' says another, 'unless Apollos is preaching.' They are far too often more taken with man than God, with man's word than God's.

We must know that if any work is accomplished, it is the Lord's doing, and he alone should be wonderful in our eyes. Whoever brings a message of mercy, it is God who sends and blesses it, and the glory should be his. These babes receive a man that stirs them as an angel of God, indeed, as Christ Jesus (*Gal.* 4:14). But after a while another may steal their hearts away, for many of them are unstable. And then Apollos is beyond Paul, and he becomes their enemy for telling them the truth, so they abandon him for another (*Gal.* 4:16-17). All this as if the men were all in all. They are won over by the men themselves, as if not Christ but Paul or others had been crucified for them; as if Christ were divided. So the apostle upbraids them (*1 Cor.* 1:12-13).

c) These babes were so carnal that some would refuse to believe a truth unless it came from the mouth of Paul; others unless it came from Apollos.

They embraced the truth for the man's sake more than the man for the truth's sake. The feet were more beautiful than the tidings, or else the tidings were not beautiful if such a man's feet did not bring them. If Paul said it was an oracle, his word was sufficient to some who would scarce believe it from Apollos. And others, for Apollos, preferred his message far beyond what they would have done if Paul had said the same thing. It is to them as if it were another thing, another gospel, another Christ, another spirit (*2 Cor.* 11:4).

And as it was then, is it not now? Some truths will not go down with some persons unless it comes from such and such a man, as if he made it more, and another less, true than it was. The truth is the same whether in Paul's or Apollos' mouth, and no more or less true for this or that man's saying it. If such a man or party of men say so, we will believe it, say many babes. This or that man is their oracle; if he says it, it must be true. If he does not say it, especially if he denies it, it cannot be true.

d) They were so carnal they fell into parties and took sides, and from there came envying and strife, factions, and confusion.

They broke out into vilifying one another, becoming proud and quarrelsome, and could not live in love and peace together. 'We say Paul is the best preacher, he preaches powerfully,' say the Paulinists. And say the Apollonians: 'Apollos is the best preacher, he preaches fluently.' And they can hardly resist fighting and crying out, Who is on our side? Who?

And alas, is this not fulfilled in our days! Who would think that babes would make so much ado? But babes are carnal. And what causes fighting and war, but the lusts of the flesh (*James* 4:1)? Oh that these babyish and carnal games may be laid aside! Granted, that God may use one man more than another for bringing in and building up. But still remember that the power is of God and not of the earthen vessel. You may love, if you do not idolize, your father Paul or call him father, as the Jews did the Pharisees. Boanerges may suit one, and Barnabas another; but remember, do not judge by personal taste. Hear your Apollos, yet receive the word not as his but as God's, or else it will not work effectually (*1 Thess.* 2:13). Do not call him your great Apollos, your oracle. Believe the truth whoever preaches it, Paul or Apollos, and do not pin your faith on any man's sleeve, be it white or black. Be of what church you will, so you are of the church of Christ. And do not glory in this, I am of Paul, and I am of Apollos, for there is no church in Scripture called this man's or that man's. It is the church of God, and the churches of Christ.

I could say more, but I intend to spare you all I can, though there are many more carnalities yet to be mentioned.

(ii) They were as carnal in that they were proud of being in church communion, though they kept fellowship with very unclean persons and their lump was leavened.

It is clear from 1 Corinthians 5 that they did so and yet were puffed up and gloried. They boasted of being in fellowship with people who committed gross sin, for which the apostle exhorted them (*1 Cor.* 5:11; *2 Cor.* 6:14).

When persons can content themselves with and be proud of such vulgar, profane, and therefore offensive communion at large, it is evidence of their being as carnal. When content with ordinances administered in disorderly fashion, they are as carnal (*1 Cor.* 11:17–34). When human divisions steal the name of a church, and when unwholesome fellowship is called communion, and Christians can please themselves with and glory in it, they are as carnal. Therefore do not be unequally yoked, and if any that is called a brother be immoral, with such a one do not eat.

(iii) That these Corinthian babes were as carnal appears by their going to law with one another before the unbelievers and unjust (1 Cor. 6:1–8).

This they were bold and daring in. Dare any of you (6:1)? This they did for toys and trifles, the smallest matters. They had cause to be ashamed, as if there had not been one wise or honest man among them. It was utterly and undeniably a fault (6:7). And yet being but babes and as carnal, this they dared to do.

All those who do such things are babes. So is everyone who refuses the hearing of the saints and goes to law against his brother, before unbelievers and the unjust. The apostle speaks angrily in this case, How dare you? Can you profess and pray, and yet not forgive, nor suffer, but wrong and defraud, and that your brethren? Oh, what a strange thing is this, there is no excuse. It is utterly a fault, it is altogether and wholly a fault; as in the Greek, it is base all over.

(iv) Babes appear to be as carnal in that they pass from one extreme to another and do not know a happy medium or moderation, they either under-do or over-do things.

For a while these Corinthians were so heedless that they did not think of casting out or censuring the incestuous person (*1 Cor.* 5). But later they were so strict that they would not forgive him, allowing him to be swallowed up with overmuch sorrow (*2 Cor.* 2). Thus they go from the extreme of defect to that of excess, not acquainted with the divine middle way among the paths of judgement.

It was similar with the Galatian babes. At the first they admired Paul and blessed him, but after a short while they turned on him as if he were their enemy (*Gal.* 1:6; 4:14–16). At the beginning they were ready to deify him; after a while, he was nobody and they were ready to defy him. Thus, they do not turn about by degrees, but swing about from one extreme to another, being tossed with every wind of doctrine (*Eph.* 4:14). They sail with the wind that blows and are carried with the last man they heard, poor weathervanes that they are.

When our Saviour began to wash the disciples' feet (*John* 13), Peter says, 'Lord, dost thou wash my feet?' He seems to put it off with scorn. What, have I no more manners than to let thee wash my feet? 'Thou shalt never wash my feet.' And yet when Christ had told him but a word or two, he says, 'Lord, not only my feet, but my hands and my head.' The one extreme was, 'thou shalt not ever wash my feet'; and the other extreme is, 'wash my head, too'. He passes from one extreme to another in a moment.

In matter of practice the Corinthians were in the extreme, at one time not casting out, at another time not taking in the incestuous person. In matter of attitude, the Galatians would at first pull out their eyes for Paul, and then pull out his eyes. And as for professing, Peter is one time for 'not at all', and soon for 'all over'. This is the way of babes, and this is their folly, for they are as carnal.

(v) They are as carnal in that they argue at little matters and will take offence at almost nothing.

If you do not agree with them they will take it ill, even forbidding to do Christ's work, as the disciples did. But they were as carnal in this, and therefore Christ forbade them to do any such thing, and on weighty reasons, too (*Mark* 9:38–40).

Many babes in Christ are of a touchy, peevish, and sour nature. So when the disciples did not receive the hospitality they looked for, they wanted to call fire from heaven. That was evidence that they knew not what spirit they were of (*Luke* 9:51–55). When the apostle Paul had promised to come to the Corinthians (*I Cor.* 16:5–7) and was disappointed, they accused him of making promises lightly, causing him to apologize for himself (*2 Cor.* 1:15–24). Surely anyone so rash and critical, who takes offence and argues without cause is as babyish and carnal as these were.

(vi) Babes are as carnal in asking many trivial or needless questions.

They are preoccupied with things that do not concern their Christian growth. Thinking it a case of conscience, they will ask many irrelevant questions. To be sure, asking questions may be of great use; but carnal men, as the Pharisees and Sadducees were, asked Christ many a captious and quarrelsome question; and the devil deceived our common mother with a query.

Babes take up a great deal of time and words with little things. The Corinthians troubled Paul about things that common discretion should have determined, and that is why he tells them so often in response, Thus say I, not the Lord (*1 Cor.* 7:6,12,25,26,40). He is saying that these are not so much matters of religion and conscience as of prudence and discretion. About marrying and about eating they seemed to be very anxious and concerned. But these things in themselves were not so important, only liberty must not be abused to the offence of others, for then it becomes more than a matter of conscience (*1 Cor.* 8:8–9). Anything sold in the markets and good for food is lawful to be eaten without a dispute (*1 Cor.* 10:27–33).

The disciples, till Christ's ascension, were also full of pitiful questions: Who shall be greatest (*Matt.* 18:1)? What shall this man do (*John* 21:21)? Wilt thou at this time restore the kingdom to Israel (*Acts* 1:6)? Alas, what poor, low way of questioning is this?

Indeed, to ask, What shall I do to be saved? What is the

will of God concerning me in my place and circumstance? How shall I attain to a more perfect state? These things are considerable and worth asking, but to be taken up with little and low things is to be as babes, and as carnal, more nice than wise.

(vii) These babes live much more by tradition and the example of men than by rule or reason.
They are dependent and unquestioning, and believe as the church or as some great wise and learned doctor believes, and in practice they imitate. This made Paul tell his Corinthians to follow him, but as he followed Christ. If you will follow and have an example of me, look on me only as I walk in the steps of Christ Jesus (*I Cor.* 11:1–3).

I fear that to this day many persons believe and practise some things more because they are believed and practised by such and such men whom they are fond of, than from any conviction or account they can give that it is the way of God. But remember, we should not walk by what is done, but by what ought to be done (*Matt.* 19:3–9).

(viii) They are as carnal in having more zeal than knowledge to manage it.
The apostle says this of the Jews (*Rom* 10:2–3) and also of the Galatian babes upon a similar occasion (*Gal.* 4:16–21; 3:1–5). They no sooner grasp a notion than they are all aflame. Like tinder, they catch fire and allow zeal without discretion to consume them. Paul himself, while carnal, was a most zealous man, but it was in days of his ignorance. Zeal, like fire, is a good servant indeed, but it is a bad master; it must be carefully watched.

The disciples who in their zeal would have called fire from heaven were unacquainted with their own spirit. And it was in such a fit that Peter drew his sword. But this is not the way of Christ, whose kingdom is not of this world and therefore does not want his servants fighting (*Matt.* 26:51, *John* 18:10,36). It is like carnal men, to think we do God service by killing those that do not deserve it, for being not of our way (*John* 16:2). Usually the zeal of such men shows itself most in the presence of their leaders and dies in their absence (*Gal.* 4:18, *2 Chron.* 24:2). I will not try to tell how many of these babes there are in our days, but I am afraid there are too many.

(ix) Babes are as carnal in that they can hardly bear a reproof or an exhortation.

Carnal men, and babes that are as carnal, look on reproof as blame or reproach and cannot bear it. They carry grudges against those who reprove them. The Corinthians were nettled when Paul dealt with them roundly and rebuked them sharply that they might be sound in the faith. They could hardly bear with him, and almost called him a fool for his kindness and love (*2 Cor.* 11:1; 12:11–15). The author of the epistle to the Hebrew babes begs them to suffer a word of exhortation (*Heb.* 13:22). I beseech you, brethren, suffer the word of exhortation, for I have written a letter to you in few words. It may be only a few words, but the babes will think it too many if they do not like what is said, though it might be most important for them. Eli's carnal sons could not bear reproof from their father; nor can babes bear any, even from a Father.

Besides this, they are unwilling to suffer for religion. They will conform to the rudiments of this world, as the Hebrews with their Jewish rites and the Corinthians with Gentile, rather than suffer persecution. It is true, the Hebrews, after they were illuminated, endured a great fight of affliction at first (*Heb.* 10:32), but they had weak hands and feeble knees. They began to be weary and falter, which was the cause for the exhortation which the writer begs them to suffer (13:22). The disciples themselves were scattered and fled at the smiting of the shepherd, so burdensome it is for babes to suffer. If thou faint in the day of affliction, thy strength is small (*Prov.* 24:10).

(x) Some of them are apt to measure God's heart by his hand. They are as carnal men, who measure love and hatred by the things before them, which is a false rule. If God's hand is open to them and fills them with his blessings, then all is well. But if his hand is shut from them or laid upon them, then like Zion of old, they think God has forsaken them. This is a weakness; for the best of this world is not good enough to be construed as a love token, nor the worst of it bad enough to be a token of hatred. If God slays their son or takes away what they love, they draw the sad conclusion that God has no concern for them. It seems the Corinthians were apt to do this when God afflicted them; and so the apostle tells them that when we are judged for a cause, we are chastened of the Lord, that we may not be condemned with the world (*1 Cor.* 11:30–32). And the Hebrew babes were comforted by a similar word, that God dealt with them as sons (*Heb.* 12:5–13), so they might not measure God's heart by his hand nor his promises and love by his provisions.

These are some of the many ways in which babes are more carnal than other saints are, at least to such a degree. These things are wicked and unbecoming. Paul threatens the Corinthians with a rod if they do not mend their ways, which were corrupted even more by the evil words of an Epicurean sort of man who had crept in among them (*1 Cor.* 15:32). Twice, if not three times, the apostle speaks to them of these things of which they ought to be ashamed (*1 Cor.* 4:14; 6:5; 15:34), shaking the rod over them again and again to make them fear being carnal any longer (*1 Cor.* 4:13-21, *2 Cor.* 1:23; 10:9-11; 12:20-21; 13:10).

BEING NEWBORN

(i) Examining whether we are newborn or not
To examine ourselves, we must first learn to tell whether we are babes or not, whether newborn or not. It is foolish to trust only our hearts in this matter (*Prov.* 28:26). Our hearts are deceitful and may make us think ourselves different from what we are. Many, such as the foolish virgins, have been falsely comforted. Many poor have thought themselves rich, as the church at Laodicea (*Rev.* 3:17), and others have been rich who thought themselves poor, as those at Smyrna (*Rev.* 2:9).

Therefore, let us examine ourselves so that we may judge rightly. To prevent objections and to clear the way to knowing whether we are converted or not, I first lay down six premises about conversion:

a) The new birth is a mystery. Conversion is a private thing, a work that begins within, out of sight. It puzzled Nicodemus, a master, a rabbi in Israel, to think what kind of thing regeneration could be (*John* 3:3-13). As in the wheels of a watch, there are motions and visible turnings, but the spring is hidden within. How the child is fashioned in the womb is a great mystery; but the forming of the new birth is a greater mystery, for it is a work wholly and altogether of God's making, and it is wondrously brought about in the secret places of the heart. The being is renewed in the spirit of the mind, which is the prime and proper seat of it (*Eph.* 4:23).

Now the work being so inward, secret, and hidden, it is hard to trace God's footsteps and to search man's heart. All the ways of God are unsearchable enough, but especially these in the great deep, as man's heart is called. The way of a serpent on a rock, of a ship in the sea, and of a bird in the air cannot be found out, much less can this way of God, unless he reveals it by his Spirit, which works it (*1 Cor.* 2:10–12). Though the outside of the new man created in righteousness and true holiness may be discerned, the inwards are like the white name which none knows but he, and perhaps not even everyone who has it. For there are only a few who can fully and exactly relate the story of their conversion. It is so secret that many things pass by unnoticed. Who knows the true workings, any more than the errors, of his heart? It is the hidden man of the heart, and the heart is hidden from the man. If men understand so little of the earthly things, which are their element and in which they profess themselves masters, how much less do they know such a spiritual and heavenly thing as this, as our Saviour told Nicodemus. Experience is the best schoolteacher in this case.

b) God takes various occasions to convert men and uses various means to bring about this work. I mention this because some are apt to think they are not converted if it has not happened with them in the same way as with others. The first and most usual way is by the preaching of the gospel, for faith comes by hearing (*Rom.* 10:14–17). Sometimes God takes the occasion when one has been reading to send a preacher, as to the eunuch (*Acts* 8:27). Whichever way the word reaches us to save us, let us reach to the saving word. Give yourself to reading and to hearing, and who knows but God may give you faith while you are reading or hearing, if he has not done it for you that way already.

Sometimes God takes occasion during a meeting or conversation, as it was between Christ and the woman of Samaria (*John* 4).

Sometimes God makes use of an affliction and a desperate condition, as he did to convert the prodigal. And David found this of use for a re-conversion (*Psa.* 119:67–71).

Sometimes he works through some mercy he has shown and deliverance which he has brought about for a person, and in that way obliged and led him to repentance by his goodness. That was how the blind man was converted (*John* 9), and one of the lepers, and perhaps the jailer.

Sometimes God uses a dream (*Job* 33:14–30).

Sometimes it is from a man's curiosity, as Zaccheus (*Luke* 19:1–10), or many that have gone to see and be seen, or to hear words as a lovely song. Some who went to hear Paul for novelty believed (*Acts* 17:19– 34).

Indeed, sometimes God waits till men are in a full career of sinning, and then meets with them as he did with Saul (*Acts* 9). But such cases are not ordinary.

Sometimes God uses the good behaviour of others. When men will not hear the good word of God, the good works even of women may lead to and be used for their conversion (*1 Pet.* 3:1–2). Oh, that there were more such preachers and preaching, for then perhaps there would be more conversion.

Sometimes God makes use of the patient sufferings of his saints, as he did that of Christ to convince a few at the time of his passion (*Matt.* 27:54, *Luke* 23:39–43). And God blessed it so much that in later ages it became a familiar saying. The blood of innocent and patient martyrs became the seed of the Church.

We must not limit the holy one of Israel, for though he ties us to means, he has not tied himself. But he works on many so indiscernibly that they hardly know the means used to do it. He waits to be gracious, for he is a God of judgement. He acts judiciously and takes what occasions he pleases; he best knows what will best take. If the work is done, we should not have misgivings as to which way it is done. But seeing the word preached is the most usual, we should wait and watch at the door of hope (*Prov.* 8:34).

And it is a great obligation upon all Christians to speak and behave in a holy manner and to suffer patiently as Christ did. God may make use of their graces to make others gracious, to convince and convert men, so they shall glorify God and say God truly is in them (*1 Cor.* 14:24-25). It is a great mercy and blessing to be instrumental to the conversion of others (*Dan.* 12:3, *James* 5:19-20).

c) Just as the occasions and means differ, so does the manner of working. Some he draws, others he drives in; promises prevail with some, and threatening with others. Boanerges works on this and Barnabas on that. Terrors most affect some, but love others. One is broken, another is melted. Some he keeps long under the pangs of the new birth and they have hard labour of it; others have a more quick delivery. Some pay but a little deposit, but a great deal of rent annually; others pay a greater deposit and less rent.

And these are but some of his ways. Who can tell all the ways that God takes with man to turn back his soul from the pit? Some he leads on by degrees; others start up suddenly and are men almost as soon as they are born, as Paul was. God frowns and smiles, speaks in thunder or a still voice, with dismal or joyful sounds, as it pleases him. The Spirit blows where and how he will: Sometimes the blustering north, and other times the benign south wind blows. Sometimes heavy rain falls, other times but a little dew; but all shall prosper. It cost Paul and the jailer dear for the time, but it was soon over. But for Matthew and others, it was but Follow me, and they followed immediately.

d) The time of conversion varies also. There are no certain set times, as not before or after such a year. But God calls at any hour of the day, as it seems good to him, some sooner and some later, as he did labourers into the vineyard (*Matt.* 20:1–7). Some are called when young, others when old. The thief was called at the last gasp, as it were. We may look to this conversion so that none might despair – and that none might presume.

e) Conversion is felt more by some than by others; and the conversion of some is more visible than that of others. Some can tell the time and manner as well as the means of their conversion, but others cannot do so. Zaccheus, Saul, and the jailer could tell the whole story in detail, but it is likely that Timothy could not do so, having been good, as I may say, from the very cradle. Some know the day of conception, the moment of new life, and can give account of the babe's stirring in their womb from time to time, when others take it for granted, or have only a vague notion.

Persons who had not previously heard the gospel, as the Gentiles at first, or those who have been notorious sinners, as Saul and the jailer, can better tell the time and manner of their conversion. But others that have heard the gospel many years or have had the advantage of better education and more civil lives, cannot give so exact an account of the change in them. Though their conversion may be as true, it is not so visible and discernible. A little sugar will sweeten wine, when a great deal must go to sweeten vinegar. Therefore well-bred people and those of good disposition are often more doubtful of their conversion than others who have been so completely changed.

f) Though conversion is a mystery and brought about by various ways and means, still it is a conversion and therefore is more or less knowable. It is being translated from darkness to light, from death to life, from the power of Satan unto God. This cannot be done without changing a person considerably, and working such good in the very best that was not there before. And though the time of conversion may not be known, it may be known that the person is converted. There are things characteristic of all converts, and only of converts, new creatures, which nature cannot imitate. Some things even the most refined nature, if not renewed, cannot do. Grace is an element above nature, and nature at the highest cannot rise so high as grace at the lowest. It is not show and appearance, but reality that makes the difference. Brass gilded over is not gold; nature, even reformed nature, is not grace. A dog may vomit, a sow may be washed, but they still retain their nature. Grace makes a new man, a new nature.

(ii) Knowing that a person is newborn

By what criteria, then, may we know that a person is newborn? It is not only by their eating of milk. There are some things found in all true converts which the best nature, with all the advantages of education, can never attain. These characterize the lowest as well as the highest Christian who has truly known the grace of God.

a) They desire heartily and sincerely not only that God may be their God, but that they may be his people. And they wish as heartily that they may have a childlike love to him, as that he may have a fatherly love to them. They are as willing to be his to serve him, as that he should be theirs to save them. They take Christ Jesus not as a physician, to make use of him when necessary, but as a husband to love and live with him. They take him not only as a Saviour, but as a Prince to rule and a Prophet to teach them. They implicitly take Christ whole, in all his offices, and not divided.

Who but a newborn soul could do this? The natural man (especially if assisted by the common principles and grace of the gospel) desires to be happy, and so he may wish God to be his God by way of privilege, but he does not desire to be God's by way of duty. But every saint, in some measure, does so, even without having yet attained the witness and seal of the Spirit that they are the children of God. For it is beyond nature at its highest, with all its attainments, to desire and endeavour to serve God as well as to be saved by him; to be conformed to him as to have salvation from him; to obey commands, as to enjoy promises and privileges; to be holy as to be happy; to have grace to glorify God, as well as to be glorified thereby; to be sanctified, as to be justified and saved; to live as well as to die the death of the righteous.

b) Newborn ones have the law of God written in their hearts, and they act from this and from the living principle to bring forth the fruits of righteousness.   When the law of God is in our hearts, our hearts will be set to do it: I delight to do thy will, O God, thy law is in my heart (*Psa.* 40:8). The people who know righteousness are the ones in whose heart is God's law (*Isa.* 57:7). Others may do some righteous acts, but these new creatures do it as their proper fruit springing from the very root, the law of God and his truth in them. And so it is an evidence of their new birth (*1 John* 2). Everyone that practises righteousness in obedience to God, whose law is in the heart, is born of God; and some, in opposition to these, practise sin (*1 John* 3:7–10).

Now this is said of the Corinthian babes themselves (*2 Cor.* 3:3): Ye are manifestly declared to be the epistle of Christ, written not with ink, but with the Spirit of the living God, not in tables of stone, but in the fleshly table of the heart. This cannot be said of any but newborn ones, and may be said of those who are just newly born.

The law written in their heart causes desires and effort for growth, and these souls will not be satisfied unless they attain it. They have tasted that the Lord is gracious and have taken into their hearts what they have tasted. They desire not only to live, but to thrive and to be lively. And though these babes do not know or see that they are growing, they know that they desire to grow and that they want not only to be planted in the house but to flourish in the courts of the Lord, and not be trees without fruit.

We would fear that those who do not desire to grow in grace, have no grace. We would wonder whether those content with only enough grace to save them, have enough grace to be saved.

Babes not only wish and desire to grow, but they also endeavour to grow. They diligently and conscientiously use all means that God has made available for their growth. Simple longings and idle wishes may be found in formalists and hypocrites, but to be as industrious as desirous is found only in the new creatures, the newborn babes. Balaam could profess and wish like a godly man, but instead of making the corresponding efforts, he practised the direct contrary. In formalists only the end is desirable, but in true saints the means are as desirable. The means are a part of their happiness as well as the way to it.

Yet true converts, though only babes, do not rest satisfied unless they attain the end of desires and efforts. They are not satisfied with the use of means without the end of means. But babes attain little, so they are restless and unsatisfied. They have the least satisfaction of any saints, because they desire much and enjoy little, and therefore desire all the more.

Others may be satisfied by their endeavours, but these cannot be. They pursue still and say as Absalom, Why am I come up from Geshur, if I may not see the king's face? Though they listen, learn, and pray as a duty, these things do not satisfy them unless they are kept up and carried on by true communion with and conformity to God. And all this is because the law of God is written in their hearts.

c) Newborn ones want their sin taken away, and not only by pardoning but by purging, even though their sorrows should continue.   If God should say to such a soul, 'I will take away all thy sorrows, and give thee a cheerful heart; thou shalt have corn and wine and oil enough,' it would still say, 'O Lord, what is that if I go graceless, if my sins are not forgiven? Take away my sins, Lord, though thou leave my sorrows and my couch is watered with tears every day, and I walk mournfully all my days. Do anything with me, so my sins may be done away. My heart will never be at ease till my sins are forgiven.'

And this is not all. If God should further say, 'I will forgive thy sin and remember it no more to charge it upon thee, but I will leave thee under the power and bondage of it,' then would this soul say, 'Oh, Lord, I bless thee for a pardon and for being kept from damnation; yet, Lord, this does not satisfy me. I desire as much to be purged and taken from sin, as that sin may be taken from me. I need as much to be delivered from sin's dominion as from damnation.'

David prays not only, 'Lord, blot out my transgressions', but 'Lord, wash me and cleanse me thoroughly from my sin' (*Psa.* 51:1–2). And it seems this was after the prophet had said, 'The Lord hath put away thy sin' (*2 Sam.* 12:13).

Who but converted ones possess this attitude? Others can be content with heart's ease, peace, and good things while they live in the love of some pet sin, especially if they entertain a notion that God will pardon them.

Purging is not heartily desired by any but gracious souls.

And though the newborn have no assurance of a pardon or any great conquests over sin, though they have little satisfaction and much sorrow, they can sincerely and truly say they are glad that other saints serve God better than they do. While they mourn that they themselves are no better, they yet rejoice that there are any better than themselves. Indeed, they do more than emulate, they suffer pangs of envy for those happy and advanced saints. And yet from their very hearts they can only be glad that God has better servants than they are, that there are sons in his house and service, though they themselves are only as hired servants.

'Alas!' says such a poor babe, 'I am a most worthless wretch, I have so little to show for my faith that I am ashamed of myself and am not worthy to be called a Christian. But nonetheless I can through grace rejoice that God has his Abrahams, Davids, Jobs, and Pauls who glorify his name better than I do.' They admire the happiness of the other saints and bless those who stand before the Lord and minister to his name and glory as the queen of Sheba did Solomon's servants.

Indeed, if they have ever in any way been instrumental to the glory of God and served his name and people they are glad of it, even if they do not yet have the reward, God seems to have forgotten it (*Heb.* 6:10), and they themselves scarcely keep it in mind (*Matt.* 25:37). But on the other hand, take hypocrites and formalists, they grudge what they do (*Mal.* 3:14) and profess Christ Jesus out of envy, vying with the saints for a reputation (*Phil.* 1:15–16).

d) Newborn ones will not depart from God. 'Let God,' they say, 'deal with us how he will, yet we are resolved, we will never leave him nor forsake him, for all the pleasures and profits of this world. No, though he kill us, we will trust in him.' God may use them like the dogs under his table and feed them with crumbs, and a knock, too, and not give them a meal of the children's bread; yet they will thank him for what they have and wait for more, as the woman of Canaan did. Will a hypocrite do this, wait and pray always? I doubt it. But these babes say to God as Ruth to Naomi, 'I will not leave thee, but will follow thee and the Lamb even to the grave, come of it what will.' In the way of thy judgements will we wait on thee (*Isa.* 26:8).

If, like Ephraim, they are under the chastening of God and for a while are like young bulls unaccustomed to the yoke, they will cry out again, 'Turn thou me and I shall be turned.' They return and repent, they are ashamed. And God hears the voices of his dear children, and remembers them, and will surely have mercy on them (*Jer.* 31:18–20). If, like Israel, they have followed other lovers, and God closes up their path with thorns, they return to their first husband and confess their foolishness in departing from him (*Hos.* 2). Though Peter failed in his promise and pledge, he wept bitterly and later proved that he would rather die than utterly forsake or deny him. And so it is with every babe in Christ. They fall yet do not fall away, but return and live.

But I caution: Do not take these words without this work, or the ideas without the feeling. Some hypocrite or formalist may hear this and pretend that he had attained it. But it is not the words of our mouth, but the attitude of our heart; it is not saying but feeling, not expression but experience, that will prove whether we are newborn. It is not being able to say these things by rote, but having them on our heart and living them out, that will do us good.

(iii) The covenant promises – effected in all saints

These are characteristics of newborn ones which distinguish them not only from common sinners but from the most refined hypocrites and those who adhere to form. I have not mentioned too many, nor have I mentioned doubtful cases.

But I have mentioned those essential to the state of the new birth, for indeed they are all promised in the new covenant and effected in the hearts of all those with whom the covenant is made. These are promised to all saints, regardless of their degrees. Let us examine the covenant and we shall find all these things (*Jer.* 31:31–34; 32:38–40):

1. 'I will be their God and they shall be my people.' This is not only promised but brought about. And as it is in God's heart to be their God, so it is in their heart to be God's people. Both are desired by them.

2. 'I will put my law into their hearts.' The law is not laid there as writings in a trunk or chest, to be idle and without effect. It is there that they may do it, that they may fear the Lord and keep his commandments, that they breathe after full obedience to it.

3. 'I will remember their sin no more.' This denotes not only forgiving, but subduing of sin (*Rom.* 6:14).

4. 'They shall not depart from me.' That is, wholly and finally; as God will not leave them totally, neither shall they leave God.

It is clear as can be that the new covenant promises and attitudes have been brought about in all saints, and in none but saints. The end of all, and of none but redeemed ones, is to be holy; that is the design of the Redeemer (*Titus* 2:14). Holiness becomes the aim and end of elected ones, and holiness is God's end in electing (*Eph.* 1:4).

God the Father, Son, and Spirit are one, and agree in one.

Election, redemption, and sanctification to salvation are all three effected in newborn ones. And these all agree in longing after the effects of the divine design of God the Father, Son, and Spirit, which no other persons do.

These things may not show themselves powerfully and visibly at all times, but they are rooted in them, their effects appearing more or less at times. Even the best of saints do not act them out alike. Some are noted for a particular grace which has appeared most evidently and run most evenly through the whole course of their lives, as Abraham for faith, Isaac for fear (and therefore God is called the fear of Isaac, meaning the God whom he feared), Jacob for prayer (and so the seekers and praying people are called his seed), Moses for meekness, Job for patience. And even these were not always completely consistent.

Saints of any class have a variety of lessons to learn, several books to read, and several exercises to perform. And when they are occupied with any one of these, the rest seem to disappear or to be dormant for that time, though that is not so in reality. But the way is to learn one lesson at a time. Sometimes saints are most concerned about their own emptiness and insufficiency; sometimes about the riches and freeness of grace; sometimes about the beauty of holiness and the usefulness of good works; sometimes sorrow and fear; at another time love and joy take hold of them.

Because of this variety and turning, some might think that they were never converted till they came to act so-and-so. But it is grace putting itself forth in another kind of growth, as the sap of a tree does first in buds, then in leaves and blossoms, and then in fruit. The fruit, too, varies greatly in form and colour till perfectly ripe.

I say these things out of tenderness to poor babes, who

are too apt to mistake and misjudge, and to let them know that to judge their state correctly, they must not judge by what is proper and peculiar to a higher class of saints, but by what is proper and essential to the new birth as such.

Next we should examine ourselves as to whether we are only babes. Perhaps many who profess and have long been in the school of Christ are yet in the lowest form to this day. It is not years and standing but experiences and attainments that indicate advance. The Corinthians and the Hebrews were still babes, though they had been long in Christ.

To know whether we are still babes, then, let us review the defects and carnalities of babes already spoken of. The beginnings of grace, and eating milk, with the other essential (covenant) characteristics recently mentioned, allow us to know that we are babes, newborn ones. In the same way, the defects and being as carnal let us know that we are still only babes.

Examine yourselves, therefore. Commune with the Word and with your own hearts and compare them. Look into the glass, as St James says, and see what sort of hearts and faces you have. Do not be forgetful hearers, as you may be, even though you might remember all these sermons word for word (*James* 1:25). Examination and prayer about these matters is close and closet work. I recommend it to you, and you to God.

Exhortation

a) To those who are not yet newborn:

To those who are not yet newborn but remain unconverted, and who cannot enter into the kingdom of God unless they are born again, as our Saviour assures us with no less than four 'verilies' (*John* 3:3–5):

Alas, how many are there yet under the condemnation of the Word and their own consciences, who do not know or profess any conversion but live a known and acknowledged sinful life? Oh, that I might yet plead with these and persuade them to consider their way and its end, which is hell, if they do not turn to God and believe in Christ Jesus. To you, poor souls, I have spoken before, when I spoke of repentance and faith. I plead with you to ponder and consider those things again, that I may not repeat them. Besides that, I have two other things to say to you by way of exhortation.

i) First, let me warn you not to offend these little ones, the least and weakest of the flock of Christ. It is a great sin, one which will be greatly punished, to offend one of Christ's little ones. If not for their sake or God's sake, yet for your own sake, take heed of this sin. There is an enmity in the heart of sinners to the seed of God. They express this by reproaches and persecution, by which they injure and offend and wrong them. But oh, that they would hear and fear, and stop this wickedness.

Jesus Christ takes notice not only of what offences are committed against his person and doctrine, but of those committed against his people, the very least of them. Consider what he said (*Matt.* 18:6–10): Whosoever shall offend, or despise, one of these little ones which believes in me, it were better for him that a millstone were hanged about his neck, and that he were drowned in the depth of the sea. Being drowned this way was looked on as a dreadful punishment, but that is nothing compared with being thrown into the depth of hell, with a millstone weight and the load of your offences about your neck.

If Jesus Christ deals severely with them that are not merciful to his people, as he will (*Matt.* 25:41–45), oh, how will he deal with those who have been cruel to his people? especially seeing it is a cruelty to himself! Of this not only their angels carry tidings (*Matt.* 18:10), but Christ himself knows it by feeling, as he tells Paul (*Acts* 9:4). And he will one day say to non-converted ones who have slain his little ones as Gideon said to Zebah and Zalmunna: 'What manner of men were they whom ye slew at Tabor?' And they will then answer, 'As thou art, so were they, each of them resembled the children of a king'; to which he will reply as Gideon: '"They were my brethren; if ye had saved them alive I would not have slain you." But now you shall be damned body and soul, I will destroy you in hell. Depart ye cursed, take them, devil.' Hear then, and fear despising or offending his little ones.

(ii) Second, take heed that you are not offended with Christ and religion because of the babes who are yet as carnal. God's people must not be as carnal, lest they give the enemies of God, as David did, an occasion to blaspheme and cause the way of truth to be evil spoken of. But the men of this world must not to be offended with and blaspheme the way of God and his people because some of them are yet as carnal and walk as men.

Worldly ones are greatly illogical and draw many *non sequiturs*. They say, 'These professing Christians are as bad as others, they are all alike. And this is their religion.' Neither is true. For though they are *as* carnal, they are *not* carnal and in the flesh as other men are; they are in Christ Jesus. They may take too many steps after the manner of men, but their whole way of living is not according to the flesh as with other men. And though some are as carnal, not all are so; there are those who are spiritual and walk in and according to the Spirit. But as for those who do otherwise, it is not their religion that is to blame, but they themselves. The doctrine of Christ Jesus does not teach them bad conduct, but the reverse: it *un*teaches them such bad conduct, and to walk as men.

It is the devil's logic to draw an argument from seeming to being, from similarity to identity; from a particular to a universal; and from the concrete to the abstract. It is the devil's logic that because they are as carnal, they must be only and fully carnal; because one is bad, they are all alike; and because professing Christians are blameworthy, religion itself is criminal!

The grace of God has taught all to deny ungodliness and worldly lusts, to live soberly, righteously, and godly in this present world. If Christians do not do it, is not grace's fault but theirs. So take heed that you are not offended with Christ and religion because of them. And you who profess Christ, learn to walk circumspectly, lest the way and name of God be blasphemed through you, and lest Christ suffer because you sin. Do not give the world any occasion to despise you and that which is better than you, the Christian religion.

b) To grown saints:

To grown saints I would say these things:

(i) *Remember what you were, not only when unconverted (1 Cor. 6:11), but what babes you were at your first conversion.* Do not be like Israel, who forgot God's work of old. Call to mind the former days. It will be worth your while and be of great use to you. Remember the time when you were but babes and sucklings, and what kinds of supports you needed before God took you by the hand and taught you to walk. Remember what kisses you had when you were little children, and how he led you forth to fight his battles when you became young men. And by fighting the fight of faith and using the sword of the Spirit, which is the word of God, you overcame the wicked one, and led captivity captive. If you are fathers, remember him whom you have known from the beginning, who has given you all the experiences and wisdom with which you are endowed. Though you can eat strong meat now, there was a time when you could eat only milk.

Remembering these things will be of great use to you in giving God the glory for your higher attainments and all your advances from step to step. It will make you greatly useful in instructing babes, which is one of your great works and duties. It will keep you humble when you see that you owe a debt to God for bringing you to this place by his grace alone and not for any worth or merit of your own. It will help you to remember that you were converted long ago, and not to think, as some are apt to do, that all the work was as nothing till they came to such or such a place. This sort of thinking leads to neglect for those who are below that place, and to ingratitude to God for what went before it and led to it. So it will it be advantageous in many ways to remember the work of old.

(ii) *Bring forth fruit answerable to your state.* At one time, fruits worthy of repentance were the fruits called for, but now you are to bring forth fruits worthy of assurance, victory and joy in the Holy Ghost. It is true, God had some little praise from you when you were babes, but now he expects much more: that you bring forth much fruit and be filled with it, that you be strong in faith, that you abound in love, that you be filled with all wisdom and knowledge, to walk worthy of God and to do all to his glory.

(iii) *Do not be ashamed of your youngest brethren that are only babes.* Paul, and even Christ himself, were not ashamed to call them brethren. But be loving, gentle, and tender towards them. You know the heart of a babe, for you yourselves were once babes, as it is said to Israel in behalf of the stranger (*Exod.* 23:9, *Lev.* 19:33–34). Some poor babes may complain that such and such do not regard them because they are not grown up to their stature. But please remember these things ought not to be so; there is an honour due to the weaker vessels and uncomely parts (*1 Cor.* 12). We should be nurses to these wilful crying babes, and as Paul among the Thessalonians, we should be gentle as a nurse that cherishes her own children or charges (*1 Thess.* 2:7).

(*iv*) *Give good examples to babes, and do not abuse your liberty to their offence.* I told you that babes pay much attention to example, and if they have bad ones given them, especially by good and eminent men, they are drawn aside by it. When Peter separated himself, the other Jews dissembled also, and even Barnabas, an eminent person, was carried away by that dissimulation (*Gal.* 2:13). And the apostle says, Take heed lest by any means your liberty becomes a stumbling block to them that are weak; for if any weak and ignorant man (which is a babe) sees you who have knowledge sitting at meat in the idol's temple, shall not the conscience of him that is weak be emboldened (Greek: *edified*)? He takes your example for sanction and thinks he is edified, when alas, it is to his loss and detriment (*1 Cor.* 8:8–13).

(*v*) *Acquaint the babes with your experiences, as Paul did* (2 Cor. *1:6–10*)) *and with Satan's devices, as he did* (1 Cor. *7:5*, 2 Cor. *2:11; 11:2*). Babes have little skill in distinguishing between good and evil, between impressions from the good or evil spirit, especially if Satan transforms himself into an angel of light. Israel was to write a history for later ages of God's dealings with them and Amalek's dealings against them, and to instruct the children how God had dealt with them; you, too, must instruct the babes. Let the little children tell stories of the Father's love, the young men of his power, and the fathers of his wisdom in carrying on the work of grace. Let the babes learn how God overthrew Pharaoh, led them through the wilderness, fought for and provided for them from heaven till they came to the good land.

c) To babes:

There are three things I would say to babes:

(i) To be glad that they are babes, newborn and in Christ Jesus. 'Glad, alas! There is no comfort for me, who am but a babe.' Yes, but there is comfort that you are a babe, though only a babe. The comfort is not yours as carnal, but as a babe in Christ. The least work of God is great consolation to the least of saints, the babes. Consider the following, and see whether it amounts to nothing:

1. You have attained to the first resurrection, from being dead and lost in sin. You are called out of Egypt and are called his son. The work is begun; you are newborn and eat milk; the foundation is laid; is this nothing? Who knows to what a great tree this little mustard seed of grace may grow? The babe that lies in the cradle may become a father in Israel; and is this nothing? He that has laid the foundation will lay the top stone, and you shall cry out with shouting, Grace, grace unto it. God is not like the foolish builder. He has counted up his cost and can finish what he has begun. He will not be laughed at and mocked as one that has laid a foundation but could not finish it. You may be a knotty piece, he will fit you for your place and perfect that which concerns you, for this work is not only that of his hand, but of his heart; and is this nothing? Pray to him and believe (*Psa.* 138:7–8).

2. You are not only brought out of Egypt, but he has drawn you into the wilderness. And though you may be in the valley of Achor, even there is a door of hope. You are bewildered, and your way is so full of twists and turns that you seem to wander rather than to progress. True, but you are on your way, and God is leading you to his

holy hill, Mount Zion. See how differently the condition of Israel is expressed (*Psa.* 107:4,7). In verse 4 it is said they wandered in the wilderness, but in verse 7 it is said he led them forth. In one it is called a solitary way, but in the other it is called the right way. First they despaired of finding any city to dwell in, but then they are led that they might go to a city of habitation. So it is with you, poor soul. And in spite of your unbelief and murmuring, he holds your soul. When you are hungry and thirsty he provides food and drink for you, and your clothes shall not wear out.

3. Your being a babe is more encouraging than discouraging. Your being a babe in Christ is more to your safety then your being as carnal is to your danger, though it must be your sorrow. Babe is the name of a saint, not of a carnal man; and it is more to your benefit that you are a babe, than against you that you are as carnal. Is it nothing to your joy that you are born, even if you are not yet clothed with a robe nor kissed by the Father? It was more for the prodigal than against him that he was alive, when he had been dead, and came home naked without even rags. It was more for the disciples that the spirit was willing than against them that the flesh was weak.

It is so with us and our babes. Their being ours endears them to us more than their wilfulness and peevishness drives us away from them. And though the elder brother blames his father for being hasty and partial to make so much of a prodigal, he still sees that it is fitting to rejoice and be glad.

4. Though you are as carnal, when convicted of your carnality you are angry with it and with yourself, and repent and abhor yourself. The Corinthian babes were no sooner convinced of theirs than they made the apostle glad by their sorrow, seeing their sorrow wrought

[169]

repentance never to be repented of, because it was to salvation (*2 Cor.* 7). In the case of the incestuous person himself (*2 Cor.* 2:4–7), the apostle, on the account of his sincere repentance, pronounces them clear and him a person to be comforted. Now the same consolation belongs to you if you also repent. And I am sure it is your new nature to do it whenever you are under the conviction of your sin. And I can safely tell you that sin repented of, as theirs was, will not be laid to your account.

5. Though you are but a babe, God has some praise from you. It is true indeed he has more from others, but he has some from you. You help to perfect his praise. One burden of these poor souls is that they are such unprofitable servants, not because they do only their duty and no more, but alas, because they do not do their duty and fall short of it and the glory of God. God is glorified when much fruit is brought forth, but as for us, they say, we bring forth little.

That is true, but your mite of grace gives a measure of glory. All the good-ground hearers brought forth fruit to the glory of God, but some more than others (*Matt.* 13:8).

The Pharisees were displeased at the hosannas ascribed to Christ by little ones. They were angry with him for not rebuking them, as if they had taken God's name in vain, for the Pharisees said with scorn, 'Hearest thou what these say?' 'Yea,' he said, 'have ye never read, "Out of the mouths of babes and sucklings thou hast perfected praise"?' (*Matt.* 21:15–16). Christ hears their joyful and glad hosannas as praise which fulfils a Scripture and helps to fill up the praise and glory of God.

A babe is one of the joints and members of the body, and contributes in praise. In nature, there is one glory of the heavens, another of the earth; one of the sun and another of the moon and stars. The heavens declare his glory and earth his goodness, for it is full of it. The sacred and royal prophet does not admire only the heavens and the sun, but the moon and stars too, and he does this in the very Psalm where he speaks of babes and sucklings, and the place from which our Saviour quotes (*Psa.* 8:2–3).

And as in nature, so in grace: Not only the greater but the lesser luminaries, not only the highest but the lowest creatures contribute something to the praise of God. The sun indeed shines brilliantly, but the stars twinkle. Though an Abraham is strong in faith and gives great glory to God, God's praise is not fully perfected without the babes' contribution, small though it may be. In the body the least member, in a house the smallest pin, has its use and completes the whole. And vessels of an inferior use help out the glory of more honourable ones.

The milk that the babes eat, every spoonful of it, gives praise and glory to God. So do repentance, faith toward God, submission to ordinances, trembling at his word, desires after growth, love of the brethren. These all praise and glorify his name, though not with so loud a voice and open a mouth as the praise and the higher attainments of children, young men, and fathers do. And the truth is that more than a little glory is given to God by these means. For it is a wonder that these poor babes who have so much corruption (and not without considerable temptation, too) should be kept from apostasy; that grace would live like a spark of fire in the midst of waters and not be extinct. It is such a wonder that, by comparison, it is less wondrous that higher saints cleave close to God. It is a wonder that the devil is conquered and baffled by the babes, but it is the greater wonder that he is defeated by them. All this is much to the praise and

[171]

glory of God and his grace, though praise is not actually given by babes as much as by others.

(ii) Babes should be humbled that they are only babes, as carnal, and not past the spoon, and so incapable of having strong meat to eat or of having any more than the alphabet of religion, such as we preach to sinners: repentance and faith towards God. And these words especially concern those old in years but still babes in understanding and practice, Christians of long standing but little proficiency. It is essential for the Christian to be low in his own eyes, under the sense of imperfections and defects, even though God is pacified towards him (*Ezek.* 16:60–63). Let babes therefore that are as carnal, though they be in Christ Jesus, be humbled by the sense of their defectiveness and worse, their carnality. Consider especially the following:

1. That you have enjoyed means and helps by which you might have been more spiritual, had you not been dull of hearing. We are all careful to use means, but we should take one care more, and that is to make use of means for being humbled. The apostle might well have taunted the Corinthian babes with this: You boast of Paul, Apollos, and Cephas, but is it not a shame to you to be carnal under such men's ministry? The more persons are privileged with means, the more improved should they be by those means. If they are not, they should be the more humbled for their non-proficiency. Many of you have not only the milk but the cream of the gospel. Are you yet carnal? Then lament and be humbled!

2. Be the more humbled considering that many of the more refined heathens would have scorned to be so carnal as some of you. The apostle upbraids the Corinthian babes and provokes them to shame by this very thing (*1 Cor.* 5:1–2): It is reported commonly that there is such fornication among you as is not so much as

recorded of any amongst the Gentiles, that one should have his father's wife, and yet you are puffed up and have not rather mourned. It should deeply humble Christians to be guilty of that which the Gentiles are not, and scorn to be.

3. Let your humility be the more, that you have been better taught (*Eph.* 4:17-21) and for a long time. Paul had spent a year and a half among these Corinthians (*Acts* 18:11), had written to them two or three times, and was yet ready to come again to correct their babyish carnality (*2 Cor.* 12:14, 20-21; 13:1-2). Our Saviour upbraids his disciples for being yet ignorant of the Father and of him after he had been so long with them (*John* 14:9). Another time he asks them, as one grieved and angry, too, How long shall I be with you? Will ye never learn? And the author of the epistle to the Hebrews upbraids them also, that for their time and standing they might have been teachers, and yet stood in need of being taught their primer over and over again (*Heb.* 5:12). When men have been planted in God's vineyard and have been often watered with the dew of heaven, and he comes year after year for fruit, yet finds none, this calls for deep humiliation. To be old men in profession but novices in knowledge and practice should lay us low.

4. Think of this also to humble you, how many that came in long after you have gone far ahead of you. Paul was born after Christ died and rose and went to heaven, yet he laboured more abundantly and outstripped many that lived in Christ's time and family. I may say by allusion (*2 Sam.* 18:23) that many like Cushi run first and yet are outrun by Ahimaaz, who set out after him but ran the way of the plain, when others, like Cushi, wander. The Gentiles came in last but outran the Jews, who were first. And is it not so with you also, that some who were

called but yesterday, long after you, have yet outlearnt and outstripped you? Be humbled therefore.

5. Let this help out your humbling, that as yet you are incapable of the strong meat which God has prepared for his own. You are fed with milk, which keeps you alive, but the choicest dainties are reserved for a second course. If you were more spiritual, he would lead you into his wine cellar, he would feed you with apples, and his banner of love would be displayed to you and spread over you. He would let you drink from his flagons, of his rivers of pleasure, and fill you with joy unspeakable and full of glory. While you are but babes you cannot bear this. You are ignorant of the choicest of gospel mysteries, of the most intimate and sweetest communion with the Father and the Son. How it should abase you that after so long a standing you should be capable of no more than the ordinary fare of the gospel, which is but milk, without bread or wine.

6. Let this help to break your heart and make it humble, that your carnality causes the wicked to decry and blaspheme religion because of you. Though it is their sin to do so, it is your sin, and should be your shame, that it is your sin that gives them occasion. Oh, say the wicked, besides profession we see no difference between Christians and ourselves; they are as peevish, as proud, as carnal as others. Alas! I beseech you be humbled, that you should cause them to speak evil not only of you, but of the way of truth, and blame your sins on your religion.

Tertullian tells us that Christians used to be known by changing their lives and being better than other men. This indeed adorns the doctrine of God our Saviour. Otherwise men bring disgrace and reproach upon it. If we do not choose to do right by religion, and ourselves, by practising it, we should not do it the wrong of professing it, and stand in the way of others coming in.

Others would be ready to enter, were they not put back by those who are as carnal. Paul says, Dare any of you go to law before unbelievers? What will they say to these things? Will they not laugh and scorn you, and your religion too? Think what became of those who brought up a bad report on the good land.

7. And lastly remember this, and do not forget: Though you go to heaven it will cost you dear before you get there, that you have been so carnal. It will bring you down with sorrow to the grave. You may be saved, yet so as by fire, as Paul tells his babes (*1 Cor.* 3:13–15). This flesh and blood of yours cannot enter into the kingdom of God, you must pass through a purgatory of water and fire, of repentance and zeal, before you have your inheritance among those sanctified by faith in Jesus. Be humbled, then, and do not leave the sense and weight of all this to come upon you when you are on your deathbed, lest your latter end know more sorrow than your beginning. Be humbled for being as carnal.

(iii) Babes must press forward to being more than a babe at the best. We should not be satisfied to be barely in Christ Jesus, but we should be ambitious to walk in him (*Col.* 2:6). We should aim not only to be and walk in him, but to abide in him and walk as he walked (*1 John* 2:6), to be rooted and built up in him, to be established in the faith, as we have been taught, and to abound with thanksgiving (*Col.* 2:7). Having tasted that the Lord is gracious should increase our appetite for the word to grow (*1 Pet.* 2:2), to grow in grace and in the knowledge of our Lord and Saviour Jesus Christ (*2 Pet.* 3:18), that we may abound in faith with thanksgiving; in hope (*Rom.* 15:13), in liberality (*2 Cor.* 8:7), in every good work (*2 Cor.* 9:8), in mutual love (*Phil.* 1:9, *1 Thess.* 3:12), in the work of the Lord (*1 Cor.* 15:58), in pleasing God (*1 Thess.* 4:1), in all grace (*2 Pet.* 1:8).

There are many encouragements, because grace has abounded towards us (*Rom.* 5:20, *Eph.* 1:7–8), and our labour is not in vain in the Lord (*1 Cor.* 15:58). But an abundant entrance shall be ministered to us, into the kingdom of our Lord and Saviour (*2 Pet.* 1:8–11). And lest we should become discouraged and fear that it is not attainable, we are to know that God is able to make grace abound (*2 Cor.* 9:8). Let us then go on to perfection, from babes to little children, from little children to young men, from young men to fathers, till we all come into the unity of the faith and of the knowledge of the son of God, unto a perfect man, unto the measure of the stature of the fullness of Christ (*Eph.* 4:13–14).

No one knows whether he may attain to more than a babe, and so should press forward. The highest saints, fathers, press forward; all the more should you. See how Paul presses forward (*Phil.* 3:8–14). Should one who had attained so much be pressing so much, and not you who have attained a little? Let the zeal of the highest arouse the lowest to zeal.

Little grace has little comfort. Though the babe has enough for being, he has only a little for well-being. To live is not merely to be, but to enjoy oneself and to be well. In this life we take care not only to keep body and soul together but to live comfortably. Shall we not aim higher in our spiritual life all the more? Little faith is full of fear and excludes present joy and comfort. In that respect, it is like having no faith, so says our Saviour: Why are ye fearful, O ye of little faith (*Matt.* 8:26)? Why are ye so fearful? How is it that ye have no faith (*Mark* 4:40)? Do you want to have less fear and more joy? Then press forward to grow in grace.

Little grace gives little glory to God. The babe does contribute something to the perfecting of God's praise, but very little. Our Father is glorified when we bring

[176]

forth much fruit (*John* 15:8). It is being filled with fruits of righteousness which brings full glory to God (*Phil.* 1:11). Abraham, who was strong in faith, gave glory to God (*Rom.* 4:20). If you want to glorify God, grow in grace.

While you are but babes, you are of little use to others. The least member is of some use (*1 Cor.* 12), but of least use. A candle may give some light, but none compared to what the sun gives. We should be, as John was, not only burning but shining lights. And our light should so shine before men, that they may see our good works and glorify our Father in heaven (*Matt.* 5:16).

GROWING IN GRACE

Be humble and lowly in mind. Humility promotes us; it is to ascend downward. Humility and a low esteem of ourselves is the ready way to grow high. The trees with the deepest roots spread most upward. Before honour is humility (*Prov.* 15:33). He that is lifted up is likely to fall (*Prov.* 18:12, *Heb.* 2:4; 10:38). But the same God who resists the proud, greatly loves and will assist, teach, and give grace to the humble. Some babes, alas, are apt to be puffed up without cause (*1 Cor.* 4:8), but pride hinders growth.

Be thankful for what is received. Ungrateful persons never or seldom thrive (*Rom.* 1:21). Because when they knew God, they glorified him not as God, neither were thankful. They became vain in their imaginations, and their foolish hearts were darkened. Professing themselves to be wise, they became fools. But he that blesses God for what he has, is likely to be blessed with more, and that which he seems to have shall be taken from him (*Luke* 8:18).

It is a great help to growth to be united one to another

in unity of mind and affection. Those who are divided in Jacob and scattered in Israel are not likely to come to much excellence, for where there are divisions there is least contribution of help and mutual assistance. When the apostle exhorts the Corinthian babes to be perfect, he joins it to the phrases 'be of one mind', and 'live in peace' (2 Cor. 13:11). For love is the bond of perfectness (Col. 3:12–14), the blessing of the God of love and peace will be with those who practise it, and his blessing makes rich (Prov. 10:22).

Read, listen to, and ponder the word of grace conscientiously and eagerly, that you may grow. Make use of ordinances for your perfection; they are designed for this (Eph. 4:11). Pastors and teachers are for the perfecting of the saints, for the edifying of the body of Christ, and every member, until we all come to a perfect man.

Get better acquainted with Christ Jesus. The apostle knew Christ Jesus well, and yet he pressed after more, the excellency of the knowledge of Christ Jesus (Phil. 3:8–14). Babes in Christ do not know the Father and are unlearned in the word of righteousness. Now the Father cannot be known but by the Son, nor can grace grow except through the excellent knowledge of Christ Jesus our Lord (2 Pet. 3:18). To grow in grace and attain assurance of the Father's love, aim for the knowledge of Christ. Be found in him and his righteousness, and know the power of his resurrection, though that means also knowing the fellowship of his suffering and being made conformable to his death. By descending, we may ascend, as he did (Phil. 3:9–10, Eph. 4:9–10).

Would you like to grow? Make use of the promises then, which are given not only that we might escape the pollutions which are in the world by lust, and so be made partakers of a divine nature (2 Pet. 1:4), but also that we might cleanse ourselves from all filthiness of flesh and spirit to perfect holiness in the fear of God (*2 Cor.* 7:1) and that we might add grace to grace, to abound and be fruitful (*2 Pet.* 1:5–8). The covenant refers to our being and birth, but the promises apply to our well-being and growth. But to enjoy what is promised, be careful to do that to which the promise is connected. For instance, if you would have God be not only a God but a Father to you; and you be to him not only a people but sons and daughters, then be separate and touch not the unclean thing (*2 Cor.* 6:17–18). And note, these promises are of most use to our perfecting. For 'having these promises' (the emphasis is in 'these'), is followed by 'let us cleanse ourselves' (*2 Cor.* 7:1), that we may enjoy what is promised.

How do we make use of promises? Some people think that the main or only way is by 'believing', as they call it. I think a greater mistake could hardly be made. When they read or hear a promise, for example that God will be a Father, or that all things shall work together for good, they think all that is required is to believe that God will do as he has promised. There is no question but that he will, for he is faithful and cannot lie. But let me tell you, lest you deceive yourselves, that it is not so much faith as obedience and practice which is necessary to the enjoyment of these promises. If you practise the duty to which the promise is made, God will make it good, whether you believe it or not (*2 Tim.* 2:11–13). But if you believe it a thousand times over and do not do the duty, God is under no obligation to make good the promise. If you do not love God, how can you expect that all things should work together for good to you, when the promise is made only to lovers of God? And if you do not separate from uncleanness, how can you expect God will be a Father to you, when it is promised only to those who separate?

Take heed, then, of an idle and dead faith. It is true,

faith is a duty, but not faith alone, faith that is idle and dead. Whatever promises are made to faith, shall be made good to faith. And whatever promises are made to love, to humility, to patience, shall be made good when these graces are acted. The apostle says, Let us draw near with a true heart, in full assurance of faith, having our hearts sprinkled from an evil conscience, and our bodies washed with clean water. Let us hold fast this profession of our faith without wavering, for he is faithful that hath promised (*Heb.* 10:23-24). By this we see that without the other qualifications mentioned there can be no full assurance of faith. I thought it good to mention this, so that no one might think that faith without obedience is enough to obtain promises.

If you wish to attain to perfection, be patient. Babes are apt to be impatient and peevish, but impatience hinders growth. To be perfect, let patience have its perfect work, then shall you be perfect, entire, and lack nothing of perfection (*James* 1:4). Patience is a completing and perfecting grace, as God says to Abraham (*Gen.* 17:1). Walk before me and be thou perfect; that is, not only sincere, but patient. Wait yet a while longer till I give thee seed by Sarah; perfect thy waiting thus far by waiting to the end. Similarly, the good-ground hearers bringing forth fruit with patience are opposed to the thorny-ground hearers not bringing forth fruit to perfection (*Luke* 18:14-15). So patience contributes greatly to bringing forth perfect fruit, and to our growing up to a perfect stature.

Patience establishes the heart, making it steadfast and immovable, which helps to abounding and growth (*1 Cor.* 15:58, *2 Pet.* 3:17-18). While persons are tossed to and fro, as babes are apt to be (*Eph.* 4:14), they are not in a condition to grow. But patience settles, fixes, and establishes the soul (*James* 5:8), whereas an impatient man is uncertain, inconstant, and double-minded, ever doubtful and in suspense, and therefore receives little, if anything, from the Lord (*James* 1:6–8).

Patience helps the soul to wait despite disappointments and sufferings. These are discouraging, they dishearten, weaken, and make us faint, rendering us incapable of thriving. But patience steels and strengthens our hearts. When hope deferred makes us sick, patience gives supports and cordials, enabling us to wait till the longed-for desire is granted, which is as a tree of life (*Rom.* 8:23–25, *Heb.* 10:35–36; 12:1). In both of these ways patience helps us onward.

Watch over your hearts and lives, and keep your accounts well, observing how you gain or lose day by day. Consider what is attained and what is lacking, that you may forget what is behind and press forward to what is ahead, as the apostle did (*Phil.* 3:13). Those who do not keep their accounts well, but let them run at random, are not likely to thrive. How can they discern the difference between what they were, are, and ought to be?

And lastly, give attention to prayer, both your own and others'. Praying saints and saints prayed for are most likely to prosper. The great apostle not only prayed himself but often begged the prayers of others, his inferiors also, for himself. All the more should you, being sickly saints who cannot pray as much or as well as you ought for yourselves. You should call in the help of Elders and the church to pray for you. Read over the prayers which the apostle made for babes, and make them for yourselves. I will give only one as an example, and will conclude with it (*Heb.* 13:20–21):

Now the God of peace, who brought again from the dead our Lord Jesus, the great shepherd of the sheep, through the blood of the everlasting covenant, make you perfect in every good work to do his will, working in you that which is well pleasing in his sight, through Jesus Christ; to whom be glory for ever and ever. Amen.

PART THREE

Little Children

From 1 John 2:13

I write unto you, little children, because ye have known the Father.

Having spoken to the first and lowest class of saints, babes in Christ, I now address the second class, who are called 'little children'. That title is not used here to name all saints, as it is in 1 John 2:1,12, 28; 3:7,18 and 5:21, which refer to all saints, fathers, young men, and little children. But in 1 John 2:13, the title denotes a particular class.

In 1 John 2:12-14, therefore, there are three sorts of saints, each characterized by their special attainments. Though many other features are included, these named are the acme, the chief excellence of each of them. The fathers' excellence is their much and long experience and wisdom, having known him that is from, and having known him from, the first or beginning. The young men's excellence is strength and valour, having overcome the wicked one. And the little children's is their assurance of God's love, having known him as their Father. We see then that little children are in a middle state between babes, whom they excel, and young men, to whose excellence they have not yet attained.

The subject of the text is little children, and it is said of them that they have known the Father. The time of their having known him is implied: You have lately known the Father, because it is not long since you were newborn and were just babes. For though every newborn one is a child of God, he is still only a babe, and not a child by degree, till he knows the Father. This some attain to later and some sooner, as the Father is pleased to make himself known to them.

THE CHILDREN'S KNOWLEDGE OF THE FATHER

To know the Father is sometimes no more than to know or to have the knowledge of God. As Christ Jesus is known by the name of Lord, so God is known by the name of the Father (*1 Cor.* 8:5–6); and Father, in general, means no more than Creator (*Isa.* 44:8). Many do not have this knowledge of God (*1 Cor.* 15:34, *John* 8:19, 54–55; 16:2–3). There are irreligious and wicked people who do not know the Lord, as it is said of Eli's sons (*1 Sam.* 2:12), nor do they know that Jesus Christ was sent of God. But the babes in Christ have this knowledge. They know the Lord; and much more do the little children. But the knowledge of God means more than this.

To know the Father is not only to know that God is a Father, that he has such a name and attribute. God is often called the Father in Scripture: the Father of our Lord Jesus Christ (*Eph.* 3:14), the Father of our faith (*Matt.* 23:9), the Father of mercies (*2 Cor.* 1:3), the Father of glory (*Eph.* 1:17), the Father of spirits (*Heb.* 12:9), the Father of lights (*James* 1:17). But knowing the Father means more than this, too.

To know the Father is not merely to know him to be the Father of all saints in general. He is the Father of whom the whole family in heaven and earth is named (*Eph.* 3:14–15). There is one God and Father of all, who is above all, and through all, and in all (*Eph.* 4:6). And for this cause Jesus Christ, the first-born among many brethren (*Rom.* 8:29), is not ashamed to call them brethren (*Heb.* 2:10–11). They are all born and begotten of God, and therefore bear not only his name but his image. You may see the Father's image in the babe's eye. Yet this knowledge of the Father is not all, either.

To know the Father is to be taught of God, or to have the anointing from the holy one, whereby they are taught and know all the things which concern their salvation (*1 John* 2:20,27). This is said of these little children (verse 13), yet this is not all that is intended. For to be taught of God is contained in the covenant and applies to all saints, babes as well as others (*Heb.* 8:11), and is part of the drawing of the Father (*John* 6:44–45) which babes partake of. The little children's knowing of the Father must therefore signify some deeper and more transcendent knowledge, beyond that of those below them in the school of Christ.

To know the Father, as it means in this text, is to know him by intimate experience. Knowing God as one's Father and knowing oneself to be his child denotes a state of assurance. It is a reciprocal knowledge, like that of the spouse: I am my beloved's and he is mine; to be able to say as Thomas, My Lord and my God. Though not every child of God can say, My Father (babes cannot), the little children can say not only Abba Father, but My Father. I will put thee among the children, and thou shalt call me, My Father (*Jer.* 3:19). Our Saviour promised his babe-disciples that when the Spirit was poured out upon them they would know their union with him, which was the same as with the Father (*John* 14:8–20). At that time he, by his Spirit, would show them plainly of the Father (*John* 16:25–26). One of the great things which the Spirit was to declare was their union with the Father and with Christ (*John* 16:13–15; 17:5, *1 John* 5:19–20), to assure them of their love.

LEARNING IN CHRIST'S SCHOOL

In knowing the Father by communion and experience
(*1 John* 1:3), they find a communication and imparting of
his fatherly love. Some do not see the king's face, though
called to court, as was Absalom's case. But these have a
knowledge of enjoyment. They find and feel his love shed
abroad into their hearts. The light of his countenance is
lifted up upon them, and they walk in the light and joy of
his salvation (*1 John* 1:3–7). They hear the joyful sound
of, My son, and My daughter, My pleasant and beloved
child in whom I am well pleased; thy sins are forgiven
thee, and thou art mine. They find the Father embracing
them in his arms and taking them into his bosom. And
this indeed is their knowledge of the Father: knowing
him by intimate experience, in union and communion.
They feast with the Father and on his love as the prodigal
did after his father had sealed his love with a kiss. How
sweet and pleasant was the entertainment and communion! They rejoiced.

HOW THE CHILDREN COME TO KNOW THE FATHER

Little children come by this knowledge by the working
and witnessing of the Spirit. I put both words together,
because though he may work where he does not witness,
as in babes, he never witnesses except where he has
worked. We observe that mortification, led by the Spirit
and being in part a spirit of adoption and prayer,
precedes the witnessing with our spirits that we are the
children of God (*Rom.* 8:13–16). Paul speaks also (*1 Cor.*
2:12–13) of the spiritual ones having received the Spirit
of God and communicating spiritual things, in spiritual
words, not in words of man's wisdom. And John (*1 John*
3:24) speaks of the assurance of these saints dwelling in
God, saying that he abides in them by the Spirit which he
has given them. But before John mentions that, he

characterizes them by their keeping of his commandments; so the work precedes the witness of the Spirit. I
will say more about this later, but first will make a few
observations about the persons that God calls from
among his babes to make them children and to give
them assurance.

(i) *The persons God places among the little children and to whom he gives assurance*

Perhaps some poor souls among the babes, for whom I
have great concern, are asking if there is any hope for
them to come to the attainment of the little children, that
they, who long after him, also may be kissed and brought
into his banqueting house. For their sakes I shall
investigate God's way in this matter. But first I must lay
down two premises.

Firstly, God is free in his choice. His Spirit blows, this
gale of knowledge and assurance of the Father's love,
when and where he pleases. It is not a trade wind, if I
may so say. God is not under any obligation, nor is he
bound to any man. As he shows mercy to whom he will,
so he shows mercy to what degrees he will. It is not in
him that wills nor in him that runs (referring to Isaac's
blessing of Jacob instead of Esau), but in God that shows
all mercy.

Secondly, God has been pleased to pick out some
persons upon whom he has fixed a special love and makes
himself known as a Father to them. Among all the
disciples, John was the one whom Jesus loved specially,
as the evangelists often mention. He loved all his family,
but John was his bosom disciple and favourite. Just as
fathers who have many children but love and kiss one
more than the rest, as Jacob loved Joseph more than all
his brothers (*Gen.* 37:3), it is so here: God is pleased to
give special manifestations of his love to some. And he

has usually done this, and has promised to do it, to certain kinds of people.

a) God shows his love to those who come into his service while young. Those who seek him shall find him sooner or later, but those who seek him early shall be sure to find him early (*Prov.* 8:17). They that love and obey him shall know the Father's love (*John* 14:21–23), and the sooner their love is manifested, the sooner is his. The reason that many give why John was the beloved disciple is that he came to Christ while very young. We love all of our children, but if one is more obedient and honest at a very early age it endears them to us. We show our special affection for them by kindnesses, small gifts, smiles; and truly God himself usually does so. God is love, and he that dwells in love of God and the brethren, dwells in God, and God in him (*1 John* 4:7,12,16). And usually, the sooner our love appears, he accordingly manifests himself to us and lets us know that he loved us first (*1 John* 4:19).

The Scripture records as special favourites those who were converted and turned to God when young. God remembers the kindness of Israel's youth, and the love of their espousals while they were young and went after him in the wilderness (*Jer.* 2:2). At that time they had wonderful demonstrations of his love. Not to mention Abel, Joseph was very gracious and tender-hearted, for he could not bear with the wickedness of his brothers, even when he was but seventeen years old, and soon God appeared to him, as to Solomon, twice (*Gen.* 37:2–9).

Samuel ministered to the Lord when he was a very young child and the Lord appeared to him. Though at first he did not understand the voice and word of the Lord, soon after he did. And Samuel grew, and the Lord was with him (*1 Sam* 3:1,4–7, 18–19).

Josiah was very good at sixteen years of age. He began

to reign at eight years old (*2 Chron.* 34:1), and in the eighth year of his reign he began to seek after the God of his father David. In the twelfth year, when he was twenty years old, he began to purge Judah and Jerusalem. How dear he was to God, and what a demonstration of love he had, may be seen from 2 Chronicles 34:26–28.

I might mention many more, as David, Moses, Daniel, the three young men in Daniel, Timothy, and others. But this shall suffice to show that God usually and signally manifests his love to those that are godly while they are yet young. This lays a great obligation upon and gives great encouragement to persons to remember their Creator in the days of their youth (*Eccles.*12:1).

b) God has been pleased to show his fatherly love to those who have been deeply humbled for sinning against God. Their humiliation would have been long, had not he made himself known as their Father. The prodigal was taken with a sense of having sinned against his father, and felt the sad effects of it. Yet the father ran to meet him, fell on his neck and kissed him; thus he knew the father and had assurance of his love.

When the spouse had undergone a hard winter of humiliation and hid herself in the clefts and secret places, ashamed to lift up her face or voice to God, she then heard the joyful sound, Rise up, my love, my fair one, my dove, and come away (*Song of Sol.* 2:10,15). And she concluded, as one that had assurance, My beloved is mine and I am his.

Manasseh had been desperately wicked, but when he was in affliction he sought the Lord and humbled himself greatly before the God of his fathers (*2 Chron.* 33:12); and God heard his supplication. Then Manasseh knew that the Lord was God, gracious and forgiving.

David no sooner confessed his sin as against God, even doubling it, 'Against thee, against thee' (*Psa.* 51:4), but

[191]

God forgave him, and told him of it, too (*Psa.* 32:5; *2 Sam.* 12:13). Other passages, such as Isaiah 57:15; 66:2 and Jeremiah 31:20, confirm what David said (*Psa.* 51:17): A broken and contrite heart, O God, thou wilt not despise, which is a diminutive expression, but full of significance. It is as if he had said, Thou wilt cherish it, revive it and make it glad with the joy of thy salvation.

This lays a great obligation upon persons as to what they should be, and gives them great encouragement when they are so, though they may be greatly humbled.

But some poor soul may object: Alas for me! I have been under humiliations a long time, sin has cost me dear. My heart has broken with sighs and groans, and I am still watering my couch with my tears. Yet I cannot obtain a smile, not a good word or a good look from God, but he seems to cast me off. Woe is me!

But poor soul, remember: God is not bound to make himself known as a Father to you. He will not be commanded into this condescension, and you must not think to bribe him by prayers and tears. Remember that though God has taken vengeance on some men's sins, he has forgiven them (*Psa.* 99:8). And he may deal so with you, and not turn you into hell nor deal with you as your iniquity deserves, though he causes you to know so much sorrow and pain. Consider, too, that perhaps your humiliation has until now been only legal and selfish, that you have been more concerned that God was displeased with you than that he was displeased by you; that your tears have been more for your own shame and pain than for the sin against God. If so, be humbled for this also, and in due time he will exalt you to a better condition, or save you at last in spite of it.

c) God usually manifests himself and his love as a Father to those that hunger and thirst after and greatly love his Son Jesus Christ.   In Jesus God is well pleased and declared from heaven that he was his beloved Son. And he is pleased to do the same for those who love his Son. God wills that we honour the Son as we do the Father (*John* 5:23). Now him that honoureth me, and consequently that honoureth my Son, I will honour, says the Lord. What honour will God confer upon them? They shall not only be, but be declared to be, the children of God; and behold what manner of love this is (*1 John* 3:1)!

When the spouse was lovesick, she was made much of. And to Mary who loved much, much was forgiven, and special demonstrations of love were given to her. Our Saviour told his disciples that the Father loved them for this very reason, because they loved him, and that shortly they would be shown plainly of the Father (*John* 16:25–27). And he promised to show himself and to abide with all that love him (*John* 14:21–23).

d) God has promised to be known as a Father to those who separate from unbelievers (2 Cor. 6:14–18). Knowing him as Father brings us more love and joy than knowing him as our God (*2 Cor.* 6:16–18, *Heb.* 1:5). Come out from them and be ye separate, saith the Lord; touch not the unclean thing, and I will receive you into my favour and embraces, and I will be a Father to you. You shall be my sons and daughters, and you shall be treated accordingly. For this reason Christ himself was anointed with the oil of gladness above his fellows (*Heb.* 1:9). And as love of righteousness and hatred of iniquity help conform his people to him in separation, the more likely they are to be anointed with the oil of gladness above their fellows.

e) God usually gives demonstrations and assurance of love to those who are about to do and suffer great things for him, and he gives these as preparation. Christ Jesus had the voice from heaven a little before he entered upon his ministry. The apostles had the Spirit sent to prepare them for doing greater things than they had done in Christ's time. And

Paul was very early assured of his election and of being dearly beloved of God because he was very soon to do great things and to undergo great sufferings (*Acts* 9:15–16). In just a few days he passed from being a babe to a little child, and then became a young-man saint, which few so suddenly do except on such an occasion as this.

By searching the Scripture, I have discovered the ones to whom God makes himself known as a Father, calls from among the babes to make them children, and gives assurance of his love. I cannot say that these are all, for there is no confining or limiting God. And I cannot say for whom of us God will do this. But it is more than probable that if we are found among these examples, we shall in due time, and perhaps soon, know the Father.

(ii) How the children come to know the Father by the witness of the Spirit

Children come to know God as their Father by the working of the Spirit in them, but beyond that, by the Spirit witnessing to them, clarifying that the work brought about in their hearts and spirits is of God (*Rom.* 8:18). Here are two witnesses: Our spirit affirms, and the Spirit of God confirms. Our spirit affirms that we have repentance, faith, and love. But our spirit by itself cannot tell whether this is brought about by God and according to the will of God unless the Spirit of God bears witness to it (*Rom.* 8:26–27, *1 Cor.* 2:10–12). From this I make two inferences.

a) This witness of the Spirit is not common to all saints, for babes do not have it. Though they have the things that assure, they do not have assurance because they do not have the Spirit witnessing with their spirit. It does not run parallel with saintship, as the work of the Spirit does. If we do not have the Spirit of Christ, we are none of his (*Rom.*

8:9); but we may still be his without having the witness of the Spirit in us. For we are his before we have the witness of it: The witness does not make us his, but the Spirit, finding us to be his, witnesses and declares that we are his children (*Rom.* 8:16). A thing must exist before it is witnessed of. To confirm this further: It is evident (*Eph.* 1:13–14) that just as they heard before they believed, so they believed before they were sealed with the Holy Spirit of promise, the earnest, or guarantee, of our inheritance, and which we had a little before we had this seal and guarantee. So we are the children of God by faith (*Gal.* 3:26) before we have the witness of being children.

It is said (*1 John* 5:10) that he who believes on the Son of God has the witness in himself, as if every believer had it. I have three things to say to this:

Firstly, St John perhaps was writing not to babes but to the higher forms, children, young men, and fathers, and all these have the witness of the Spirit in themselves. But secondly, if we do include babes, it may be said that they have the thing which witnesses and the witness of their own spirits. But it will not follow from there that they have the witness of the Spirit, or assurance, which is what I am speaking of. The three witnesses in earth agree in one, as the three witnesses in heaven are one (*1 John* 5:7–8). Yet the three do not give out their witnesses all at once; the water and blood may and do witness before the Spirit does. And thirdly, this witness is most properly understood, I think, as the witness that God has given us eternal life by and in his Son (5:11–12). He that believes has both the Son and eternal life in himself. It is already begun in every believer, though not everyone has the assurance of it, as is implied in verse 13.

I infer next that this witness of the Spirit is not only the working of grace by the Spirit in our hearts, but is something added beyond the gracious qualifications which are called the fruits of the Spirit (*Gal.* 5:22–23). It may be by a light shining upon their graces and making them clear; it may be by visibly honouring some promise that addresses such graces; it may be by some immediate beam of love from God upon the soul; or it may be by all of these ways.

Let me illustrate. The working of the Spirit is like the heat and influence of the sun, which reaches all things. But the witness of the Spirit is like the light of the sun, which does not shine on all places at once. The work and influence of the Spirit reaches all the saints, but the witness of the Spirit does not shine upon all saints at once, or upon all in the same degree.

I am inclined to believe that assurance is very rare, and enjoyed less than is claimed or talked about. I have read of one island where the sun shines more or less every day of the year. There may be some such island-saints, but I am inclined to think there are not many of them. Because, as I have mentioned before, the greater part of God's children have not, I fear, yet attained to be children, to know and have assurance of the Father's love. The fathers have; but how few are they? and the conquering young men have, but how few are they? the little children have; but how few are they? There was but one John among the many disciples.

However, this much is clear: Those of this class, whether few or many, have attained to assurance. It may be said of them, Blessed are the people that know the joyful sound: they shall walk, O Lord, in the light of thy countenance (*Psa.* 89:15–17). In thy name, which is gracious (*Exod.* 34:6), shall they rejoice all the day, and in thy righteousness, the Lord our righteousness (*Jer.* 23:6), who is Christ, they shall be exalted, for thou art the glory of their strength, and in thy favour our horn shall be exalted.

b) This witness is clear, sure, and powerful. This witness of the Spirit, by which we know we are the children of God is clear and plain. It is not dark and cloudy but bright and distinct. This brings evidence and demonstration with it, as in the case of the man who at first saw men walking as trees, but at the second touch saw all things clearly (*Mark* 8:23–25). This witness is not like that of our own hearts, which often excuse, yet often accuse, leaving us to doubt which to take for truth. It is not a conjecture, a perhaps, but is as clear as the sun in its midday strength. This witness is not like the spirit of the world which is ambiguous, or the pagan oracles which may be interpreted for or against, but like the oracles of God, clear, certain, and assuring. He that is running may read it, it is written so legibly, in golden capital letters. It is that we may know (*1 Cor.* 2:12).

The witness is also a sure testimony, true, faithful, and infallible. This witness cannot be otherwise, for the spirit which bears testimony is the Spirit of truth, and therefore a spirit of consolation, the Comforter. To lie or deceive would be against not only his name but his nature. It is the devil who is the deceiving spirit and father of lies. No lie is of the truth, nor of the Spirit of truth. This Spirit guides into all truth, and nothing but the truth. He never bears witness to hypocrites or formalists, but only to newborn ones, that they are the children of God.

As the Spirit of truth cannot deceive, so he cannot be deceived. He knows the deep things of God and men: what is in God's heart to us (*1 Cor.* 2:10–11) and what is in our hearts towards God (*Rom.* 8:26–27). It is vain as well as wicked to lie to the Holy Ghost (*Acts* 5:3). He cannot be deceived, he will not be mocked, and he cannot be mistaken. This witness of God is true and sure. If we receive the witness of men, the witness of God is greater. It was Paul's great comfort that God was his witness (*Rom.* 1:9, *1 Thess.* 2:4–5). And as he was approved of God, so he expected his justification from him (*1 Cor.* 3:4–5, *2 Cor.* 10:17–18).

It is a powerful witness, for it gives a man a settled, quiet and assured spirit and carries the soul above bondage and fear (*2 Tim.* 1:7). It is like an oath that puts an end to strife and controversy and so affords strong consolation (*Heb.* 6:16–18). The soul rests because the Lord has dealt bountifully with it, and it is upheld by his Spirit which has set it at liberty and filled it with glory (*2 Cor.* 3:17–18).

c) The witness affects and influences the children in several ways. The soul that has received this witness is filled with a great deal of joy. It is joy unspeakable and full of glory, though the person may be in the midst of afflictions, temptations, and sufferings. Yet the Spirit of God and of glory rests upon the soul and dwells there (*1 Thess.* 1:4–6, *1 Pet.* 1:6–8; 4:14). This work cannot be expressed in words. All the eloquence in the world cannot make you taste the sweetness of this honey. As none knows it but he that has it, so he who has it cannot make it known.

If a single witness, that of a man's own conscience, gives joy (*2 Cor.* 1:12), how incomparable must be the joy flowing from a double witness: the Spirit bearing witness with our spirit, that we are the children of God! This is the joyful sound, music to make the soul leap and dance for joy (*Hos.* 2:14–16). They were babes and under bondage in Egypt, but now they sing like the children that had heard the joyful sound of the silver trumpets, proclaiming love and peace. In their youth they sang when God had proclaimed them his sons and firstborn, and called them out of Egypt.

Notwithstanding this joy, they are genuinely and

deeply ashamed of their former sinfulness, which made them unworthy of such favour, worthy to have been children of wrath forever. No sooner had the father kissed the returning prodigal than he uttered his first words: Father, I have sinned against heaven, and in thy sight, and am no more worthy to be called thy son (*Luke* 15:20–21). His father understood that this confession was a great part of his gratitude, and they feasted and rejoiced together.

This openness results from this assured reconciliation (*Ezek.* 16:62–63). I will establish my covenant with thee, and thou shalt know that I am Jehovah (gracious and merciful), that thou mayest remember thy ways and be ashamed – but when is this? – when I am pacified toward thee for (or notwithstanding) all that thou hast done, saith the Lord.

Because of this testimony the little children have a great deal of confidence and boldness towards God. If our hearts condemn us not, we have confidence towards God (*1 John* 3:21). But how much more, when by the Spirit which he has given us we know that he dwells in us and we in him! Assurance is the perfecting of love, which gives us boldness not only at the throne of grace, but in the day of judgement (*1 John* 3:21–22; 4:17; 5:14–15). For there is no fear in love thus made perfect, but it casts out fear and fills us with confidence and boldness, familiarity and freedom.

Having received this testimony, the little children yearn to be with their Father, not only to have their thoughts and affections in heaven, but to be personally there. Few babe-saints, who do not know the Father, are willing to die. And if God did not take them to heaven before they were willing and desirous to die, I fear that heaven would be very thinly peopled with that class of saints. But when children have the assurance that God is

and heaven shall be theirs, they say with the good old
man Simeon, Now lettest thou thy servant depart in
peace, for mine eyes have seen thy salvation.

Not only Paul (*2 Cor.* 1:8, *Phil.* 1:23) but all who have
received this testimony, the first fruits and guarantee of
happiness, sigh and groan and long, and think it a long
time till they will be set free (*Rom.* 8:23). Here they are
absent from the Lord, and it is only with some self-denial
that they are willing to stay here. But while they must be
here they are greatly ambitious to be acceptable to God
(*2 Cor.* 5:9) and to serve the churches' good (*Phil.*
1:23–24). They are sure that though they suffer with
Christ, yet they shall be glorified together (*Rom.*
8:16–17). And so they want to hasten his coming and
pray, as they are told, Come, Lord Jesus, come quickly.
And surely they shall have their wishes: Either Christ will
come to them, or they will go to Christ within a very little
while. But yet remembering that they are not their own
and that they serve God not only for their own advantage, but for his glory, they are made willing to wait all
the days of their appointed time, though it is warfare as
in Job, till their change comes (*Rom.* 8:23–25).

*d) We may distinguish the testimony of the Spirit from
delusions of Satan and the presumptions of our own hearts.*
Some people may yet be fearful and suspicious lest they
should err and be deceived, and so meet with the true
miseries of false joys. It is all the same to the devil
whatever way people go to hell, so long as they go there,
whether through the common road and dirty highway of
profanity, immorality, and irreligion; or through the
fields and pleasant walks of a form of godliness. This
has its joy, raptures, and ecstasies, too, for the evil spirit
impersonates the good one, and to deceive more readily
and indiscernibly he clothes himself as the angel of light.

How then can we discern whether the testimony which

we think we have is sound and good, or false and counterfeit? It is good to watch and to be circumspect because our adversary, the devil, is seldom more our adversary than when he pretends to be our friend, as he did to Eve and to Christ himself. Still, those who have the testimony of God's Spirit are secure and safe. But those who do not have it cannot be safe, whatever presuming confidence they may entertain.

I shall therefore try to explain, so that no one is hardened through the deceitfulness of sin, or Satan, or their own hearts. But first I lay down this premise: Those who do not have the work of the Spirit cannot have the witness. And consequently, those who do not have the witness of their own spirits, or the testimony of a good conscience, cannot have the witness of the Spirit. For if our hearts condemn us upon just grounds, and we do not bear false witness against ourselves, (which is the sin of many an otherwise tender-hearted Christian), God is greater than our hearts.

But if our hearts do not condemn us, here begins our confidence towards God: if we love not only in word but in deed and truth, then we know, in part, that we are of the truth, and shall assure, or persuade, our hearts before him (*1 John* 3:18–21). And the apostle tells us that the Spirit bears witness with our spirit (*Rom.* 8:16). It follows, then (*1 John* 3:24), that we may have our own witness without the Spirit's, but we cannot have the Spirit's witness without our own. To make the testimony complete, both witnesses, both spirits, must agree without contradiction. The three that bear witness on earth agree in one (*1 John* 5:8).

Using three rules, we can discern the difference between the true and the pretended or presumed witness of the Spirit.

Firstly, the witness is known *from the rule according to*

which it speaks. To the law and to the testimony: if they speak not according to this word, there is no light (Hebrew: no morning) in them; no, not so much as the dawning of the day (*Isa.* 8:20, *1 John* 4:1–6, *2 John* 2:7–10, *Gal.* 1:6–9, *2 Cor.* 11:1–4). The Spirit of God acts by the same rule that we are to act and walk by, and that is the Word. If the Word and the Spirit do not agree, we must question either whether the Word is of God, or whether the Spirit is of God. And we are at a woeful loss if they do not both agree: If the Word says one thing and the Spirit another, how shall we reconcile them? But God's Word and God's Spirit always agree and are of the same mind. The Spirit of God who gave the holy Scriptures cannot say one thing here and another in your heart. That would be to bear witness against himself. And how can a divided kingdom stand?

The infallible conclusion is that when and wherever the Spirit of God bears testimony, it is always according to the written Word, contained in the Old and New Testaments. This is the foundation upon which the Spirit builds both us and his testimony (*Eph.* 2:18–22). The Spirit of God gave the Scriptures (*2 Pet.* 1:20–21, *2 Tim.* 3:14–17, *1 John* 2:20–27). The unction, or anointing, is according to what they had heard from the beginning; so that they were taught the same thing by the unction within, as they were by the Word (also called unction).

In all times the Word was the rule of trial. Our Lord Jesus Christ himself opposed and conquered the devil by this sword of the Spirit, the Word of God. He proved himself to be the Messiah more by the Scriptures than by miracles. He told his listeners that if the Scriptures did not testify of him, they should not believe him, and therefore charges them to search the Scriptures (*John* 5:39). Our Saviour confuted the errors of the Pharisees and the Sadducees by Scripture. He said that his Spirit would not bring us a new doctrine, but would apply what he taught (*John* 14:26). The apostles commended the Bereans, who searched the Scriptures to see if the apostles spoke the truth (*Acts* 17:10–11). And Peter calls it, in relation to the Jews, a more sure word of prophecy (*2 Pet.* 1:16–19). It is clear, then, that what is not according to the sacred Scriptures cannot be the witness of God's Spirit.

Secondly, the witness of the Spirit is distinguished from any other *by the grounds on which it witnesses*. The Spirit finds this groundwork laid, that you are newborn, though only a babe in days and experience. This always precedes the witness. The Spirit cannot witness to those who are dead in sins (*Eph.* 1:1–3), nor to those who have a form of godliness but are hypocrites, that they are the children of God. It is when and because you are sons, that God sends forth the Spirit of his Son into your hearts, crying, Abba Father. The work is always begun before the witness comes. That which is not wrought cannot be witnessed to. If you are not newborn, your believing yourself to be a child of God is a delusion, not the witness of the Spirit.

The Spirit of God bears witness that one is the child of God not on the ground of works and self-righteousness, but upon the ground of grace through redemption by Christ Jesus. It witnesses upon the account of mercy, not of merit. Though there is a work brought about, the witness attributes this to grace. All is of grace, and on this foundation is the witness laid. It is called sonship by adoption; the Spirit bears witness that we are the children of God, but that we are so by adoption and not by nature. For by nature we are children of wrath (*Eph.* 2:3). We were children of disobedience and enemies by wicked works (*Col.* 1:21). As for our good works after the new birth, they do not make us children of God, for they are the result of our being first the children of God – and that not from our own worth or will, but his grace and good will. On this account and this alone does the Spirit bear witness.

The witness of the Spirit is known *by the ends it aims at and attains*. The design of the Spirit is that we would be abased, while the love, grace and righteousness of the Father and the Son would be exalted in our eyes; that we may be nothing, that God and Christ may be all in all; and that we may praise and honour the God of all grace and glorify his Son Jesus forever. Ignorance is the mother of poor and feeble devotion, but that which flows from knowledge and assurance is strong and vigorous. And therefore the Spirit bears witness, giving assurance, so that our devotion and adoration may be strong. The witness makes God the more dear to us – not only dearer for his mercy, but dearer than his mercy – that we may love and serve him better. Then may we live to the praise and glory of God in righteousness and true holiness in this present world and for eternity.

This witness designs also to wean us from this world, that we may live above its pride and pleasures, having our thoughts and affections in heaven. St John tells the fathers, young men, and little children (*1 John* 2:15) not to love the world, neither the things that are in the world, on this very account. If anyone loves the world, the love included in the knowledge of the Father is not in him; he does not know the Father. And if any imagine themselves to be children of God, and yet are proud, wanton, and worldly-minded, they are deceiving themselves, for they do not have the witness of the Spirit. God's children are of another world while living in this one (*Psa.* 73:25, *Phil.* 3:20, *Heb.* 11:13–16).

THE PRIVILEGES AND ENJOYMENTS OF THE LITTLE CHILDREN IN KNOWING THE FATHER

The privileges and enjoyments of those who have assurance must be more than ordinary, because knowing the Father is more than ordinary knowledge. And the better the knowledge, the better the enjoyment, whether in kind or only in degree. One great privilege, dignity, and honour is being able to cry, Abba Father, by the Spirit of adoption received into and witnessing in ourselves. I will speak mainly to this, comparing Romans 8:14–16 with Galatians 4:1–7.

Now, whether the Spirit of adoption whereby we cry, Abba Father, is the same as the witness of the Spirit whereby we know the Father, or whether that is something preceding or following it, is a great question. About something so critical and wonderful we need to be cautious. But with all humble submission, I shall say what I think is most clear and evident in this case: that the Spirit of adoption may by a little precede the witness of the Spirit, as the dawning of the day precedes by a little the sun's rising to our view. More of it may come and appear together with the witness, but most of all, as to use and comfort, the Spirit of adoption flows from the witness after its reception. That is, the children of God act most by the Spirit of adoption crying Abba Father, after they have received the witness of the Spirit, whereby they know the Father and that they are his children.

From Romans 8 and Galatians 4, we can extract five points which will help to show this.

(i) These texts, with several others, show the great advantage and dignity of the gospel state beyond that of the Law. Under the Law they were sons and heirs, but underage, *i.e.,* babes, which is the word used (*Gal.* 4:1,3). They were

sons by adoption, or by grace (*Acts* 15:11), for none have been the sons of God any other way since the fall of Adam.

But under the Law, they were under a spirit of bondage more than of adoption, and were no different from servants under bondage. They did not receive the Spirit of adoption till their redemption by Christ. And until they received the sonship by adoption, they did not have the Spirit of the son, crying Abba Father; and after this they ceased to be servants. That is, they ceased to be sons and heirs as babes only, which differs nothing from a servant, and became sons and heirs of God through Christ (*Gal.* 3:23–29).

The state under the Law was a law of bondage. The Law is called a yoke of bondage (*Gal.* 5:1), and those under it were under a spirit of bondage. It is a weak, slavish, and cowardly spirit of fear, the opposite to that of power, love and a sound mind (*2 Tim.* 1:7). This spirit of bondage is usually interpreted to signify a slavish frame of heart, whereby the Jews, like slaves and superstitious persons, served God out of fear. And this I shall not deny. Their religion, at the best, was called The fear of the Lord. Yet I add that they did not serve God only out of fear; but their service did not free them from fear. They were afraid of suffering death and hell, notwithstanding their services and sacrifices.

Jesus Christ took flesh to free them from this fear (*Heb.* 4:11) and to bring in the Spirit of adoption (*2 Tim.* 1:7, *Gal.* 4:4–5). It is spoken of to bear them up against sufferings which they were under (*Rom.* 8:15–18), and is mentioned also to encourage Timothy in the sufferings of others and his own (*2 Tim.* 1:7–8). And it is observable that since the death of Christ and the pouring out of this Spirit, many saints have been as willing to die as they had been afraid to die before, under the Law.

In general, the gospel state is as far advanced beyond that of the Law as liberty is beyond bondage, and courage beyond fear, for those who have received not simply the adoption but the Spirit of it.

(ii) The Spirit of adoption is an addition to sonship. Under the Law they were servant-sons, but now they are son-servants; they have the Spirit of sons, says the apostle. Now ye are no more servants, but sons, you who have received the Spirit of his Son (*Gal.* 4:6–7).

They are sons, as all babes are, before they have this Spirit of sons to cry Abba Father. Indeed, when God is pleased to translate a babe into a higher form and to place him among the little children, this Spirit of sonship or adoption begins to exert himself before having a clear and full witness. Ordinarily among babes, though they are sons, there is little of the Spirit of adoption, but much of bondage appearing in them.

So the Spirit of sons is an addition to sonship. They received the adoption, and after that the Spirit; and by degrees they came to call, Abba Father. So they are called the sons of God, and upon being sons receive the Spirit of sons or of adoption (*Rom.* 8:14–15).

(iii) The witness of the Spirit of God comes not upon the adoption itself, but upon the Spirit of adoption. For it bears witness with our spirits (those who are adopted). But it is not our natural spirit that bears witness that we are the children of God; our Spirit of adoption does that, and it is this Spirit with which the Spirit of God bears witness.

The babes are sons, but do not have the Spirit of sons, and therefore do not have the witness of God's Spirit, or assurance. But as soon as the Spirit of sons begins to show forth, then usually the witness of the Spirit joins itself to it.

(iv) Upon the witness of the Spirit, these souls cry out with freedom and boldness, My Father, Abba Father. With only

the single witness of their own spirit, they had some hope and might faintly and brokenly endeavour to lisp out Father; but now, with the assurance from the Spirit that they are the children of God, they open their mouth wide and say, My Father.

The Spirit of adoption whereby we cry Abba Father is also called the Spirit of his Son (*Gal.* 4:6). Such was in Christ, who always (except once, when it was My God, my God) addressed God as Father, and once Abba Father (*Mark* 14:36). And all these were after he had received the witness of the Spirit that he was the only and beloved Son of God (*Matt.* 3:17). So, when we have the witness, we do not only think or hope that God is our Father, but with confidence and assurance we draw near to God and cry Abba Father. We cannot do so freely before we know the Father to be ours and that we are his children.

The Spirit of sons and the witness of the Spirit of God belong not to the babes, then, but to the children, young men, and fathers. They have been taken from being servants into the glorious and noble liberty of the children and friends of God (*Rom.* 8:19–21, *Gal.* 4:7, *John* 15:9).

(*v*) *To have the Spirit of adoption and the witness of the Spirit by which we cry, Abba Father, is a choice and incomparable privilege.* The adoption itself seems to be an advance beyond sonship under the Law (*Gal.* 4:5), when it was as if they, though sons, were sons of another nature, servants or servile sons.

But to have the Spirit of adoption is more than adoption; and to have the witness of the Spirit is more than the Spirit of adoption. For from these come our boldness to call, Abba Father. It is the height of gospel glory to converse with, to enjoy and to obey God as children do a father. Though the sons under the Law were under bondage, it was a state of more freedom than other nations and peoples had. But this is a state of liberty, glorious liberty.

It is a great advance to pass from servants to friends (*John* 15:15), to pass from babes to children, from as carnal to spiritual; yes, and to have not only the Spirit of Christ, without which we are none of his (*Rom.* 8:9), but to have the unique Spirit of his Son (an emphatic distinction!) whereby as he did, we cry, Abba Father. Others, who are Christ's and have the Spirit of Christ, cannot do so without this special gift of the Spirit of his Son.

(vi) To know the Father, as I have spoken of it, is a great attainment and a glorious privilege. It is prophesied of in the Old Testament as the glory of the New. The prophecies of the Messiah or gospel dispensation were far more glorious than were then realized. And when the day dawns and the daystar arises in our hearts, it supersedes the prophecies, because it has become reality. Many believed because of the prophecies which testified of these things, but more believed because of his own word (*John* 4:39–42). And now they may say, We believe not only because of their sayings, but because we have heard and felt him ourselves (*1 John* 1:1–3), and that this is indeed the Spirit of his Son, which bears witness with our Spirit of adoption.

Now, among many other prophecies of the glories of the gospel saints, one is that they should know God as a Father, and as their own Father (*Psa.* 89:26). This is spoken of David, and of Christ, who was more a David than David was. He shall cry unto me, Thou art my Father (*Isa.* 64:8). And it is spoken that they should say in time to come, Doubtless thou art our Father (*Isa.* 63:16). I said, How shall I put thee among the children? And I said, Thou shalt call me, My Father (*Jer.* 3:19).

Again, in the New Testament, knowing God as our Father is shown as a greater glory than knowing him as our God: I shall be their God, and they shall be my people; but if they come out from among them, and be separate and touch not the unclean thing, then I will receive them, and will be a Father to them, and they shall be my sons and daughters, saith the Lord Almighty (2 Cor. 6:16–18). God is the God of angels, but to which of them said he at any time: Thou art my Son, this day have I begotten thee? And again, I will be to him a Father, and he shall be to me a Son (Heb . 1:5). The apostles call God the God and Father of our Lord Jesus Christ (2 Cor. 11:31, Eph. 1:3, 1 Pet. 1:3). So it is apparent that it is sweeter that God is our Father, than if he were only our God.

The great, if not the greatest, disclosure which Christ promised to make, by sending the Spirit to do it, was to make known the Father. The disciples had heard him speak much of the Father and of knowing the Father (John 14:1–7). Philip said, Show us the Father, and it suffices us. Our Saviour took that occasion to speak more of the union that was between him and the Father. He said that in knowing him they might know the Father also, and that whoever loves him shall be loved of the Father. And the Father would send the Holy Ghost to be the Comforter, a name under which he had not yet been so clearly known. Therefore they should rejoice, because he went to the Father. And the time is coming, he said (John 16:25), when the Comforter comes, that I will show you plainly of the Father; and he places even more comfort in this than in his own intercession for us, which itself is one of the greatest comforts we have (Rom. 8:34, Heb. 7:25, 1 John 2:1). Accordingly, the good news which he sent his disciples after his resurrection was that he was ascending to his God and their God;

and not only this, but to his Father and their Father
(*John* 20:17).

To have the witness of the Spirit, and so to know the
Father, is an honour that was conferred on Christ
himself. As the Spirit is the Spirit of his Son, so the
glory is the glory of his Son, such as he had when he
received honour and glory from God the Father (*Matt.*
3:17; 17:5, *2 Pet.* 1:17). And when the like testimony is
borne by the Spirit of God to our spirits, we receive
honour and glory from God the Father; for if it be so
great an honour to be known of God, how much is it to
know him, and to know him as our Father (*Gal.* 4:9, *1
Cor.* 13:11–12, *Phil.* 3:12)! All these things show what a
great, glorious, and sweet privilege it is to know the
Father by the witness of his Spirit.

(vii) It is a glorious and sweet privilege.   The children
have a great deal of freedom, boldness, and assurance in
their addresses to God at the throne of grace and in the
day of judgement, and it is expressly on account of their
intercessor and high priest (*Heb.* 4:14–16). And indeed
the Spirit becomes a Spirit of prayer, an intercessor, in
them (*Rom.* 8:26–27). The Spirit's knowledge is more to
their advantage and comfort than their ignorance is to
their detriment. They go to God as to a father, as
children go to their fathers. But they go with a much
greater assurance (*Matt.* 7:11), as the prayers of Christ
are heard always (*John* 11:41–42) and by his prayers he
can obtain and do mighty things (*Matt.* 26:53) because
they are addressed to his Father. So it is also with these
that know the Father (*1 John* 3:21–22; 5:14–15).

God always had his favourite sons and daughters, who
had his ear and heart and hand, almost at their
command. Such were Noah, Daniel, Job, Moses, Joshua,
Samuel, Abraham, Jacob and others. And now these
little children, the Johns that lie in his bosom (*John*

13:21–26), prevail with and obtain much from the Lord, as our Saviour said they would do after he was ascended and had sent the Spirit to make known the Father to them (*John* 14:12–13; 15:7; 16:23–24).

As they have great boldness at the throne of grace, so in the day of judgement also, because of their perfect love and full assurance. As he is, so they in this world are (*1 John* 4:17); that is, he is declared and witnessed to be the Son, and these, too, are to be the sons of God. They shall have confidence at his coming (*1 John* 2:28).

Another advantage in knowing the Father and being able to cry, Abba Father, is the great relief it affords in the saddest times and conditions. It was Christ's standing consolation that God was his Father, and so it is theirs. It is sufficient to know the Father, who is all-sufficient, and whose grace shall be sufficient for them, come what may. This is great and strong consolation.

It consoles us when we are misjudged and misinterpreted, as it did Christ himself (*John* 8:15–19; 47–55): Whatever you think or say, it does not matter; my Father witnesses to me, and my Father honours me. It was Paul's comfort that the God and Father of our Lord Jesus Christ (and in him, our Father) knew that he did not lie, though some were to apt to think that he did (*2 Cor.* 12:31). It is a small thing to be misjudged in man's day, when our Father will be our judge and judge righteously (*1 Pet.* 2:23).

It is great and strong consolation when we fear want. We are all too prone to be anxious for tomorrow and to pour out many and long prayers to God. But to deliver us from vain repetitions and troubled thoughts, our Saviour offers the remedy to ease our hearts (*Matt.* 6:7–9). He bids them pray briefly and succinctly, and to make applications to God as a Father who knows better than they do what they need and what is fit for them.

It comforts us if we are forsaken and forgotten by friends and nearest relations. Though father and mother forget us, God our Father will not, and therefore the church pleads it: Doubtless thou art our Father, though Abraham be ignorant of us, and Israel acknowledge us not: thou, O Lord, art our Father (*Isa.* 63:16). This supported Christ himself when the disciples fled and left him alone. Yet he was not alone, for his Father was with him (*John* 16:32).

When suffering comes not only from men but from God himself, knowing the Father brings about patience and submission. When a person was lanced and cut by a surgeon, who was her father, she was asked how she would endure it. 'Oh,' said she, 'it is my father, and he loves me.' Our Saviour took the cup because his Father gave it to him to drink (*John* 18:11). And the apostle presses us to endure chastening upon this account (*Heb.* 12:5–10).

In times of desertion, death and judgement, this is a cordial. A child of light, when walking through darkness, may lean on the staff that God is his God, and that would be enough (*Isa.* 1:10); but how much more that God is his Father (*Isa.* 64:7–8). When our Lord Jesus cried out, My God, my God, why hast thou forsaken me?, he concluded, in almost the same breath (which was also his last), Father, into thine hands I commend my spirit (*Luke* 23:46). This casts out fear in the day of judgement.

It is great comfort that we know the Father and are known of him when no one knows the good we do, because it has been done in secret (*Matt.* 6:4–6). Though we ourselves forget the good we have done, our Father will remember it and bless us for it: Come, ye blessed of my Father, inherit the kingdom prepared for you, who fed me and clothed me. They say, O Lord, when did we do this? (*Matt.* 25). Though they had forgotten, the

Father had a book of remembrance written for them that loved his name, and showed it in ministering to the saints (*Heb.* 6:9–10).

It is a great comfort, when it is difficult for us to pray and we cannot express our own needs, that our Father knows and concerns himself for all our affairs (*Matt.* 6:7–9, *Rom.* 8:26–27). The Spirit that witnesses assists in the prayers of those who have the Spirit of adoption, commending their thoughts, sighs, and groans to God, for he searches the hearts.

It is a great comfort that at times when we have particular things that we pray for, our heavenly Father will not withhold any good thing. If he withholds anything, that thing is not good for us. If it is good, and good now, we shall have it soon, for no earthly father can be so ready as our heavenly Father is to give good things, even the Spirit, to them that ask aright and according to his will (*Matt.* 7:11, *Luke* 11:13). They have all that they would ask (*1 John* 3:22) that is according to his will (*1 John* 5:14). A child of God would neither have nor ask anything knowingly that is not according to his will. They are sure to have all that is good, and it is best to be without what is not good and is denied. His denial and their disappointment; the evil they undergo as well as the good they do; the good they are without as well as the good they enjoy – all work together for their good who love God, and that they do, dearly, who know the Father and have assurance of his love.

THE ATTITUDE OF THE HEART AND SOUL, AND THE
MANNER OF LIFE OF THESE LITTLE CHILDREN

These little children, who know the Father by experience, are of a very loving (which is a very lovely) disposition, and consequently are of a very affable, obliging, and winning manner. Love is the whetstone and lodestone of love; and being beloved of the Father, his love being made known and assured to them, they cannot but inwardly and outwardly love and show their love to their Father and to their brethren (*1 John* 4:19–21). Under the influences of his smiles and kisses, they cannot but be enamoured and inflamed with love. The love of God shed abroad in their hearts causes their love to be shed and spread abroad toward him and his. Their love is second to his first love and bears a relationship to it.

In their love-fits they express many pretty, innocent, and harmless fondnesses, as I may call them. They do many things which would not seem so decent and becoming; but that love not only excuses, but warrants them, sets a gloss and beauty upon them. Mary and Martha were two of his special favourites (*John* 11:5). This Mary especially: As she was loved, so she loved much (*Luke* 7:47). And in the zeal and ecstasy of her love, she anointed the Lord with ointment and not only washed his feet with her tears, but kissed them with her lips and wiped them with her hair (*John* 11:2, *Luke* 7:37–47). Others murmured at this, but Christ commended her for it, and even upbraided Simon for falling very short, though he had made him a feast.

No danger will frighten the children from him whom they love. When the other disciples fled, John (the disciple whom Jesus loved) was found and observed by Christ himself, standing by the cross (*John* 19:26). But to take Mary Magdalene especially as example, oh, how she was carried beyond, above, and out of herself by love to Jesus, who loved her first! She stood by the cross and was not frightened away by the soldiers, rude and unruly though they were, when others were doubting. She went to the sepulchre early, and (as it is noted) while it was yet dark. This did not frighten her, having been made bold by love, though she was of the weaker and more fearful sex. And she did not go empty-handed, but carried sweet spices. She ran to tell Peter and John how it was (*John* 20:2), and when they had seen they returned; but she stayed weeping. As she wept, she stooped down and looked. And when the angels asked her why she wept, she said, 'Alas, do you ask what ails me? They have taken away my dear, dear Lord, and I do not know where they have laid him. Though he is as one that is not, I cannot but love him!' And love at that time was so much a passion that she did not know her Lord when she saw and heard him, and thought it was the gardener. But when Jesus called her by name, oh, how she is transported! 'Rabboni, oh my Lord, is this so? Am I in a dream? Rabboni!' And it seems she would have embraced him, but as love knows how to obey as well as to enjoy, she went away as she was commanded.

Children love the Father in keeping his commandments without regret or grief (*1 John* 5:1-3). Love desires not only to be beloved, but to be commanded; and it is so greatly inclined and obliged to do good and well, that it thinks itself either wronged or suspected if it is not put to the highest and most difficult services. Love never says, This is a hard saying, who can bear it? Love never repines; neither doing nor suffering is grievous to it. Therefore it is remarkable that when our Saviour was about to tell Peter what he must do and suffer, he first of all made sure of his love (*John* 21:15-19).

When the Father gives out commands, love wings the soul, to fly to obedience with speed and pleasure. Love has an ambition to please to the utmost (*2 Cor.* 5:9,14), to do something worthy of the Father's love (*1 Thess.* 2:11-12). Therefore the apostle, having prayed that they might know the unparalleled love of God and Christ, such as passes knowledge, presently exhorts them to walk in a manner worthy of their vocation (*Eph.* 3:18–19; 4:1).

Little children are modest and humble. They do not seek after greatness or great things in this world, for they are weaned (*Psa.* 131:1–2). Being past the stage of babes, they are not concerned to grasp at things which are not suitable to their state. While the disciples were but babes they were often querying who should be greatest. But our Saviour called a little child unto him and set him in the midst of them, and said, 'Verily I say unto you, unless ye be converted and become as little children, he shall not enter into the kingdom of heaven.' That is, you shall have no abundant entrance there (*2 Pet.* 2:11).

And further, 'Whosoever therefore shall humble himself as this little child (the emblem of God's little children), the same is (one of the) greatest in the kingdom of heaven' (*Matt.* 18:4). They were converted before, but they needed to be converted from being as carnal and but babes. Conversion is continued and advanced in growth, both in degree and in passing from one state to another, as from babes to little children. For till we are thus converted we are not weaned from being as carnal, nor can we strengthen our brethren, as Christ told Peter to do.

The little children are full of compassion, very tender-hearted. God as a Father is so, and in being so, we are his children (*Matt.* 5:44–48, *Eph.* 5:1, *Col.* 3:12). And this is pure religion before God as a Father (*James* 1:27). It was upon this account that our Saviour committed his blessed mother to the beloved disciple John, who of all was the most likely to be tender of her (*John* 19:27).

And the children are very tender-hearted in this respect: if at any time they do anything which grieves their Father, or the Spirit by which they are sealed to the day of redemption, their heart smites them and they are more angry with themselves than their Father is, for they will not forgive themselves, though he forgives them. Though God has told David (the beloved one, and the weak babes are not yet as David), that his sin is forgiven, yet he repents and abhors himself in dust and ashes, as Job also did (*Job* 42:5–6).

Children are full of imitation. They tread in their Father's steps, making the Father their example (*1 Pet.* 1:14–17, *Eph.* 5:1). And children are very teachable: babes are not so. The child state is a learning state; the babes are dull of hearing (*Heb.* 5:11, *2 Cor.* 3:2, *John* 16:12). Great things cannot be taught to babes (*Isa.* 28:9), but 'hear ye, children' (*Prov.* 4:1); and 'come near, my children, I will teach you' (*Psa.* 34:11). These are capable of strong meat, for they are spiritual, having received the Sprit of adoption and the witness of that Spirit by which they bring forth all the fruits of the Spirit (*Gal.* 5:22–26).

Before I continue, one question will require an answer. The question is whether those that have assurance do always, till their dying day, lie in the enjoyment and powerful influences of this assurance. May this sun not be eclipsed? May this child of light not walk in darkness, after the light and sight of God as a Father? May the witness of the Spirit not be suspended and withdrawn?

The answer is that some of them may and do live in a continual enjoyment of their assurance (*1 John* 5:18–20), especially if they grow to be fathers after they have been young-men conquerors; for the fathers are spoken of as persons who have, without interruption, known him that is from the beginning. And little children, those who continue as little children, may also, as John did, lie in the bosom to the very last. But those who become young men indeed are tempted to call their sonship into question; but by the word and witness abiding in them, like Joseph's bow in strength, they overcome and conquer, as Christ Jesus did.

As to the influence of assurance in respect of joy, rapture, and the like, I humbly conceive that it does not abide with anyone in so great a measure as when it came at first. My reason is this: Their spirit would fail, for the vision is too strong and the light too bright to be borne always. Beside, if it should continue long, they would be unfit for any of these lower affairs of their particular calling in which they are to serve the will of God in their generations. For this would so possess and take them up (as the prophets of old were during the time of their visions) that they could not attend to anything else.

As, when wrath is upon anyone, the spirit would fail if God should contend forever (*Isa.* 57:16–18); so indeed, if God should continue the bright light of glory always, as it is when the assurance comes at first, they would faint under the weight of glory and beg God to forbear a little, lest their spirit should fail. Now as wrath due to sin is not always so strongly perceived as it is at first conviction, so it may be with love. Still, the influence of this sun may operate much when the clouds intervene; and accordingly the little children, when in that state, have a sedate peace and calm serenity for the most part, and so can cheerfully serve their God and Father and be pleased with his will in all conditions.

The Spirit they have received never witnesses against them, to deny or contradict the former witness. It never revokes it, though it should suspend it; nor reverses it, though it should witness bitter things against them. For though it never says to such a soul, Thou art a child of wrath, yet possibly in a time of desertion and darkness it may say, Thou art under wrath; and so send home terrible things, to the great affliction and deep humbling of the soul.

Application

(i) *An exhortation to babes*

My exhortation is first to babes, *that they would be much in prayer to God that he would place them among the children* and give them the Spirit of adoption and the witness of the Spirit, that they may know the Father to be their Father and themselves to be his children, and so cry, Abba Father. Beg and beg again that he would fall on your neck and kiss you. For your help I present you with a number of arguments which you may breathe and sigh out before the Lord, not in these very words, but as the Spirit may help you.

In the first place, be sure to bless God for what you have received. Do not despise the day of small things, or think any of his consolations little, seeing you are less than the least of all. Bless him that he has proclaimed his name, the Lord gracious, of which you have tasted; that the saying is faithful and worthy of acceptance that Jesus Christ came into the world to save sinners; that you have taken in the milk of this gospel, the first principles of the doctrine of Christ, repentance from dead works and faith towards God and Christ; and that you are taken into the family, though you have only a little of the children's bread, and are fed with crumbs.

The best way to be blessed with more is to bless God for what we have. To him who has been thankful shall be given, and he shall have more abundantly. Bless him, and tell him you will bless him even though he should never do any more for you than what he has done. Seeing he has convinced you of the sinfulness of sin and of the excellence of a state of grace; and has given you desires to grow; and has made with you an everlasting covenant, well ordered in all things and sure, you will bless him for that as for your salvation – though your house is not with

[220]

God as you could wish it, and though he is not making it grow.

Yet humbly tell him that this is not all you desire, but you have, with your thanksgiving, a request to make: that he would place you among the children, that you may cry, Abba Father. For the taste you have had of his grace has set your soul to longing, as it did the spouse (*Song of Sol.* 3:1–2) after the good fruit and growth of the land. Tell him that you hope, seeing he found you when you were not seeking him, that he will make himself known to you as a Father, now you enquire after him. Tell him that is a desire of his own begetting, and beg him that it may not be disappointed or denied by him, a God who hears prayers and encourages all flesh to come unto him.

Say, O Lord, thou not only bringest to the birth, but bringest forth and then bringest up. Wilt not thou, who art the same today as yesterday, be merciful as to them that love thy name, which, my dear Lord, thou knowest I do? Urge yet again for the light of his countenance and his loving kindness, which is to you better than life.

If he still does not answer, go on and confess that you are unworthy of so great a favour as when the father kissed the prodigal, yet you pray him to remember that all others were unworthy, too; and if he pleases to do for you as he has for some others, that you will give him, as they do, the glory of his grace, and say, ' 'Tis not my merit, no desert of mine, 'Tis only thy pure love hath made me thine.'

It is a favour too great for you to beg, but not too great for him to give, who is the God of all grace and has promised that if we confess our sin, he is just and faithful to forgive us. They fare best, who confess their unworthiness and ill-deserving, as the prodigal and others did.

But if he yet does not smile upon you, tell him what a

great grief of heart it is for you to see how poor and low you live, how unserviceable you are to his glory, and that you would gladly do him better service. You have heard of the affable and dutiful dispositions and fruitfulness of the little children, and you long to be one of them, even though you may not experience their joys and raptures. Tell him that you come not merely to have more pleasure for yourself, but to please him more, that you may walk worthy of him.

Tell him that the Lord Jesus said he had more of the Father's heart-love to display, which would be done by the Spirit. He would enable them to bear these things who before could not do it; and if he pleases, he can advance you to this honour also. Oh Lord, strengthen me and perfect that which concerns thy servant!

If yet he does not make himself known, tell him further that Jesus Christ promised that whatever of this nature and concern we ask in his name, it should be done, and pray him to remember his own Son and promise. Surely he will be as good as his word, who is faithful and cannot deny himself! Is there not much more put on the heavenly Father, as to giving good things, even his Holy Spirit, to them that ask it?

Add that you are lovesick, so sick that if he does not shine on you it will cost you your life, and he will see you die in a love fit! 'He whom you love is sick' and 'He who loves you is sick' are the two engaging arguments; and though you cannot say the former, you can say the latter. So pray to him, who is love, to have compassion on you in your sickness, seeing love has made you so. The spouse had no sooner pleaded this than she was embraced in the arms of love, his left hand was under her head, and his right hand over her heart (*Song of Sol.* 2:5–6). Oh dear Lord, let it be so with me!

If he still seems not to regard you, tell him then that if

he persists in denying you, it may prove a great temptation and snare to you to turn aside. Ah Lord, Satan and
flesh and blood have often hinted: Why do you wait on
one who does not care for you, and does not provide you
bread or give you a good word or look? O Lord, it goes to
my heart like a sword that they say, Where is your God?
Oh! Lead me not into temptation, but give me one kiss at
least, that I may tell Satan from experience how good it is
to draw near to God and that I do not seek his face in
vain.

Go on and tell him that you are resolved never to give
him over, but to cleave to him with full purpose of
heart. Tell him that you will be an importunate suitor,
that you will give him no rest but will continually pursue
him and beg others to pursue on your behalf, till he
establishes you a praise in the earth by saying, Is he not
my dear son, a pleasant child? I will surely have mercy
upon him.

Tell him that though he may lame you as he did Jacob,
you will not let him go till he blesses you and gives you a
new name. He may call you dog and beat you with
frowns, yet for all that you will love him and lie at his
feet.

If he begins to speak against you, as he did to Ephraim
and the woman of Canaan, take hold of what he says and
plead, for it will be to your advantage at last, as it was to
theirs. If he tells you that you are not yet able, answer
him humbly that no one ever was till he was pleased to
make them so, and that you come to pray that he will
make you fit. If he tells you that you will abuse it by being
puffed up, tell him that he can prevent it by his grace. It
is true, your heart, alas! is deceitful, but you do not
intend any such thing. But you hope that if he will give
you this pearl, it shall not be cast before a swine who will
trample upon it. You also pray that you may never

receive this grace and favour in vain, or sin because his grace abounds.

If he tells you the time is not yet come, reply to him that you will wait his pleasure and not awake him till he pleases, but wait all your days, if at last this happy change may come!

Conclude by telling him that if you have been bold, it is in the name of the great high priest who sits at his own right hand and is touched with the feeling of your infirmities, by whom you have been emboldened to come with your petitions and present them to the throne of grace, that you might obtain the mercy and grace for your relief. And therefore, though you cannot call him your Father, you can call upon him as the Father of Jesus Christ, who hears him always.

Speak to him and call him Father, though you cannot do so confidently. Say, Oh my dear Lord, though I am as carnal, thine apostle calls me not carnal, but a babe in Christ. And I am told by them who think better of me than I dare think of myself, that they see thine image in my eye. That makes me the more inclined to say, Father, look upon me and see if there is not something of the spirit of a son in me. Oh, send thy good Spirit, the Comforter, to witness with this spirit that I am thy child. Dear God and Father, do this for your poor babe!

Thus plead with God, and who knows but he may be gracious to you? Delight yourself in him and he will give you your heart's desire. Commit yourself and way to him, and he will bring it to pass; he shall bring forth your righteousness as the light, and your judgement as the noon day, unto victory. He will not quench the smoking flax, nor break the bruised reed. But as he has done for those who have thus pleaded with and submitted to him, so I believe he will do for you. He will revive the heart of the humble, and they shall live. You may soon hear the joyful sound of 'Son, be of good cheer, thy sins are forgiven thee; thou art a pleasant child, be it unto thee as thou wilt.' You shall no longer sit trembling at the door of hope, but have an abundant entrance into the family and be placed among the children, to eat their bread and drink their wine, and to enjoy the fruit of righteousness, which is peace and assurance forever.

(ii) An exhortation to the little children

To those who know the Father, who by the witness of the Spirit are assured that they are the children of God:

a) Do not be proud and puffed up through this abundance of revelation. You must expect to be set upon by Satan, as Christ was when he had received the witness of the Spirit that he was the Son of God (*Matt.* 3:16–17; 4:1). When Paul was advanced to paradise, and inclined to be puffed up, a messenger of Satan was sent to buffet him (*2 Cor.* 12:7). Buffeting is common to this state, but especially if there is puffing up, therefore beware. High fortunes, as the world speaks, are the way to high minds; but high minds and mountainous spirits are more liable to tempests and storms from Satan's wind and weather than the humble valleys. Those who are lifted up are most likely to be brought down.

Indeed, God is very gracious in giving the witness of his Spirit and manifesting himself as a Father before the tempter comes, so that when we must enter the field and fight with him (in this case, about our sonship), we may be better armed and able to defend ourselves. Yet the devil takes this opportunity to tempt us, and our hearts too often give it to him. Beware and take heed not to become lifted up by this advancement.

b) Now you know the Father and his everlasting love towards you, take heed you do not neglect the Son of his love and the righteousness which is by him. God expects that you honour the Son as you do the Father (*John* 5:23), for you are not justified by the Father's grace and love, but in conjunction with and through the redemption that is by Jesus Christ (*Rom.* 3:24). The Father indeed chose you, and he blesses you with all spiritual blessings, but it is in Christ Jesus he does this (*Eph.* 1:2–5). And the everlasting consolation is not from the Father only, but from the Son also, who has loved you (*2 Thess.* 2:16). Be sure, then, that you are not so focused on the love of the Father as to look away from the Son, who is jointly engaged with the Father. When the butler was advanced, he forgot Joseph; and some are apt to do the same by Jesus Christ, though it was by him they came to all their honour.

c) *Do not grieve the Holy Spirit of God,* whereby you are sealed to the day of redemption (*Eph.* 4:30). If you are not kind to one another, tender-hearted, forgiving one another, you not only forget God and Christ, for whose sake God forgave you, but you grieve the Spirit, who brought you this good news. This too, if you do not edify one another, and minister grace to them that hear you.

If God should, as it were, call back the witness of his Spirit and leave you to walk in darkness, what a woeful state would you be in! It would, in some respects, be far worse with you than it was before, when you were but a babe. Oh, then, do not grieve the Spirit, or cause God to put you under a state of desertion.

d) *Honour your Father.* It is the sin of some that they do not glorify God as God, but it may be your sin not to glorify God as your Father (*Mal.* 1:6). A son honours his father not only as a man or a man above him, but as his father. The father has compassion on the son that serves him, and the son should honour and serve the father that has compassion on him. Be, as Christ Jesus was, always about your Father's business, and bring forth much fruit by which his and our Father may be glorified. Live up to the manner of living of the children: Be loving, be humble, be tender-hearted, be teachable, and imitate your Father, to be perfect as your heavenly Father is perfect. The more you abound in these things, the more communion and joy will be yours; you will know the dignity and enjoyment of assurance, and what it is to call upon and live with God as a Father.

e) And lastly, let the Word of God dwell richly in you in all wisdom, that if the Lord calls you, as he does some of your class, to be young men and fight his battles, you may be strong and overcome the wicked one by the word of God abiding in you. Perhaps such little ones as you are reluctant to leave your rooms and go into the field, and I cannot altogether blame you. Yet, if God calls you to undergo trials and be tempted, remember that love's commands are not grievous. You need to hide the Word in your heart and to spend some time, as our Saviour did, in fasting and prayer, in case you must enter into the battle. And do not entangle yourselves with the affairs of this life, that you may please him, who shall choose you to be soldiers and endure hardship as the good soldiers of Jesus Christ (*2 Tim.* 2:3–4).

PART FOUR

Young Men

From *1 John 2:13–14*

I write unto you, young men, because ye have overcome the wicked one.

I have written unto you, young men, because ye are strong, and the word of God abideth in you, and ye have overcome the wicked one.

In these two verses, the young men are mentioned twice, and we may observe: that the young-men saints are strong; that the Word of God abides in them; that they overcome the wicked one; that they overcome the wicked one by strength; and that a great part of their strength is from the Word of God abiding in them.

Among very good authors and historians, the word *neanischoi* is used in a military sense, to signify soldiers, and it is also used in that sense in the Scriptures. Indeed, it is used not only for a common soldier but for the choicest soldiers. When the two armies of Ishbosheth and David, under their two generals, Abner and Joab, met together by the pool of Gibeon, Abner said to Joab, 'Let the young men now arise and play before us,' as if war were but a sport and pastime; and the field where they fought and fell was called Helkath Hazzurim, the field of strong men (*2 Sam.* 2:12–16). Accordingly, in a moral sense, the young men in our text are said to be strong men in that they had fought with and overcome the evil one.

These young-men-saints, then, are the soldiers, the worthies of Israel. It is as much as if St John had said, 'I write to you, the soldiers, warriors, and champions.'

Indeed, the babes may pass for common soldiers; but these are the choice young men, the good soldiers of Christ Jesus, as Paul would have Timothy be, in being strong in the grace which is in Christ Jesus (*2 Tim.* 2:1–5). They are the valiant ones of Israel.

As the babe-saint is taken out from sinners and becomes a middle state between the carnal and spiritual, of the first degree; and as little children are taken from among babes and are a middle state between babes and young men; so young men are taken from little children, and are a middle state between them and the fathers. These young men, having known the Father and received the witness of his Spirit that they are the children of God, are new prepared for the battle with Satan the tempter. Our Saviour, too, when he had received the witness of the Spirit from heaven, was led into the wilderness to be tempted of the devil. God does not take his young men from among babes immediately, but from little children, who are made strong by the word and witness of God abiding in them. And the glory of these young men is their strength.

THE YOUNG MEN'S STRENGTH

(i) *What is meant by their being strong*

The text tells us that these young men are strong. It denotes the strength preceding the victory and by which they overcome; not that which follows and abides after conquest and victory. Ye are strong, *i.e.*, ye are mighty, and were so before the dispute and fight, as well as after, or else you would not have overcome. The strength of the young men marks them as men of might and valour, men fit to undergo labour and to endure hardship, as the good soldiers of Jesus Christ.

You shall find that in the Scripture, the most difficult

undertakings have been assigned to and performed by young men, because they are strong and fit for such service. The glory of young men is their strength (*Prov.* 20:29). It is said that Jeroboam was a mighty man of valour; and Solomon seeing that the young man was industrious (Hebrew: that he did work), he made him ruler over all the charge (Hebrew: burden) of the house of Joseph (*1 Kings* 11:28). He is described by might, valour, work and burden-bearing. In 2 Timothy 2:1–5, strength, enduring hardship, and being a good soldier are all joined together. Joshua sent young men to spy out the land (*Josh.* 6:23). The porters (*1 Chron.* 26:6–8) are said to be mighty men of valour, strong and able for the service.

As it is naturally, it is also morally the glory of young men that they are strong.

(ii) Where their strength lies

It is said that Samson's strength was in his hair, and the behemoth's in his loins, his force in the muscles of his belly (*Job* 40:16). But where does the strength of these young men lie? It is originally in the Lord and the power of his might (*Eph.* 6:10), or the grace which is in Christ Jesus (*2 Tim.* 2:1). It is not the grace that is in us, but that which is in him, that is sufficient for us (*2 Cor.* 12:8–9), and it is of his fullness that we receive grace for grace, as we have occasion to use it (*John* 1:16, *Heb.* 4:16). God has laid our help on him who is mighty to save, and who goes forth conquering and to conquer, till all his enemies be made his footstool and subdued under his feet.

But beyond all the grace communicated to them, their strength is in faith, for this is the victory whereby we overcome the world, even our faith (*1 John* 5:4–5). And as we overcome the world, so we also overcome him who is in the world, that is, the devil. And therefore, though

[233]

every piece of God's armour is of great use, we are advised above all to take the shield of faith, by which we quench the fiery darts of the devil (*Eph.* 6:11–16).

Abraham was strong in faith; in the strength of faith David encountered Goliath (a type of the devil); and it was by faith that the heroes worked such wonders and obtained victories (*Heb.* 11:32–34).

So these young men are strong in the Lord, strong in the faith that is in them. They go out in his name and prevail. It is not in their own but his strength (*Phil.* 4:13), for it is not they of themselves that conquer, but he that lives in them by faith and makes them conquerors (*Rom.* 8:37). These young men are Christ's armour bearers, and they slay after him, as it is said of Jonathan's (*I Sam.* 14:13). It is Jesus Christ who teaches their hands to war, so that the devil's bow of steel is broken by them, and they bring down the devil under their feet. Through the strength of Christ living in them by faith (*Eph.* 3:16–17), they are almost omnipotent, for they are able to do all things: not only to abound, but to be abased and to endure hardship (*Phil.* 4:11–13). By the power of his might all things are possible to them.

Abraham conquered doubts, fears, and naturally impossible things by strength of faith. He could live by faith when his own body and Sarah's womb were dead. The things which bound up his hope were no more obstacles to him than the strongest were to Samson before his hair was shaved and his strength departed. By his strength Jacob prevailed with God and had his new name given, Israel, a prevailer with God.

It is by this strength that the young men overcome the evil one and every one of his evils – for so his temptations are called, and the day of temptation is called 'the evil day' (*Eph.* 6:13). Be strong in the grace which is in Christ Jesus, says the apostle (*2 Tim.* 2:1). Now that may well refer to faith which is in Christ Jesus, for though it is *from* him, this is *in* him; we believe in him. And accordingly, the same apostle charges the same Timothy fight the good fight of faith (*1 Tim.* 6:12).

Faith is the armour which is proof against the devil's darts, and if we will resist the devil so that he flees from us, it must be by being steadfast in the faith (*1 Pet.* 5:8-9). Though the devil roars dreadfully like a lion, a strong and steadfast faith will make this king of terrors run away. And therefore the apostle says, Watch ye, stand fast in the faith, quit you like men, be strong (*1 Cor.* 16:13). These are all military terms and appropriate for these young men. Be courageous like men, like young men-soldiers, like men of war; and that you may do so, stand fast and be strong in faith. Look to Jesus, the captain of our faith. He has conquered the devil; be his armour bearers and slay after him, by faith following him, your captain and rear guard. And as he overcame the evil one, so shall you, if you are truly young men.

(iii) How they come by this strength

The Word of God abides in these young men. This may be understood to mean that their hot and sharp fight with the devil did not weaken them. But I believe it more properly shows us the means by which they were strengthened to overcome: For if the Word of God had not been abiding with them, they would not have been strong enough to overcome the evil one. The weapon by which the young men overcome him is the sword of the Spirit, the Word of God. As their enemies are not carnal only but spiritual (*Eph.* 6:12), so their weapons are not all carnal but spiritual, and so mighty through God (*2 Cor.* 10:4-5).

But first, what is meant by the Word of God? In general, by the Word of God we are to understand the mind and will of God revealed and made known in the holy Scriptures, which are so often called the Word of God, as held forth in its doctrines, prophecies, promises and precepts; but especially as it is written and imprinted in their hearts according to the new covenant. This Word of God in whole and in every part is very useful for enlightening, comforting and strengthening, that we may overcome the wicked one. It is to make the man of God perfect (*2 Tim.* 3:16–17). It is the sword of the Spirit, and by it Christ himself overcame the wicked one.

Yet more particularly, this may refer to Christ himself, who is the original Word of God the Father, by whom he made the world and has spoken to the world not by diverse fashions, as of old, but clearly, plainly and fully (*Heb.* 1:1–2). Now by Christ Jesus abiding and dwelling in us are we strong (*Phil.* 4:13), or by the grace that is in him, of which he is full, and without whom we can do nothing (*John* 15:5).

The Word of God may refer to the promises of God which are so often called 'the word', 'thy word', 'the word of promise', which is all one with the Word of God. It was this that Abraham's faith referred to and wherein he was so strong (*Rom.* 4:20). Truly the word of promise abiding in us contributes more than a little to our strength and victory. By these we are not only made partakers of a divine nature (*2 Pet.* 1:4), but we are obliged, assisted, and quickened to perfect holiness (*2 Cor.* 7:1) despite temptations from without or within.

The Word of God may here be understood as the witness of the Spirit bearing witness with their spirits that they are the children of God. This testimony abiding in them, as it did in Christ, strengthens them to overcome the evil one. When they were little children they received this testimony, and being now called to the war, this word as well as work of God abides in them and makes them strong for the battle. So that here is Father, Son, and Spirit, the Word of God in each respect, standing by them and abiding in them to strengthen them, to deliver them out of the mouth of the lion, to keep them from every evil work, and to preserve them to the heavenly kingdom (*2 Tim.* 4:17–18).

Next, what is meant by God's Word 'abiding' in them? It denotes not only that the word is there in their heart and inner man; not only that it is called into mind and kept in their memory; not only that it lodges with them as a guest or friend that is to depart. Instead, the phrase denotes a settled abode or dwelling in efficacious power and influence. It is said of Timothy's mother and grand-mother that faith dwelt in them (*2 Tim.* 1:5). The apostle prays both that the Ephesians may be strengthened and that Christ may dwell in their hearts by faith (*Eph.* 3:16–17). And it is said of the happy ones who are reproached for the name of Christ, that the Spirit of God and of glory rests upon them (*1 Pet.* 4:14). Our Saviour tells his disciples that there is no great thing to be done merely by being in him, but they must abide in him and he in them (*John* 15). The great promise of the Holy Ghost was that he should abide with them. So the sense of this expression can signify no less than that the Word of God remains in them in the fullness of assurance, joy, and power, by which they are strengthened and enabled to overcome the wicked one.

THE WICKED ONE; TEMPTATIONS

(i) *Who or what is meant by the wicked one*
If read in the neuter gender (*to poneron*), this expression is meant of more evils than one, indeed, of all evil. It may be understood that way in the prayer which our Lord

taught (*Matt.* 6:13), and in the prayer which he prayed (*John* 17:15); also in Romans 12:9 and 1 John 5:19.

But here it seems to be of the masculine gender (*ho poneros*), and refers to one, him who is eminently and principally the evil one, or the wicked one, whether spoken of a man or of the devil. It is used to set out a notoriously wicked man that has no equal in wickedness, a devil incarnate, an Antichrist. But it most usually refers to the devil himself, who is *ho poneros*, the wicked one, so eminently as no other is (compare *Matt.* 13:19, *Luke* 8:12, *Eph.* 6:16, *1 John* 3:12).

Now this is the evil, or wicked one, not excluding others, that these young men have overcome by being strong, and by the Word of God abiding in them. The devil being the captain-general, the master of misrule and mischief, the rest fall with him. In telling us that they have overcome the wicked one, it is implied that there was first a fight, a hot and sharp encounter between the devil and the young men. The devil set upon them and tempted them sorely, and they had a lot to do to win the field and day of him. And surely it was not common temptations, but some exceptional ones, that these young men were under. The babes meet with common ones, but these with special ones (*1 Cor.* 10:13). As Christ Jesus would not teach the babes doctrine which they could not bear, so he would not lead them into temptations which they could not overcome. But these young men, his champions and worthies, encounter giants, as David's did. They war not against flesh and blood, weak enemies, but against principalities and powers (*Eph.* 6).

(ii) What the dispute is about; what the temptations are
It must be remembered that these young men are taken out from among the little children, who have received the

witness of the Spirit, that they are the children of God. And about this very issue is the dispute between the devil and them: whether they indeed are the children of God or not. That is the way some understand that passage, which speaks in military language, as if it properly referred to the state and condition of these young men (*Eph.* 6:12), reading the phrase we render 'in high or heavenly places' as 'about heavenly things', that is, our title to sonship and heaven. This is what the Spirit witnessed to their spirits, and it is this the devil calls into question and offers arguments against. But all these arguments the young men overcome by the Word of God abiding in them, which strengthens their faith to give glory to God and his Spirit as the faithful and true witness, despite all the cunning insinuations and wiles of the devil.

To make this a little clearer, I humbly offer this for consideration: The saints, members of Christ's body, are all more or less conformed to his image and to the several states in which he was. Now such was the condescension of our great Lord Jesus that he not only took on flesh and blood, human nature, but he was found in our fashion and tempted like us in all things, yet still without sin. He went through all our states. He was once as a babe, made under the Law, and was in the likeness of sinful flesh, and so judged as carnal. He was under tutors and governors and was obedient to them (*Luke* 2:46–51). He increased in wisdom as in age, which argues, without any disparagement, that his attainments, as in the flesh, were gradual. After a while, being baptized and praying, he had the witness from heaven that he was the Son of God (*Luke* 3:21–22). And then was Jesus led up by the Spirit into the wilderness to be tempted of the devil (*Matt.* 4:1), and so passed from a child's to a young man's state.

So then, in accordance with this, I believe that the

temptations which the young men undergo are the same, and about the same issue, which Jesus Christ underwent when after the witness of the Spirit he was tempted by the devil. The Spirit first witnessed; then the devil called this into question and challenged Christ to prove it. Christ answered and conquered by the Word of God abiding in him. And it was just so with these young men; the phrases and things agree so well that it seems to me beyond question.

The saints, in conformity to Christ Jesus, are but babes at first, under the Law, in the likeness of sinners, as carnal, and are in subjection to tutors and governors. After this God is pleased to make himself known to some of them as a Father by the witness of his Spirit, and so they arrive to the state of children. God then singles out some of these to be tempted of the devil about their sonship, and they become young men and brave soldiers who are taught to draw and wield the sword of the Spirit, the Word of God, against the devil, as Christ also did.

God was pleased to make this law for Israel: When a man has taken a new wife he should not go out to war, nor should he be charged with any business, but he should be free at home one year and cheer himself with his wife (*Deut.* 24:5). So, by way of allusion I may say that when the saints marry a new wife, the Father's love, they are often privileged for some time to lie in his bosom and to cheer themselves with his love.

But then some of them are called out to war (*John* 21:18–22), and though they endure a time of hardship they become conquerors, which is a greater glory than not to fight at all, as it is in some sense to conquer death than to be immortal. In the sense and strength of his love, they go forth conquering and to conquer, and so live in the triumph of their assurance, as our Saviour did. They become his squires or armour bearers, fighting under his banner of love against the evil one, if he returns again to make new assaults upon them. He did so upon Christ himself; he departed only for a time. But then the after-temptations are of another nature, that is, persecutions and sufferings, as our Saviour's were. On the whole, I conclude that the temptations of the wicked one which the young men have overcome are such as Christ's were when tempted of the devil after the witness of the Spirit.

(iii) The temptations of Christ and the young men
The young men having been proclaimed, as Christ was, that they are the sons of God and heirs of God and glory, the devil puts in his objections against this title. He would have them believe that this is but enthusiasm, the work of their own imagination, without any true grounds. He comes, then, and calls it into question, first labouring to make them doubt; and if he cannot attain that, then endeavouring to bring them to presume upon it and take advantage.

His first design is to make it doubtful: 'If thou be the Son of God, command that these stones be made bread'(*Matt.* 4:3). This was after our Lord had fasted forty days and forty nights and was hungry. What the devil slyly insinuates is this: You think yourself the Son of God, and suppose yourself to have witness from heaven. But if God were your Father and loved you, would he let you be so poor and hungry? And could he find it in his heart to put on you so much hardship as fasting? and so long, too! Would he leave you in the wilderness among the beasts? Fathers provide for their children, and if you were his son, surely he would maintain you at a better rate than this. Look at your condition: Can you believe yourself to be the Son of God?

The devil pleads with and against the children of God

in the same way when they are not well off in this world. It has pleased God to choose many of the poor of this world to be rich in faith and heirs of the kingdom (*James* 2:5). Many of these who have this assurance are hard put to it in the world, and by Satan too, because of their poverty, as if it were inconsistent with the riches of faith and the title of heir to a kingdom.

But as Christ answered and conquered, so do they by the Word of God abiding in them. One answer serves them both: Man does not live by bread; a man's life does not consist in the abundance of things enjoyed, but by every word that comes out of the mouth of God, anything that God shall appoint. His Word can do without anything else. These things here below are not good enough to be love tokens. As hatred, so love is not known by external low or high conditions. Some may have bread and no love; and others have love, though they have no bread. God can and will provide in due time. And what is it to you, O devil, if I am contented with the will of God and have meat to eat which you know nothing of? Thus being strong in faith by the Word of God abiding in them, they overcome the wicked one and will not question their sonship because they are poor and low in this world.

The devil's first argument being invalidated, he takes a far different one. He would now have Christ be as confident and presuming, as before he would have had him wavering and doubtful. He deals in the same way with the young men. He says, 'If thou be the Son of God, cast thyself down from the pinnacle, for it is written, He shall give his angels charge concerning thee, and in their hands they shall bear thee up, lest at any time thou dash thy foot against a stone' (*Matt.* 4:6). It is undoubtedly true that this promise belonged to Christ in a special manner; and the devil, perceiving how precious the written Word of God was to Christ Jesus, fills his mouth with Scripture and a promise. But he leaves out the condition to which the protection is attached. And he cunningly insinuates is: If you are the Son, will you not trust your Father's promise and power? Can you have a better security than the power of a faithful God, and the faith of a powerful God? Has he not appointed you a life-guard of angels to bear you in their arms? Are you afraid?

He often sets on the young men in this way. Why need you be so troubled and concerned about means? Do you not have promises of teaching, protection, preservation, and other things? What, will you not trust your Father and take his word?

But again, one answer fits both: Thou shalt not tempt the Lord thy God. Indeed, to trust in means is to despise God, but to neglect means is to tempt God. There is no need to cast myself down, to make such daring attempts, for there is a way down, and the longest way about is the nearest way home. Thou shalt not tempt the Lord thy God. That means you shall not go out of his way, which is your way, and only in that way is preservation promised. While there is an ordinary appointed way and means, I must not attempt nor presume on extra-ordinary ones. That would be to seek after signs and miracles when there is no need of them, which is no less than to tempt God. You, O devil, are tempting me to tempt God, which is not for his sons to do, though you would have me do it as his son. No, though you tempt me, I will not tempt the Lord my God by going out of my way and neglecting the means he has appointed.

Having been defeated in dispute, the devil takes another course and falls to offering terms and making bargains. 'All these things' (the kingdoms of the world and the glory of them), he says, 'will I give thee, if thou wilt fall down and worship me' (*Matt.* 4:9). Here are fine

[243]

and brave things, grandeur and gallantry, pleasure, prettiness and pomp. Here are the lusts of the eye, the flesh, and the pride of life, the things which the young men in the world are enamoured of. These are the things which the Alexanders and Julius Caesars of this world, the Nimrods and hunters after glory, pursue with might and main and ambition.

Do but fall down and bow the knee to worship me, and all shall be thine. This seems to be the devil's last hope. If he cannot prevail this way, he despairs. He has choked many a forward and far-gone professor with this bait, as he did our first parents even in innocence. St John immediately after his having spoken to the young men, adds: Love not the world nor the things thereof (*1 John* 2:14–15).

But let us hear the answer from the Word of God, written not only in the Bible but in their hearts: Then Jesus (and the young-man-saint) said to him, 'Get thee hence, Satan, for it is written, Thou shalt worship the Lord thy God, and him only shalt thou serve.' No man can serve two masters, God and mammon, God and the devil. God is too good a master to be left, and the devil too bad a one to be served. Go away, wretched and wicked one! Do you think I will leave heaven for hell, God for the devil, the kingdom and glory of God, for the kingdoms and glory of this world, which are all just vanity and vexation of spirit? Are God and heaven, and my soul worth no more than this? Do you think I will sell my soul for a paltry vanity, and love what will make me the enemy of my God, and make a god of my enemy? No, Satan, get hence.

After this the devil leaves him and runs away. He cannot stand before the Word of God. If he is resisted by being steadfast in the faith, he will flee. And if he flees he is, for the present, conquered. And he is put to flight and conquered by the 'It is written', the Word of God abiding in power and efficacy in the young men, as he was by our Saviour.

(iv) One temptation more

There is one argument which the devil could not make use of against Christ, who was without sin, but often makes use of against the little children and young men to make them call their sonship into question. It is that they are not without sin, but offend in many things, either by doing evil, or by omitting good, or by falling short of their duty and in giving God the glory due his name.

Says the devil, You cannot be a child of God or know him as a Father, for such do not and cannot commit sin. Just read 1 John 3:4–10, and tell me what you can say to these things. And if you say you do not sin, I will prove you do; if you say you have no sin, you lie and sin in saying so. And if you do sin, how can you say that you are born of God, when the Scripture says that he who is born of God does not commit sin? This is a two-edged sword, an argument that cuts on both sides. It seems to put these poor souls in a dilemma.

But yet by the word of God abiding in them, they defeat this also.

They follow the example of Christ Jesus and oppose truly quoted and rightly understood Scripture, to the Scripture which is falsely quoted and misapplied. The devil wrests and wrongs the Scripture and knows it, though it is to his own confutation and confusion. Again, they say, as our Saviour did, 'It is written.' The devil knows that the seeming contradictory Scriptures may be reconciled, but he cannot endure that they should be reconciled. He would rather answer nothing, as when Christ opposed his half quotation by a whole one.

[245]

Thus then may the young man answer: Satan, you know that Abraham, Moses, David, and others were born of God and had the witness of his Spirit that they were his children, and yet they were not without sin, but sinned after their new birth. And you know that if we (those who have fellowship with God) say that we have not sinned since conversion, we make him a liar and his word is not in us (*1 John* 1:10). This the devil either cannot or will not reconcile, though he knows it is compatible with the above texts and they are misapplied.

The young men say: The texts which you have quoted do not seem to speak of any sin in any degree, but of a special sin, hating or not loving the brethren, which they that are born of God cannot be guilty of (*1 John* 4:20). But you know, Satan, to your vexation, that I love the brethren and am passed from death to life. Or else it may refer to the sin unto death (*1 John* 5:16–18).

And if the text may not be restrained to that, I can say further, that I do not live in sin or make a trade of sin as you do. I am no sin maker as you are, and I do not sin as those who belong to you. You work in the children of disobedience that they may fulfil the lusts and wills of the flesh (*Eph.* 2:1–3). You cannot deny this, for the quoted texts speak of them.

I can say even more in a true sense, as the apostle does (*Rom.* 7:15–20), that it is not I, who am born of God, but sin that dwells in me. Though I with my flesh may - alas, I do! - serve the law of sin, still, thanks be to God through Jesus Christ our Lord, with the mind I myself serve the law of God (*Rom.* 7:25). There is therefore no condemnation to me, since I am in Christ Jesus and walk not after the flesh, but after the Spirit (*Rom.* 8:1). Though I, wretch that I am, may be sin's captive, I am not its subject that I must obey it. Sin may domineer, but it has no dominion over me, because I am not under the

Law, but under grace (*Rom.* 6:1–18). You know, Satan, that I am not one of sin's servants.

I confess my sin and have my pardon, and what do you, Satan, say to this? or what can you say against it, that God should forgive my sin? According to 1 John 1:8–9, I have reason to be of good cheer, though because of you, my warfare is not finished. But God has spoken to my heart and said, 'Son, be of good cheer, thy sins are forgiven thee.' It is not against you that I have sinned, but against God, which goes most to my heart, and if God pardon me, what is that to you? Are you jealous because God is good and gracious? May he not do, without your leave, what he will with his own?

Satan, to stop your mouth, I have an advocate with the Father (both his and mine), Jesus Christ the righteous, who is the propitiation for my sin (*1 John* 2:1–2). You have nothing to lay to the charge of God's elect, for he justifies (*Rom.* 8:33). Can you condemn, seeing Christ has died and is risen again? He died for our sin, and is risen for our justification (*Rom.* 4:25). And he is at the right hand of God, and appears in heaven for us, and lives forever to make intercession for those who come to God by him, and so saves perfectly and to the utmost. What do you have to say to this? Go away, Satan, for I have heard a voice saying from heaven, Now is salvation, and strength, and the kingdom of our God, and the power of his Christ, for the accuser of the brethren is cast out, which accused them before our God day and night; but they overcame him by the blood of the Lamb, and by the word of their testimony, and loved not their lives unto the death (*Rev.* 12:10–11).

LEARNING IN CHRIST'S SCHOOL

THE YOUNG MEN'S VICTORY

(i) What is meant by their overcoming the wicked one
To 'overcome' is a law term, and a term of war. In a legal
sense, it is to overcome by right and justification, to be
cleared and justified of any charge and indictment laid
against them. To be justified is to overcome (*Rom.* 3:4).
Now in this sense not only the young men but all the
saints are conquerors and do overcome. That is, there is
no condemnation but justification for them (*Rom.* 8:1,
33–34, 38–39). Though condemned by men they are
justified by God, as Christ was put to death in the flesh
but justified in and by the Spirit. Though the devil
accuses, Christ as their advocate pleads to their justification. And they are freed in God's court, so that nothing
separates them from the love of God in Christ. 1
Corinthians 15:57 and 1 John 5:18 also speak to this sense.
To overcome in a military sense is to conquer by
might, by dint of sword, which in an academic sense is to
overcome by force of argument. And it is in this sense
that we are most specially to understand the conquest
and overcoming of the young men in our text. They have
overcome by mere strength of the Word and faith, so
that they not only overcome the evil one by being
justified from his indictment, but overcome his temptations by dint of sword, *i.e.*, by strength of argument from
the Word abiding in them. If the devil pleads sin and
guilt, they plead Christ and his satisfaction; if the devil
witnesses against them that they are not the children of
God, they produce the witness of the Spirit that they are,
and so overcome him. So the young man is a double
conqueror, by right and might; by work and sword; at
the bar and in the field. They overcome by strength of
faith or believing in Christ, or rather by the strength of
Christ believed in.

How and how far have they overcome? The devil is not slain; he is still active and has the power of temptation. How then is it said that they have overcome the wicked one? May not the devil rally and recruit again? May he make more assaults on the young men?

To this some answer that the past tense is used for the future, meaning that you shall as certainly overcome as if you had overcome. While the word of God abides in you, you shall never be overcome, and so do overcome, and may be said to have overcome. In the same way, those called of God are said to be saved because they shall be saved (*1 Cor.* 1:18, *2 Tim.* 1:9). So Christ says that he has overcome the world (*John* 16:33), though his conquest was not complete till his resurrection and ascension, nor is fully so till his enemies are made his footstool. He also said, I have finished the work which thou gavest me to do (*John* 17:4), when as yet he had not died, which command he was yet to obey, having received it from the Father. Many other passages use the past tense to denote the certainty of what shall be; it is said to be done because it shall be done.

And so it is said here that the young men have overcome the wicked one. That is, they are to fight, and though the dispute might be so hot and fierce that a stander-by may doubt whether the young men will overcome, still it is so sure that they will do that it is said they have overcome.

But though this is often true and is true here, I do not doubt that it is a reality, and not only a figure of speech, that they have overcome: They are conquerors and have obtained victory already. When the devil is resisted he flees, and so is for the present conquered, as he fled from Christ and was conquered in that battle (*James* 4:7, *1 Pet.* 5:9). He who succeeds in doing what he is exhorted to, attains that for which he was exhorted. So resisting the

[249]

devil as they are exhorted, he does flee and so is conquered for that time. Moreover, they stand their ground, which is a further expression of victory. This resistance and standing is by faith (*1 Pet.* 5:9, *Eph.* 6:16). And thus by resisting, standing firm and maintaining their ground, they have till now overcome the wicked one.

The sum of it amounts to this: I write to you, young men, because ye are strong, and have overcome the wicked one. That is, you have thus far resisted and kept your ground and have not given place to the devil. You have stood it out against all his wiles and subtleties, you have made him flee by the power of the Word of God, which makes you strong in faith, the grace which is in Christ Jesus. And this your strength abides with you, as it did with Caleb (*Josh.* 14:11). So if the devil attacks you any more, you know how to conquer by the same Word again. Go on, thou mighty man, in this thy might, for the Lord of Hosts is with thee. Go on conquering and to conquer; go and prosper. Keep on your armour, do not lay aside your sword or your shield, for perhaps the devil will rally his scattered forces and fall on you again. Or he may be preparing other kinds of temptations for you, sufferings and death, as he did for Christ. But you, as he, shall rise again and live forever and be where Satan has had no place for thousands of years, and never shall, in heaven. And by not loving your lives to the death, you conquer the devil again, as Christ also did (*Rev.* 12:11, *Heb.* 2:14–15).

(ii) How the Word of God strengthens, and how strength leads to victory
We would faint, or falter, if we did not believe (*Psa.* 27:13), and faltering would prove our strength of faith to be very small (*Prov.* 24:10). But our faith would faint were it not upheld and quickened by the Word of God.

It is observable how David, who was one of God's worthies, celebrates the Word of God (*Psa.* 119:9). The young man clears and cleanses his way by taking heed thereto, according to God's Word. And therefore he hides God's Word in his heart, that he might not sin against him (verse 11). He begs for quickening, or renewing, according to his Word (verses 25, 107, 154). And it is comfort in his affliction that God's Word has quickened him (verse 50). When his soul melts for heaviness, he prays to be strengthened according to God's Word (verse 28). His Word is a light unto his path and a lamp to his feet (verse 105). And he has the wherewithal to answer him that reproaches him, the accuser of the brethren, because he trusts in his Word (verses 41–42). God is his hiding place and shield, for he hopes in his Word (verse 114) and prays that his steps may be ordered in his Word, so that no iniquity may have dominion over him (verse 133).

The Word of God is true; indeed, it is truth. And truth is strong, stronger than the devil, who is a liar, and a lie is weak (*1 John* 4:4). This Word of truth exposes the devil's devices, sophistries, methods, and all his deceits. Thus, the Word of God strengthens by taking away hindrances such as doubts, fears, and distrusts, that the soul is no longer under a spirit of bondage again to fear (*Rom.* 8:15, *2 Tim.* 1:7). And it comes in with counsels, comforts and quickenings, as in Psalm 119, all of which are strengthening.

Thus the young men's eyes being opened and enlightened, as Jonathan's were, by tasting this honey, they are strong for the battle. And by faith they see, as the prophet's man did, that there are more for them than against them. Therefore they do not waver out of fear, especially while they look to invisible things (*2 Cor.* 4:16–18) and see a great recompense of reward, and all things co-working for their good and glory. As the sight and speech of a general often encourages and animates his soldiers, so a believing sight of Jesus (*Heb.* 12:2) and his Word puts life and courage into them (*Acts* 27:23, 2 *Tim.* 4:16–17). And Christ conquers the devil by his Word. Our own words and reasonings are weak and will not do it, as in the case of the sons of Sceva (*Acts* 19:13–16), but when the Word of God speaks it is effectual, and the devil cannot stand before it.

As the Word strengthens faith, so strength of faith obtains victory. The reason is that where faith is, God is; and where God is, there is strength against which none can prevail. From this the heroes and martyrs (*Heb.* 11) had all their success and victory. When Gideon had expressed a little faith, not without some doubting, the angel yet said to him, Go in this thy might, the Lord is with thee, thou mighty man of valour (*Judg.* 6:12–14). If God is with us, it does not matter who is against us. That is why some of the saints of God have out-braved men, devils, dangers, and death (see *Psa.* 4:6, *Isa.* 8:9–10, *Mic.* 7:7–9, *1 Cor.* 15:55–57, *2 Cor.* 12:9–10).

So, faith is of great use for conquest, for seeing the victory afar off, as the eagle sees her prey, and is sure of victory even in the midst of the battle (*Rom.* 8:37).

(iii) The greatness of the victory

The enemy that is overcome is formidable. This is no puny pygmy that is conquered, but a huge giant, a man of war from his youth, who has slain many a ten thousand in his time. It is an easy matter to tread a worm underfoot, and man is but flesh and blood, which is weak. But to tread Satan underfoot (the prince of the air and the god of this world, as some understand *2 Cor.* 4:4) is a conquest with a witness – an extraordinary one! To enter a city such as Laish was, without gates and bars, is no great achievement. But to attack the gates of hell and to put the devil to flight from his strongholds, is a miracle of victory! Stronger is he that subdues this spirit as well as his own, than he that takes a fenced city (*Prov.* 16:32).

Alexander's conquests and Julius Caesar's *Veni, vidi, vici* were nothing to this; Job's conquest excels them all. I might have illustrated it by the types of the wars of Israel, and noted especially how Amalek and Goliath were overcome by Joshua, Caleb, and David, the young-men-saints of their generations. But instead, I shall look at that great foe, the devil, and will note five points about him.

a) Let us consider him in his *strength*. He is the strong man and the strong man armed, and he that overcomes him needs to be strong indeed (*Luke* 11:22–23). He is the roaring lion, both strong and fearsome, and cannot be resisted but by being strong in faith (*1 Pet.* 5:8–9).

Besides, he has many legions, and therefore they are expressed in the plural and by words that signify strength: principalities, powers, spiritual wickedness, and rulers of the darkness of this world, against whom we must go armed with the whole armour of God and the power of his might (*Eph.* 6:10–13).

They are spoken of in the abstract, and as invisible and in the dark, which makes them all the more terrible. And yet these principalities and powers are not able to achieve their end; but over them the young men are more than conquerors, or as the word may be read, they *over-overcome* (*Rom.* 8:37–39). And therefore the victory is great and glorious.

b) Let us consider the devil in his *malice, revenge, and envy*. Who can stand before envy? He is the adversary, the envious one (*Matt.* 13:28), and from this envy and enmity accuses the brethren; and to be sure, malice will

[253]

do its worst. He reproaches and throws darts. And contrary to the law of arms, he fights with poisoned arrows, with fiery darts, which are set on fire of hell, poisoned with the venom of envy and malice (*Eph.* 6:16).

His slanderous accusations would burn up the saints, were it not for the shield of faith which quenches them. He challenged God to afflict Job without a cause, he slandered Job. He threw fiery darts to enflame his spirit against God and to cause him to curse God. But they were quenched by faith and overcome by faith and patience. Oh, what a glorious victory it is to conquer envy and malice itself, whetted by revenge and enmity!

c) Let us consider him in his *subtlety*. He is not only malicious, which makes him yet stronger, but he is subtle too, which strengthens his malice. He is the subtle serpent; and if he were so subtle when he was but young as to deceive Eve and Adam in innocence (*Gen.* 3, *2 Cor.* 11:3), what is he now he is grown old? The old serpent, which has deceived the whole world in all ages (*Rev.* 12:9–11). He is improved in subtlety by long practice; he is a chameleon that can turn himself into any colour.

Rather than fail he will – though he cannot endure the light – turn himself into an angel of light, and has got the knack of speaking Scripture. He will talk in Scripture language, filling his mouth with good words and fair speeches to deceive. He goes about to circumvent and get the advantage by the many devices which he has (*2 Cor.* 2:11), which he has studied and practised these many years. He has windings and turnings, methods and wiles; he is an old fox. He has so many arts and tricks (*Eph.* 6:11); he is a master craftsman.

Though an enemy, he pretends friendship and good-will (*2 Cor.* 11:2–3). He will pretend himself much concerned for us, indeed, more than we ourselves are, as if he were troubled with scruples of conscience for our sakes. He will offer queries, and ask us if perhaps we misunderstand God, and so take less liberty and enjoy less good than God allows us. We may enjoy a little more, if we will only take a step in the way that he will show us, that we may be gods; but he means such gods as himself and his fellows, that is, devils.

He has lying wonders in readiness to ape God's true miracles as in Egypt. He can juggle and play sleight-of-hand to purpose (*2 Thess.* 2:9). We read, too, of the depths of Satan (*Rev.* 2:24). Now to conquer such a one as this requires strength (*Eph.* 6:10–11), and the young men are the ones who conquer him. And it is a great victory!

d) Let us consider him in his *constant and unwearied industry.* The Pharisees and Jesuits, though very near of kin to him, and well acquainted with him and following him in crossing sea and land to make proselytes, do yet fall short of him. For he is walking about night and day, seeking whom he may devour (*1 Pet.* 5:8). He takes no rest in the night nor will allow others to rest night or day. Now add this industry to his strength, malice, and art, and it enhances the victory not a little.

e) *Conquests and victories* he has obtained in all ages: Alas, how many have fallen down at his feet! He has deceived and destroyed a world of men (*Rev.* 1:8, *1 John* 5:19, *2 Cor.* 4:4, *John* 14:30, *Eph.* 2:2), yet this devil has been defeated in his own kingdom, even where his throne was, and that by these young men (*Rev.* 2:13). And this victory is the more glorious, considering the advantages the devil has over us as a spirit thus qualified with strength, malice, and art, thus fleshed with success.

(iv) The tokens and signs of this victory
Perhaps some will be apt to say that this is but a romantic

[255]

story, only for talk and discourse. Where are the erected pillars and the trophies of honour that should witness this victory? Where is Goliath's sword and head? Where are the spoils and booty, the signs of their victory?

But we have not brought to you a fiction or cunningly devised fable, but words of truth and power. And as we paralleled above the temptations of Christ and those of the young men, we shall now parallel the signs and tokens of their respective victories.

When our Saviour was tempted and the devil's thrust deflected and his argument defeated, he wholly waived the assumption and shifted his ground, no longer able to stand upon it, which is one sign of his being so far conquered. He attempted the second time another way, but with no better success, and therefore tried to negotiate, which is another sign that his forces failed him. When he could do no good (that is, no evil!) this way either, he not only retreated but ran away ashamed, as one that flees in battle.

So the field was left to Christ Jesus, and the angels came and ministered to him. They did homage to him as to a great conqueror, singing and celebrating his praise, as we have cause to believe. After this our Saviour went in the power of the Spirit into Galilee like a conqueror that had won the day and could go where he would (*Luke* 4:14-15). Though the devil attempted to invalidate the witness of the Spirit, he went in the power of the Spirit and that testimony ever after, it being not at all weakened by the encounter. He went up and down teaching his gospel and giving forth his laws, delivering captives, and healing (*Luke* 4:18; 11:22).

But it seems the devil departed only for a time, for he came again (*John* 14:30), it is true. But observe that he never attempted with the former weapons again, never disputed Christ's Sonship again, but fell to downright persecution without finding anything in Christ to accuse or any reason to condemn him – as the devil's own judge, even Pilate himself, declared in open court.

But here also, Christ was too much for him, for though the devil bruised his heel, Christ broke the devil's head, according to the first promise (*Gen.* 3:15). By dying he destroyed him that had the power of death, the devil (*Heb.* 2:14); and accordingly he keeps the keys to this day (*Rev.* 1:18). So the devil, ever since he was a devil, was never so much defeated as now. For when Christ was crucified he spoiled principalities and powers, triumphing over them (*Col.* 2:14–15).

So now the saints need not fear either law, death or devil (*Heb.* 2:14–15, *I Cor.* 15:55–57). Yet further, our Saviour not only rose from the dead and so was declared to be the Son of God, despite the devil's guarding the sepulchre; but he ascended on high and rode in triumph through the devil's principality, the air, of which he is prince. And as the devil could not hinder him from ascending to the Father, so he cannot prevent his gifts descending on men, another token of Christ's victory and triumph. And then it was that he led captivity captive (*Eph.* 4:8–9).

There are similar tokens of the victory of our young men, the armour bearers of Christ, who slay after him. They stand firm and fixed, losing no ground or strength, For ye are strong, says the text, and the Word of God abideth in you after this war. And in the power of the Spirit and his word of witness, they, as our Saviour did, go about their work which the Father has given them to do, and so glorify him on earth. The very angels become ministering spirits to them (*Heb.* 1:14).

They have their journals to show how and where they conquered: Satan's broken weapons and defeated arguments they carry away as spoils and come out of the battle enriched with experiences. These they distribute as so many gifts to their brethren, as Paul did (*2 Cor.* 1:4–7). And these are no small signs of their victory; not to mention the devil's flight.

As to what may come afterward, the sufferings which come to them from the envy of a defeated devil, these too they overcome by not loving their lives, but being faithful to the death (*Rev.* 12:11; 2:10). None of these things move them (*Acts* 20:23–24), for in as well as after these things, they are more than conquerors. They are of so great and noble souls and spirits that they do not accept deliverance, but expect and shall obtain a better resurrection (*Heb.* 11:35). This perseverance to the end is often called overcoming in the epistles to the seven churches.

(v) The result of the victory in the young men's lives
Besides what flows from their having the witness of the Spirit which is the same as that of the little children, a further influence from this victory almost doubles their joy, love, and obedience: It is another witness, as it were, or a confirmation of the former, an assured assurance.

It fills them with joy and rejoicing in the Lord. They make their boast in him, and to him they give the glory all the day long. They rejoice not only as the disciples did, that the devils are subject to them, but that their names are written in the book of life (*Luke* 10:17). They triumph in the praises of God and say, Thanks be to God who hath given us the victory through our Lord Jesus Christ. When they erect an altar, the name and motto is *Jehovah nissi*, The Lord my banner, and the Lord my strength. It was he who taught me to fight and gave me the victory. Not to us, not to us, but unto thy name be all the glory. They sing the eighteenth Psalm.

The Lord having given them rest and settlement,

which is the consequence of victory, they not only rejoice and sing songs, but they consider what to return to the Lord for all his benefits. They dedicate all the spoils to God. They want, as David did, to build a house for God, and lay up all they can as a preparation for it. With their lives they assist in this great work. They do not court the Delilahs of this world's pleasure, as too many Samson-like conquerors do, or turn young ones to lust after their great successes. They strive to walk with God and to please him, and by doing so to abound more and more till they walk worthy of him to all well-pleasing. They do not put God off with words and a song, and then forget his works; but they give and live thanks to God, the fruit of their lips and of their lives.

They are exceedingly humble and lowly towards their weak brothers. They dare not lord it over the Lord's inheritance, their brethren, though they may be only babes. But they give them a helping hand and tell them of their own experiences to encourage them, as Paul did (*2 Cor.* 1:4–7). If any is overtaken, they endeavour to restore him with a spirit of meekness, for these soldiers are not proud and lifted up like others. But being spiritual, they know tenderness and are acquainted with the heart of tempted ones, having been tempted themselves. And so they are conformed to their great high priest and captain-general of their faith and victory; and this conformity is always an obligation to meekness and moderation, not a spur to ambition or a stirrup to pride. Though some babes are apt to envy their attainment and glory, they have compassion on them, and bear (as well as bear with) their infirmities.

They keep strict watch, always standing and walking in their armour, that of God. They do not turn their swords into ploughshares or their spears into pruning hooks as if all were over, but they keep strong guard because of their adversary the devil. They do not know but that the devil may fall on them again. They are not secure and do not lay aside their weapons as if they should know war no more.

From the experiences they have had, they take courage and good heart of grace to trust in God for the future, not in their sword or in their bow, though, like Joseph's, it abides in strength. Though some young men faint, and youths fail by reason of presumption, yet these wait on the Lord and renew their strength; they mount up with wings as eagles, they run and are not weary, they walk and do not faint (*Isa.* 40:30–31). They look on past deliverances as the promise of and security for future deliverances, as Paul did (*2 Cor.* 1:10, *2 Tim.* 4:17–18).

They do not entangle themselves with the affairs of this life, that they may please him who has chosen them to be soldiers (*2 Tim.* 2:4). They live above the lusts of the eye, the lusts of the flesh and pride of life, the love of these things being inconsistent with the love of God. They make the choice of Moses, being come to age as he was (*Heb.* 11:24–27). They will not stoop to take up with these things which are below. This earth is for their feet to tread on and not to set their hearts on. No, this is the victory whereby they overcome the world, even their faith, which looks to higher and better things than this world has (*1 John* 5:4–5). These charming and bewitching things have no power over them, but they go on from strength to strength till they appear before God in Zion, and say with David, 'Whom have I in heaven but thee, there is none on earth that I can desire in comparison of thee' (*Psa.* 73:25).

I have attempted to describe the young men's conditions, as I have the others', not by guess and conjecture, but as they are represented in the Scripture.

[260]

I have chosen not to address other things, as intermissions and desertions, which our text did not mention at all.

Application: Encouragement for Fighting the Good Fight

As for you, little children, who have thus far lived in the Father's house enjoying his love without doubts or disputes, let me warn you to look for and prepare for temptations. Satan makes challenges, and desires to winnow you and sift you as he did Job and Peter and others (*Luke* 22:31).

Therefore watch and pray lest you enter into temptation, and beg God either not to lead you into temptation, or, if he does, as the Spirit did Christ Jesus, that he will not allow you to be tempted above your strength, but that he will deliver you from the evil, or the evil one. Tell your Father that you have heard what a potent and subtle adversary the devil is, that he throws fiery darts to inflame the hearts of God's children against their Father and tempts them to worship devils, which are such horrid things that you would not willingly be acquainted with them.

But if he chooses to glorify his name this way, as he has done before, then say, 'Father, thy will be done,' as your Saviour did; and conclude that your Father will not forsake you or leave you to be a prey and captive to this mighty one.

If any of you should be called out to this war, take these encouragements to help you:

(i) *The cause is good, called the 'good fight of faith'.* The devil would turn you out of house and home and deprive you of your right and title to heaven. It is about heavenly things, this dispute, and whether or not you are sons of God. In other wars the cause is not the best, and often

[261]

very bad. But it is clear and without exception that we should fight against the devil and all his works, which war against our comforts, souls, and happiness. Do not fear, then, but fight, for your cause is good and just. It is to defend your own rights and liberties.

(ii) The battle is the Lord's. This Goliath defies not only Israel but the living God. In calling your title into question, he calls the truth of God and witness of his Spirit into question, so that God is engaged with you; he will plead his as well as your cause and will be jealous for his name and for his people. You fight for God, and therefore God will fight for you. As you may be said to help the Lord against the mighty, so the Lord will help you against their might. 'This day,' said David to Goliath, 'will the Lord deliver thee into my hands, for the battle is the Lord's' (*1 Sam.* 17:46–47). If the Lord be with us, it does not matter who is against us, the gates (power and policy) of hell shall not prevail. No, not death itself, for that is what Grotius understands the 'gates of hell' to mean.

(iii) You fight under a captain-general, Jesus Christ, who never turned back, was never foiled, but always went on conquering and to conquer. Look to Jesus, who is the leader and rear guard, the author and will be the finisher of your faith (*Heb.* 12:2–3). This great commander says, 'Go and fight, but follow me.' It is always a great encouragement to bear arms and fight under the conduct of a successful general.

(iv) You are to fight with an enemy that has been conquered by Christ Jesus and by many of your brothers. The devil is not so dreadful as he was before Christ died (*Heb.* 2:14–15); the prince of peace has conquered the king of terrors. And many of your brothers have contended and defeated him many times. It is true, his wiles are his worst weapons, and his wit is more than his might, and

his ill will and malice more than his wit. But he has been fooled many a time, despite all his cunning devices, and put to shame for his malicious lying, as in the case of Job and many others.

(v) You are provided with armour of God's making as well as of God's appointing. And there is none other like it. You have the same sword by which Jesus Christ and the young men, your brothers, have conquered the devil, and the same shield of faith with which to quench his fiery darts. This armour is mighty through God (*2 Cor.* 10:3).

(vi) God will take care for your pay, you shall not war at your own expense (1 Cor. *9:7*). Beside the glory of overcoming, you shall have a crown of glory after you have overcome (*2 Tim.* 4:7-8). To him that overcometh, God will give honour, for they that honour him will be honoured. Their labour shall not be in vain in the Lord (*1 Cor.* 15:58).

(vii) God has promised you success and victory. He will tread Satan under your feet shortly (*Rom.* 16:20). He shall be cast out, and you shall overcome him (*Rev.* 12:9-11). Read Isaiah 41:8-17, and through the comfort of that and other Scriptures written for our encouragement, you may have hope and strong consolation.

(viii) Well then, be strong in the Lord and the power of his might, for by no other strength can any prevail. Though it is said that by strength shall no man prevail, yet by strength do all men prevail: It is an orthodox paradox. By strength no man or devil can prevail against God (*1 Sam.* 2:8-10). Let no man, therefore, provoke the Lord to jealousy, for he has no match. He is stronger than all, and none shall take his saints out of his hand. Whoever fought against God and prospered? But there is a strength of faith and prayer, like Jacob's, by which some prevail with God. They are princes, the true Israelites (*Hos.* 12:3-4, *Gen.* 32:24-28). When God yields we prevail with him; and

[263]

when we do not yield but are strong in the Lord, resisting the devil, we prevail over him. It is not by strength, but by Christ strengthening us, that we can do all things (*Phil.* 4:13). It is not by strength of wit or reason, not by strength of hands or legs, or by strength of our spirit and courage; but by the strength of God, of his Word, grace, and Spirit abiding in us that we prevail.

As for the young men, I have no more to add, but to exhort them to make good everything that has been said of them. Show that you are strong, that the Word of God abides in you, that you have overcome the evil one, which will prove that God is your God and Father (*Rev.* 11:7) and that none shall separate you from the love of God in Christ (*Rom.* 8:39). Show the tokens and signs of your victory; let the disposition and manner of young men be apparent in you. Hold forth the word of life and power in the works of your lives, that so you may grow up to be fathers in Israel and grey-haired in righteousness. This will be to you a crown of glory, as strength is your glory while you are young men. Live and thrive as those who prepare, eat, and digest strong meat, who feed on the eternal love of God and on the priesthood of our Lord Jesus Christ, which belongs to the little children, to you and to the fathers, who, in different measures, are practised at discerning good and evil (*Heb.* 5:14).

PART FIVE

Fathers in Israel

I write unto you, fathers, because ye have known him that is from the beginning (verse 13).

I have written unto you, fathers, because ye have known him that is from the beginning (verse 14).

THEIR CHARACTERISTICS

The fathers, it seems, if I may venture to say anything of them, are usually marked by age as well as attainments. They are the ancients and elders of Israel, whose grey hairs are wise and found in the way; they are filled with the fruits of righteousness, which is their crown of glory. The Word of God dwells richly in them in all wisdom and spiritual understanding, in sense, experience and judgement, by which they discern different persons and things. They are spiritual and perfect in the superlative degree. They have gone through all the former states, having, like Enoch, a continuous communion with, as well as a knowledge of, him that is from the beginning, from the first to last.

THEIR ABILITIES

And by reason of their knowledge and wisdom born of experience (*James* 3:17–18), they are able to speak to all the cases of conscience and to the various dispensations which belong to the whole Christian course. They can divide the word aright and speak words suitable to all, giving everyone their portion. They bring out of their treasures things new and old. They know how to speak to the faint and weary, to the broken-hearted and the downcast, to the deserted and tempted ones. They know also how to discern between form and power, hypocrisy and sincerity, pretensions and realities.

Of this state let days speak and multitude of years teach this wisdom (*Job* 32:7). I am but few of days and dare not give you my opinion (if I may borrow more of Elihu's words) concerning this state beyond what I have now mentioned in general.

PART SIX

Conclusions

To conclude, my design being to help Christians discover their states, attainments, and growths, I shall add only a few things more.

CLASSES OF CHRISTIANS

(i) A Christian may know what class he is in.   As it may be known whether a man is in the faith (*2 Cor.* 13:5), so it may also be known how far he has proceeded in the faith. As for some 'random' saints, who are not fixed but fleeting, most of these also may be placed in one or another class according to their state in general.

It is a great advantage in many respects to know where one is, to know one's place, rank and station, as it is for a servant in a family or a soldier in an army. Those who do not know what their work is do not know how to do their work. But if we know our station, and it is clear what our work is and how it is to be done, we may set about it.

(ii) Though a saint should be content with his present state, he should desire and pray, endeavour and labour after progress and advancement.   Though he should not forget to bless God for what he has, he should forget what is behind, not rest in what he has, and not think that he has attained so much or were already so perfect that there were no more to be attained.

Reaching and pressing forward, as Paul did, is the duty of all, till they attain to the resurrection of the dead.

There is no state on earth so satisfying that it should divert anyone from looking and hastening to the coming of Christ, that we may be always with him and altogether like him (*Phil.* 1:23, *1 John* 3:2, *2 Pet.* 3:11–13). The good and bad things in this world call upon us to long to be above in heaven; for if it is bad to be here, it is good to be there; and if it is good to be here, it is better to be there, to be sure. Though we may have enough sometimes to say it is good to be here, we never have enough to say it is best to be here.

(iii) We should all take heed where we place our growth and advancement, and beware that we do not place them only in knowledge, head- and book-learning, or only in gifts and parts, or only in common graces; no, or in going from one opinion to another, or one form of church government to another, from one profession to another. This, I fear, has been a great mistake, to suppose it is a going on to, when, alas! if this is all, it is a going away from perfection. For to be tossed to and fro with every wind of doctrine is but babyish (*Eph.* 4:13–16). Alas! what is it to be Episcopal, Presbyterian, or Congregational? Our religion, much less our perfection, lies not in these or any other opinions or forms of government. I do not doubt that there are saints in all these forms, yet I believe and affirm that none of these forms makes them saints. And a person may be in any of these and yet be only a babe, or even carnal. This is like those who go up and down the city streets collecting old satin and ends of gold and silver but never grow rich or gain any considerable estate.

(iv) We should be as careful to mind and discharge the duties as to enjoy the privileges and dignities of our state. And take care not only to be in Christ but to walk in him and as he walked. Study commands as well as promises, and look for light that you may walk in the light. For if we walk in

the light, as children of light, we (God and we) have fellowship one with another. Thus as God glorifies us, we glorify him. We should have a great ambition to glorify him and to let our light so shine before men, that they also may glorify our Father which is in heaven (*Matt.* 5:13–16).

LIVE IN LOVE; WALK WORTHY OF GOD

Let us live in love and speak the truth in love. For oh how good and pleasant a thing it is for brethren to dwell together in unity! Let us not be like Ephraim and Judah, envying and vexing, biting and devouring one another, but let us love one another with a pure heart fervently.

Finally, let us make it our business, and our pleasure too, to adorn the doctrine of God our Saviour and to walk worthy of God to all well-pleasing. To this end, 'Let us grow in grace and in the knowledge of our Lord and Saviour Jesus Christ, that to him and to the Father by him, there may be thanks and glory given, both now and forever.' Amen.

ANALYSIS

PART ONE
INTRODUCTION

1 General design and scope of the treatise

2 Ranks of saints – not measured by age

3 'Little children' – all true Christians

4 Fathers, young men, little children

5 Babes

General Application
 (i) Words to all
  a) Love one another
  b) Do not compare yourself with others
  c) Be thankful for attainments
  d) Aim for the best
  e) Do not envy or despise others
  f) Each has a share in sermons and epistles
  g) Make the best use of any sermon
 (ii) A few words to each in turn
  a) To fathers: Lay aside childish things
  b) To young men: Be strong
  c) To children: Be obedient
  d) To babes: Desire milk

6 Further clarification
 (i) The difference between saints and the unconverted

    (ii)   The difference between saints and saints
   (iii)   Things common to all saints
   (iv)   Things specific to each state
    (v)   The difference in graces
   (vi)   The grace of God working in us
  (vii)   Many members in one body
 (viii)   The states have an appointed measure
   (ix)   Everyone has grace sufficient to his state
    (x)   Few are eminent in all graces
   (xi)   Some grow up faster than others
  (xii)   Each grows to his appointed measure
 (xiii)   Variations in the states
  (xiv)   Aim at the highest state
   (xv)   God builds by his Word and Spirit

PART TWO

BABES

From 1 Corinthians 3:1-2 and Hebrews 5:11-14

1 The state of babes, and their attainments
     (i)   Some Christians are only babes
    (ii)   Some may be only babes for a long time
   (iii)   Babes eat only milk
   (iv)   Babes are called brethren

2 Their feeding on milk

3 Growth in babes

4 Babes' attainments, in general (from Hebrews 6:1-2)

5 Repentance from dead works
     (i)   Repentance, the babes' first milk
    (ii)   Babes better at repentance than at other virtues
   (iii)   Repentance includes: the sense of sin, sorrow
           and confession, and reformation

Application
    a) For those who have not repented
        (i) Common principles will condemn you
        (ii) God has long waited to be gracious
        (iii) If you die in your sins, you are damned irrecoverably
    b) For babes, who have repented
        (i) God has put a stop to your uncleanness
        (ii) Many have not come so far as repentance
        (iii) You will be preserved
        (iv) God is pleased with that little grace in you
        (v) Your soul is secured

6 The babes' faith
    (i) How their faith acts towards God
        a) Babes believe that God is, and that he rewards
        b) Babes believe that God can save them
        c) Babes look to God's promises
    (ii) How their faith acts towards Christ Jesus
        a) They believe that Jesus Christ is the Son of God
        b) Babes believe that God sent his Son to save sinners
    (iii) How their faith acts towards God and Christ
        a) They resolve to go to God
        b) They pray
        c) They obey and submit to ordinances

Application
    a) To those who are not babes
        (i) You are not yet convinced of the sinfulness of sin

      (ii) You have long had the means of faith: preaching and hearing

      (iii) You may die in your sins and be damned forever

   b) To babes who are discouraged

      (i) You have gone farther than you are aware of

      (ii) You have gone far enough to be saved

      (iii) The gates of hell shall not prevail against your faith

      (iv) Your experiences can be had only by a true saint

      (v) There is joy in heaven that you have come to God

      (vi) You lack only the knowledge of your happy state

      (vii) Press forward

7 Their submission to baptism and other ordinances
   i) How babes follow ordinances
     a) Using them much but making little real use of them
     b) Confining religion to certain duties
     c) Placing more in ordinances than God has placed in them
     d) Thinking they deserve something from God by what they do
     e) Valuing ordinances according to who administers them
     f) Not sensing their own inward defects

Application
   a) Words of exhortation for babes
     (i) Consider how you ought to do things
     (ii) Consider the true design of ordinances

    (iii) Do not confine religion to certain days and duties

    (iv) Observe the proper times of ordinances and duties

    (v) Act out of love and thankfulness

    (vi) Serve God even without encouragement

    (vii) Cast yourself on Jesus Christ

  b) Words of consolation for babes

    (i) God will pick out the best and make much of it

    (ii) You have an advocate with the Father

    (iii) There is a resurrection and eternal judgement to come

8 Their belief in the resurrection of the dead and eternal judgement

  (i) Which resurrection is here meant

  (ii) What attainment results from this belief

Application: Encouragement to babes concerning the judgement

9 Their tasting that the Lord is gracious, and their desiring the milk of the word (from 1 Peter 2:1-3)

10 Their love to the brethren

11 Summing up the attainments and characters of babes

12 Their defectiveness and falling short compared with other saints

  (i) They little understand their communion with God and Christ

  (ii) They are unskilful in the word of righteousness

    a) For justification

    b) For sanctification

- (iii) They listen a great deal but are unable to bear much
- (iv) Babes have not developed the habits of grown saints
- (v) Babes' senses are not developed
- (vi) They are apt to be tossed to and fro by winds of teaching
- (vii) They serve God more as servants than as children

13 Their being as carnal and walking as men (taking the Corinthians as example)
- (i) There was envy, strife, and division among them
  - a) They were more taken with the gifts than with graces
  - b) They confined themselves and God to a particular man's ministry
  - c) Some accepted truth only from certain men
  - d) They fell into parties and took sides
- (ii) They kept communion with very unclean persons
- (iii) They went to law with one another
- (iv) They pass from one extreme to another
- (v) They argue over little matters
- (vi) Babes ask many trivial questions
- (vii) Babes live by tradition and the example of men
- (viii) They have more zeal than knowledge
- (ix) Babes can hardly bear a reproof
- (x) Some measure God's heart by his hand

14 Being newborn
- (i) Examining whether we are newborn or not
  - a) The new birth is a mystery
  - b) God converts by various means
  - c) His manner of working also differs
  - d) The time of conversion varies

    e) Conversion is felt more by some and is more visible in some than others

    f) Conversion is more or less knowable

(ii) Knowing that a person is newborn

    a) Desiring that God may be their God and they may be his people

    b) Acting from the law of God written in their hearts

    c) Wanting their sin taken away, not only by pardoning but by purging

    d) Not departing from God

(iii) The covenant promises effected in all saints

Exhortation

    a) To those who are not yet newborn

        (i) Do not offend Christ's babes

        (ii) Do not reject Christ because of carnal babes

    b) To grown saints

        (i) Remember what babes you were

        (ii) Produce fruit in keeping with your state

        (iii) Do not be ashamed of your youngest brothers, babes

        (iv) Give good examples to babes

        (v) Acquaint babes with your experiences and with Satan's devices

    c) To babes

        (i) Be glad that you are newborn and in Christ Jesus

        (ii) Be humbled that you are only babes, as carnal

        (iii) Press forward to being more than a babe

15 Growing in grace; helps for growing

PART THREE

LITTLE CHILDREN

1 The children's knowledge of the Father

2 How the children come to know the Father
  (i) The persons God places among the little
      children
    a) Those who come into his service while young
    b) Those who have been deeply humbled for
       sin
    c) Those who hunger and thirst after Jesus
       Christ
    d) Those who separate from unbelievers
    e) Those about to do and suffer great things for
       God
  (ii) The witness of the Spirit
    a) Not all saints have the witness
    b) This witness is sure
    c) The effects of this witness
    d) Distinguishing true and false testimony

3 The privileges and enjoyments of little children
  (i) The gospel state beyond that of the law
  (ii) The Spirit of adoption an addition to sonship
  (iii) The witness of the Spirit; the Spirit of
        adoption
  (iv) Little children say, Abba Father
  (v) The Spirit of adoption an incomparable
      privilege
  (vi) Knowing the Father a choice privilege
  (vii) It is a glorious and sweet privilege

4 The attitudes and life of little children

Application
- (i) An exhortation to babes: Pray to be among the children
- (ii) An exhortation to the little children
  - a) Do not be proud
  - b) Do not neglect the Son
  - c) Do not grieve the Holy Spirit
  - d) Honour your Father
  - e) Let the Word of God dwell richly in you

PART FOUR

YOUNG MEN

1 The young men's strength
- (i) What is meant by their being strong
- (ii) Where their strength lies
- (iii) How they come by this strength

2 The wicked one, and his temptings
- (i) Who or what is meant by the wicked one
- (ii) What the dispute is about; what the temptations are
- (iii) The temptations of Christ and the young men
- (iv) One temptation more

3 The young men's victory
- (i) What is meant by their overcoming the wicked one
- (ii) How the Word of God strengthens; how strength leads to victory
- (iii) The greatness of the victory
  - a) The enemy's strength
  - b) His malice, revenge, and envy
  - c) His subtlety
  - d) His ceaseless activity
  - e) His conquests in all ages

  (iv) The tokens and signs of this victory
  (v) The result of the victory in the young men's lives

Application: Encouragement for fighting the good fight
  (i) The cause is good
  (ii) The battle is the Lord's
  (iii) Your captain-general, Jesus Christ, is a
    conqueror
  (iv) Your enemy has been conquered
  (v) You are provided with armour
  (vi) You shall not fight without reward
  (vii) God has promised victory
  (viii) Be strong in the Lord

PART FIVE

FATHERS IN ISRAEL

1 Their characteristics

2 Their abilities

CONCLUSIONS

1 Classes of Christians
  (i) A Christian may know which class he is in
  (ii) Be content, but labour after progress
  (iii) Take heed how growth is measured
  (iv) Discharge the duties of your state

2 Live in love; walk worthy of God

SOME OTHER
BANNER OF TRUTH
TITLES

THE SINFULNESS OF SIN

Ralph Venning

We cannot understand the Christian gospel until we know what sin is. Yet modern secular counsellors urge us to ignore both the word and what it tells us about our rebellion against God and his law. Sadly the church too often echoes this cheap and short-sighted wisdom. First published in the aftermath of the Great Plague of London and entitled *Sin, The Plague of Plagues*, this book gives a crystal-clear explanation of what sin is, why it is so serious, and what we need to do about it. Here is reliable medicine for a fatal epidemic.

ISBN: 0 85151 647 5
284pp. Paperback
£3.50/$7.50

HEAVEN ON EARTH

Thomas Brooks

Assurance of salvation is one of the most important elements in Christian experience. There is no higher privilege than to be a child of God *and to know it*, for assurance brings joy to worship and prayer and provides strength and boldness in witness. Failure and weakness in these areas can often be traced to a lack of assurance. This work, first published in 1654, deals with all these aspects of assurance. 'The being in a state of grace', says Brooks, 'makes a man's condition happy, safe and sure; but the seeing, the knowing of himself to be in such a state is that which renders his life sweet and comfortable. The being in a state of grace will yield a man a heaven hereafter, but the seeing of himself in this state will yield him both a heaven here *and* a heaven hereafter.'

ISBN: 0 85151 356 5
320pp. Paperback
£4.50/$8.99

ALL THINGS FOR GOOD

Thomas Watson

Thomas Watson's exposition is always illuminating and rich in practical application. In this work he explains that both the best and the worst experiences work for the good of God's people. He carefully analyses what it means to be someone who 'loves God' and who is 'called according to his purpose'. *All Things for Good* provides the biblical answer to the contemporary question, 'Why do bad things happen to good people?'

ISBN: 0 85151 478 2
128pp. Paperback
£2.25/$4.99

For free illustrated catalogue please write to
THE BANNER OF TRUTH TRUST
3 Murrayfield Road, Edinburgh EH12 6EL
P O Box 621, Carlisle, Pennsylvania 17013, USA